The Sermons of Jonathan Edwards

The Sermons of Jonathan Edwards

A Reader

Edited by

Wilson H. Kimnach, Kenneth P. Minkema,

and Douglas A. Sweeney

New Haven and London Yale University Press

Funds for editing *The Works of Jonathan Edwards* have been provided
by The Pew Charitable Trusts, Lilly Endowment, Inc.,
and The Henry Luce Foundation, Inc.
Published with assistance from The Exxon Education Foundation
and the Annie Burr Lewis Fund.

Designed by Sonia Scanlon. Set in Adobe Caslon type by
The Composing Room of Michigan, Inc.,
Grand Rapids, Michigan.
Printed in the United States of America by
Vail-Ballou Press, Binghamton, N.Y.

Library of Congress Cataloging-in-Publication Data

Edwards, Jonathan, 1703–1758
[Sermons. Selections]
The sermons of Jonathan Edwards : a reader / edited by Wilson
H. Kimnach, Kenneth P. Minkema, and Douglas A. Sweeney.
p. cm.
Includes bibliographical references (p.) and index.
ISBN 0–300–07766–1 (cloth : alk. paper)
ISBN 0–300–07768–8 (pbk. : alk. paper)
1. Congregational churches—Sermons. 2. Sermons, American.
I. Kimnach, Wilson H. II. Minkema, Kenneth P. III. Sweeney, Douglas A.
IV. Title.
BX7233.E42 S47 1999
252′.058—dc21 98–46145
CIP

A catalogue for this book is available
from the British Library.

The paper in this book meets the guidelines for permanence and
durability of the Committee on Production Guidelines for Book
Longevity of the Council on Library Resources

10 9 8 7 6 5 4 3 2

To Richard D. Edwards, John H. Edwards, Debra A. Edwards,
Janet Edwards Anti, and Mary Edwards Foster
for their interest in Jonathan Edwards
and assistance in making his writings available

Contents

Editors' Introduction

In 1722 Jonathan Edwards, arguably America's greatest religious genius, began a list of "Resolutions" by which he intended to live. He was then just nineteen. The first resolution read: "Resolved, that I will do whatsoever I think to be most to God's glory, and my own good, profit and pleasure, in the whole of my duration, without any consideration of the time, whether now, or never so many myriads of ages hence. Resolved to do whatever I think to be my duty, and most for the good and advantage of mankind in general. Resolved to do this, whatever difficulties I meet with, how many and how great soever." More than any other genre of his writings, the sermons of Jonathan Edwards tell us how he attempted to adhere to this credo and "to live with all my might, while I do live."[1] His sermons reflect the stages of his busy life—a life of profound importance for understanding the formation of American religious thought, a life of great successes and bitter disappointments, a life caught up in the period of dramatic social, political, and religious change between the Salem witchcraft trials and the American Revolution, but a life, above all, dedicated to the understanding and experience of spiritual truth, and to conveying that experience and understanding to others.

Among the writings of Jonathan Edwards, both published and unpublished, his sermons are by far the most numerous. Indeed, sermons alone make up well over half his literary corpus. Nearly 1,250 have survived—an impressive figure that surprises even those familiar with Edwards, particularly since only about seventy sermons were available in print before the Yale Edition of *The Works of Jonathan Edwards* began publishing additional sermons from the manuscripts. This fact alone makes a volume of his selected sermons, drawn both from his published works and his manuscripts, long overdue. Of the fourteen sermons and

1. *Works of Jonathan Edwards, 16, Letters and Personal Writings*, ed. George S. Claghorn (New Haven, Yale Univ. Press, 1998), 753.

discourses offered in this volume, five have never been previously published. But the sheer mass of Edwards' sermons also says something about the importance of the sermon to his life and work. Edwards was first and foremost a preacher and pastor leading souls to the truth as he saw it and interpreting the religious experiences of his listeners. His primary tool in achieving these goals was the sermon, the spoken word of God, which in the Reformed tradition that shaped him was the centerpiece of worship and religious edification.

This volume therefore has a specialized focus. It is not an introduction to Edwards' entire life or to the impressive range of his thought. Rather it recognizes the crucial role of the sermon in the life and art of Jonathan Edwards, and is intended as an aid to understanding Edwards as a preacher, sermon writer, and pastoral theologian. The texts presented here focus on the major themes upon which Edwards consistently preached as a way of guiding souls through spiritual pitfalls toward eternal joy. Thus the sermons have a sense of progression to them that reflects the pilgrimage of the soul, as Edwards conceived it, from its sinful earthly state to a pure heavenly existence.

In this introduction we seek to familiarize the reader with Edwards the preacher: first, by discussing the sermon itself as a literary form and showing Edwards' artistry in that form; second, by placing Edwards' sermons within their social and cultural contexts; and third, by examining the contents of these sermons and Edwards' theological aims in preaching them. We hope thereby to give the reader a fuller appreciation of the richness of Edwards' sermons and their great significance for American literature, history, and religion.

The Homiletical Tradition and Edwards' Preaching

Words have different resonances in different ages, even though their basic definition may remain the same. At times in the past, the word "sermon" has excited anticipation not only among religious zealots or Puritans but also among worldly sophisticates whose main interest was in the latest trends in taste and the intellectual fads of the day. During England's Restoration (1660–1700)—a period noted for anti-Puritanism and moral skepticism—a representative establishment intellectual like Samuel Pepys records in his diary not only casual sexual promiscuity but also excursions—in parties of men and women—to hear the latest sermons of the most stylish preachers. Piety plays a small role in this picture; the idea of entertainment, albeit on a relatively high intellectual level, is much more prominent. Of course, Pepys' town was London, not Boston. In contemporary Boston during the second half of the seventeenth century whole communities would hang upon the words of important preachers for provocative readings of the times. So daily life has often been defined primarily through sermons for large and diverse communities.

Today it may be difficult to imagine the average American—especially a "sophisticated" one—waiting excitedly for a preacher's next sermon. "Sermon" has for many a dreary sound. Yet we still use the word evocatively: when the local football team retreats at half-time with defeat in their eyes but returns in the second half to triumph, we observe knowingly that the coach "must have preached them a sermon" in the locker room. The idea persists that the sermon, while not exactly entertaining, is speech that mysteriously moves people, enabling them to change their attitudes and even, perhaps, the very terms of their reality. Moreover, that notion of the sermon still emerges from time to time, perhaps most tellingly in the now-classic "I Have a Dream" address of Martin Luther King, Jr., a piece that most people would properly recognize as a sermon despite its outwardly secular context and message, and not merely because its author was an ordained minister and a martyr in his calling.

The word "sermon," derived from the Latin *sermo*, means little more than "a talk," yet it acquired in ancient times an association with the idea of privileged, sanctioned, even divinely inspired speech. Over time, this *genre*, as the sermon is classified in rhetorical terms, has acquired formal definition, though like all genres it constantly evolves and is modified by its best practitioners. As in the case of the drama—a genre that has flourished in Western civilization from ancient times until the present, encompassing such diverse periods of activity and creativity as those of the Greek and Shakespearean tragedies—different styles or "schools" of homiletics have emerged in different periods, and inevitably certain periods have assumed in retrospect the reputation of "great ages of preaching." In

England the period encompassing Lancelot Andrewes and John Tillotson (virtually the entire seventeenth century) is generally considered to be the high point, though there were other great moments as well. In America most people are likely to think first of the age of the New England Puritans—essentially the period between 1630 and 1690—though others would argue for the era of Jonathan Edwards and the Great Awakening in the mid-eighteenth century or that of Ralph Waldo Emerson and William Ellery Channing in the early nineteenth as being equally distinctive and important. Of course, on a microcosmic level, nearly every denomination, society, and region has its local heroes among preachers who have critically shaped a community or a church at some point in its history.

At any moment in time, the sermon embodies a number of conventions of style and form that enable its audience to anticipate and thus more readily absorb its message. These conventions define the genre for a certain period or sect, and the preacher is constrained to operate within them, much as an artist assumes certain conventional limits on the medium in which he or she works. Paradoxically, the most confining conventions sometimes elicit the most creative efforts.

Perhaps the most important convention of the sermon is the idea that it is an act of mediation: between the present moment and eternity, between the secular and the sacred, and between humans and their God. This act of mediation involves a dramatic reconceiving of the context of secular activity, and it is in this conjunction of radical opposites that much of the impact of the sermon lies. Beyond this fundamental element the sermon has innumerable stylistic variations, largely depending on denominational taste—the importance of biblical exegesis, for example—and the more general conventions of the age—such as the degree of respect given to human reason or to mystery. Moreover, since virtually all sermons are occasional in their inception, referring to a particular group of people in a particular situation at a particular time, sermons reflect their historical contexts more directly than do most belletristic genres.

Beyond these more general conventions, the sermon is shaped by the conventions of each sect. For Jonathan Edwards, this was New England Congregationalism in the years immediately following the last days of the Puritans (or "the Old Dissenters," as Edwards called them), the church founders. The form of the sermon was generally that used by the Puritans, although important stylistic changes were already being made as the eighteenth century began. As in England within the Anglican church, the eighteenth century demanded a less elaborate sermon form than the baroque forms popular among both Anglican and Puritan congregations during the seventeenth century. For Edwards this meant a formal simplification of the sermon of his father (the Reverend Timothy Edwards of East Windsor, Connecticut), wherein he reduced discursive subheads drastically, permitting a fuller development of each point and facilitating a more focused overall line of argument.

The resulting Edwardsean sermon consists of three clearly defined divisions: the Scripture text and a brief commentary or interpretation; the statement of a doctrine (the thesis or thematic motif for the entire sermon), followed by numbered argumentative heads collectively called "reasons"; and the "application" of the doctrine, through various numbered "uses," to the immediate personal and social context of the auditory. The Text-Doctrine-Application structure is the defining form of the sermon for Jonathan Edwards; he never varies from it, though he sometimes compounds it (without altering the external structure) by the insertion of multiple doctrinal statements and corresponding uses. The only real variation in Edwards' sermon form is known as the "lecture." Unlike the regular pastoral sermon, in which the Doctrine and Application roughly divide the sermon between them—with a tendency to a longer Application if anything—the "lecture," designed for propounding more abstract theological arguments, has only a few brief points by way of application and frequently has no formal Application division. An example of the lecture form in this volume is *A Divine and Supernatural Light* (1734).

The formal structure of the sermon gives Edwards and his auditory a shared set of expectations since, as in a sonnet, the form itself identifies the genre, subject, and structure of argument. In Edwards' sermon, the initial biblical text with its explication asserts the priority of the Bible as the source of understanding and all ultimate truth; Edwards asserts nothing in a sermon without the claim of scriptural sanction, and the initial text symbolizes this posture. The statement of doctrine and its substantial elaboration through numbered "reasons" again formally symbolize an important aspect of Edwards' attitude and practice, namely, the necessity of applying analysis or human reason to the words of the Bible so that general principles may be deduced and grasped by human understanding. This emphasis on rational religion is one of the badges of Protestantism, if not of Puritanism in particular. Finally, the application of principles derived from the Scripture to the practical affairs of life through the sermon's "uses" symbolizes the stress on conduct and the strict practice of religion in everyday life that is most often associated with the Puritan aspect of Edwards' heritage.

Together the formal elements of the Edwardsean sermon link reading the Bible with intellectual rumination and a practical, affectional response in the context of daily life; eternity enters the mind to impact upon the momentary act; the reality of God is translated through intense personal reflection into a system of committed practice. This is embodied in the very form of Edwards' sermons and, like those of all great literary artists, Edwards' statements are wholly harmonious with his genre, his form with his meaning.

Thus far we have examined the sermon formally, but readers do not read forms alone; inevitably, the issue of the substantive scope of sermons arises. For instance, readers are often introduced to Edwards by way of *Sinners in the Hands of an Angry God* (1741), his most frequently anthologized sermon, and the question arises: "Is this what he believed?" Unless you want to claim that Edwards was a writer of fiction or a liar, the answer is "yes." But this is not the real question, anyway. A better way to phrase it would be: "Is this *all* he believed, or is this a fair representation of the gist of Jonathan Edwards' religion?" The answer in this case, as in the case of any one sermon, would be "no," for the sermon is a short form, like the essay, and is not intended for grand summary statements of systematic thought. It is not, however, lacking in depth or subtlety because of this, merely in length or breadth.

The practical situation of the preacher is generally that of one who speaks repeatedly to the same audience. Only the wandering friars of the medieval period or revivalists of the modern period (beginning with the itinerant George Whitefield in Edwards' time) had the option of changing auditors rather than sermons. Moreover, even the friars and revivalists were tacitly in league with settled preachers who would presumably explain the full scope of religion to the people once they had been "awakened" by the shock troops on the street or in the field. The regular sermon is thus a single installment of a religious doctrine, however deep and complete a statement in itself. In the case of Edwards in particular, preaching from the cultural context of New England's Puritan heritage, the notion that there were stages of progress in religion was a given, from the moment of awakening through various steps to full participation. A responsible preacher addressed all of these stages of personal religious preparation, as well as acknowledging the major public events and issues that impinged on the congregation for which he was responsible. At the least, this means that a preacher gave a more or less systematic course of sermons, or a "round of preaching," in order to meet the minimal requirements of pastoral responsibility.

Only once in his life did Jonathan Edwards publish a collection of sermons, his *Discourses on Various Important Subjects, Nearly Concerning the Great Affair of the Soul's Eternal Salvation* (1738), which he offered as a memorial to an extraordinary period of religious interest described in *A Faithful Narrative of the Surprising Work of God in the Conversion of Many Hundred Souls* (1737).[2] Since the sermons do not pretend to be a collection that reflects the ordinary course of his preaching year in and year out, it is particularly noteworthy that Edwards explains in a preface to the reader that, although four of the five sermons included in the volume were requested by his congregation as being among the most stimulative to their interest in religion, he appended one additional sermon himself (namely, *The Excellency of Christ*, included below) to "properly follow others" correlating with earlier stages of the soul's preparation. For Edwards, a sermon's significance was in part a matter of what preceded and followed it, and if there were only two basic sermon forms, the pastoral sermon and the lecture, there were many functions for the sermon, several of which are illustrated in the selected sermons of this volume.

A final observation is suggested by the contents of the *Discourses on Various Important Subjects*, namely, that the first sermon has been ex-

2. *Works of Jonathan Edwards, 4, The Great Awakening*, ed. C. C. Goen (New Haven, Yale Univ. Press, 1972), 144–211.

panded to a point where it would have been impossible to deliver it in one preaching session, or for that matter in less than five or more sessions. This sermon, *Justification by Faith Alone*, was transformed into a brief treatise without losing the essential form of the sermon. This construct is what Edwards and his contemporaries called a *discourse*, a sermon that had been expanded beyond the scope of "a talk." Such lengthy pieces were delivered on the installment plan, discourses being preached in sections over several sabbaths or on a combination of sabbaths and lecture days.

The discourse on justification as published by Edwards, however, was never actually preached in its printed form, and this calls attention to an increasingly significant development during Edwards' lifetime: the rapidly expanding printing industry. Sermons had been printed or at least copied in manuscript for centuries as a means of broadcasting beyond the range of the preacher's voice, but the printed sermon was mainly a memorial of the speech act of the original. Edwards saw the beginning of the vogue of the sermon as a work of literature. As literature, the sermon is not "a talk" or even primarily the record of a talk, but a reading: less immediate or intimate than a talk but more persistent. The eighteenth century proved to be the great age of the printed sermon in America, and Edwards was clearly aware of the literary opportunity in the printed format, despite the fact that he lived at the beginning of the age and his work was not nearly so comprehensively printed as that of many later preachers, like his disciple Nathanael Emmons.

The sermons in this volume represent a spectrum of Edwards' preaching, including sermons for both his English and his Indian congregations. The sermons have been arranged to reflect the various stages in a hypothetical cycle of preaching addressing various spiritual conditions assumed by Edwards' religious culture, from an introduction to religious experience through various levels of instruction and discipline to the ultimate vision of the soul in heaven. This format is significant in calling attention to the theological structure implicit in what has been referred to as the "round," or cycle, of preaching, a point that cannot be overemphasized in any consideration of the art of preaching as Edwards understood it. But the literary, historical, and theological dimensions of his sermons are also significant and will be addressed in turn.

The Way of Holiness (1722) is the product of a teenaged preacher in his first (temporary) pastorate. He has not yet mastered the sentence but focuses clearly upon a foundational concept of his theology, the necessity of alignment with God so that "there is a likeness in *nature* between God and the soul of the believer." The beauty of holiness is not only Edwards' earliest but one of his most persistent messages, emerging as an aesthetic stratum in much of his lifelong theological and moral expression. But Edwards apparently realized that he was preaching in an age of reason, and another early sermon, *The Pleasantness of Religion* (1723), attempts to defend the Christian religion by employing a calculus of pleasure and pain to demonstrate that it always fulfills rational virtue and enhances earthly life. Such early emphases are more expressions of Edwards' private religious attitudes than systematic efforts to turn sinners toward salvation, however. His is the religion of a meditative, poetical, even mystical personality—today we would say "romantic"—which emphasizes such religious concepts as a unique relationship, a new quality of experience, and an indwelling principle, rather than the more externally structured experiences of the Puritan conversion regimen. As a more experienced preacher, however, Edwards learned that many people are not intuitively spiritual but are locked in bodily "lusts" (greed, ambition, and the like) and bounded by sense impressions of present life. For them, passing beyond the visible and the momentary is like a sleeper's efforts to achieve clarity and rationality in dreams: there is no relief short of waking up. And so despite a personal experience that may have tended otherwise, Edwards took up the practices of his fathers in dealing with the recalcitrant offspring of Adam and Eve. For this reason, his theology retained a tension between the *nature* of religious experience and models of how it might be *structured*.

The most famous of Edwards' sermons, *Sinners in the Hands of an Angry God*, functions as a homiletical slap in the face to get the attention of those who have no sense of their investment in religion or have otherwise shown themselves "sermon proof" (to use Edwards' expression). It is remarkable for its concentrated message and the rhythmic incantation driving home the precariousness of the human condition. Although *Sinners* is usually referred to as a "hellfire" sermon, it is actually focused on this life rather than the afterlife in hell. As such, it is more aptly called an eschatological sermon: one depicting the inevitability—and the temporal unpredictability—of death and judgment. Most people have no real belief in their own mortality, at least until a brush with death makes them feel their vulnerability. This sermon is Edwards' attempt to construct a verbal correlative to such a brush, and it is unremitting in the pursuit of its effect. He gives only the briefest attention to the ultimate solution of salvation through Christ, because it is enough for one sermon to get the attention—or "awaken"—a complacent or cynical listener.

Most of the sermons in this sampler, however, are devoted to the medial ground of theological instruction concerning the workings of faith and grace in life, for such was the actual proportion of Edwards' preaching. Readers will note that although Edwards is undoubtedly dedicated to an affective religion of the heart, this does not eliminate the need for considerable intellectual substance, for as he observes in *The Importance and Advantage of a Thorough Knowledge of Divine Truth* (1739): "There is no other way by which any means of grace whatsoever can be of any benefit, but by knowledge." One cannot have faith without knowing what to have faith in. For Edwards this stance implied the acquisition of substantial and specific learning, much of which he attempted to disseminate in sermons like the ones composing the bulk of this selection. Perhaps most striking in this respect is his effort to enlighten his Indian congregation at Stockbridge—preaching through an interpreter—with sermons which effect an astonishing compression of doctrine, commonly taken from previous versions to his white congregation in Northampton. The linear arguments of the Indian sermons telescope the more complex arguments yet omit no important points, extending even to a two-preaching-unit, morning-and-afternoon sermon, like *He That Believeth Shall Be Saved* (1751). The Indian sermons also nicely illustrate Edwards' ability to adjust his sermon to his listeners through brief references to their condition and interests.

In the course of instruction, Edwards employs a variety of rhetorical resources as pedagogical aids. Noteworthy are his clear definitions, in *The Way of Holiness*, for example, where an entire sermon is focused upon the key concept of holiness, or in *Knowledge of Divine Truth*, where essential terms and relationships involving the understanding and the heart are set forth, or in *The Reality of Conversion* (1740), where Edwards critically evaluates the revivalism current during the Great Awakening and observes, among other points, that conversion is not so much a matter of a certain order or structure of experience as it is of an altered "nature"—a point that has been little noticed. Yet another example of definition is *A Divine and Supernatural Light*, a remarkable lecture presenting a seminal concept in Edwards' vision of religion that stands as his most elegant exercise in definition. Perhaps a more entertaining method of definition is that illustrated in *Much in Deeds of Charity* (1741), where Edwards employs exemplary lives as patterns, some taken from the Scripture and some from the contemporary scene.

In all his regular pastoral sermons, then, there is an element of instruction not unlike that of most other pastors of his time and culture. But there is a quality in Edwards missing in all but a very few preachers, a pursuit of the implications of doctrine which reaches into new dimensions of thought and realization. Although professedly the most orthodox of New England preachers, Edwards employed a radical rhetoric that suggests that he should be placed within a tradition of Christian writers generally identified as "metaphysical." Some of his contemporaries in fact accused him of being "metaphysical," but for them the term seems to have implied only what we would recognize as "philosophical." Of course, Edwards *is* one of our most significant philosophers, and he does have a metaphysic through which he interprets the Scripture, but this is not what is implied here by "metaphysical"; rather, it is the literary preoccupation with capturing spiritual experiences in all their passionate intensity, representing *the spiritual* in concrete language implying an almost physical tangibility, that distinguishes Edwards' homiletics. Edwards thus belongs to the international coterie of preachers and poets that includes the seventeenth-century John Donne and George Herbert, as well as Edwards' near contemporary Edward Taylor, though unlike Taylor's, Edwards' technique does not hearken back to an earlier age so much as extend the approach into a new dimension of psychological realism in religious rhetoric.

No better introduction to Edwards' technique need be adduced than

God Glorified in the Work of Redemption (1731), Edwards' own debut in the clerical world of the Boston ministry (before whose assembly he preached it) and his first publication. In this important sermon, enunciating one of his most cherished positions on the religious issues of the day, Edwards abandons the plain style—now identified with the easy rhetoric of John Tillotson of the Church of England rather than with the Puritans—and employs a kind of verbal emphasis identified in the seventeenth century with Lancelot Andrewes and other "ornate" preachers. The sermon's stress on "universal dependence" upon God is dramatized by Edwards through a play on prepositions, of all things: "of," "by," "through," and "in." Similarly, Edwards differentiates *objective* and *inherent* in a rather fine distinction. Of course the sermon has an overall rational argument and plenty of biblical proofs, but the arresting intensity of argument and the impression of inevitability in it depend in large part upon that learned, metaphysical "word play."

A similar strategy of analytical division and juxtaposition is brilliantly employed in *The Excellency of Christ* (1738), but here a more substantive division is represented emblematically by the lion and the lamb. First of all, the word "excellency" represents in Edwards' vocabulary a union of the highest ethical and aesthetic values, and thus the title anticipates an enumeration and exaltation of many diverse qualities.[3] Rhetorically, the sermon does not disappoint: in the tradition of metaphysical exploitation of paradox and hyperbole to suggest the nature of divine mystery, the sermon joins diverse qualities identified with the emblematic figures—justice and grace, glory and humility, majesty and meekness, reverence and equality, worthiness and patience, authority and obedience, sovereignty and resignation, self-sufficiency and entire trust in God. For the most part, Edwards employs these paradoxical conjunctions to define Christ and his acts on earth and (in the Application) in heaven, at times compounding the lion and lamb images in moments of greater intensity. The attentive reader may observe, incidentally, that Edwards sometimes betrays the imagistic enthusiasm or inventive inconsistency of earlier

3. For an extensive discussion of the concept of excellency and related ideas, see Roland A. Delattre, *Beauty and Sensibility in the Thought of Jonathan Edwards* (New Haven, Yale Univ. Press, 1968).

metaphysicals when he suddenly shifts the image of the lion to Satan, then back to Christ. But as a whole, the sermon is a remarkably intense effort to realize the wonder of the Redeemer in his many dimensions, and in the inevitable context of human experience.

A very different kind of meditation characterizes the *Farewell Sermon* (1750) Edwards preached after a tragic dispute with his Northampton congregation brought about his dismissal, but it is in its own way equally metaphysical. Subtly echoing the word "peculiar"—indicative of "personal" or "unique"—the sermon makes explicit the implications of the bond between pastor and people. He and his congregation will be judged ultimately in terms of this unique Christian relationship, Edwards insists, and he then proceeds to enumerate the logical implications of that relationship with metaphysical specificity. The Doctrine division of the sermon particularly dramatizes the radical pursuit of the entire ethical context of the Day of Judgment. There is little of the self-referential pathos that one might expect in a farewell sermon, nor is there self-protective dignity or superiority; rather, Edwards presents the searing pain and indignation of his predicament in an exalted theological context which elevates the issue but does not eliminate the human context that tragically united the pastor and his flock in their "peculiar" relationship.

Relationship is also the primary preoccupation in one of the most radical of Edwards' sermons, *Heaven Is a World of Love* (1738). Originally composed as the culmination of a fifteen-sermon series on practical Christian ethics (published after Edwards' death as *Charity and Its Fruits*), this sermon constitutes a metaphysical poet's "beatific vision" expressed in the genre of the sermon. That is, the content is metaphorical rather than a purportedly literal mystical vision; but it nevertheless represents Edwards' finest attempt to represent in the concreteness and specificity of metaphysical statement the fulfillment of the Christian life in an afterlife. As has been indicated above, Edwards appreciated that people are "body bound" and therefore respond to images (imagined sense impressions) more than to abstractions. As he observes elsewhere, they can agree that abstractions are true, but only images seem real. Hence, like many of the great metaphysical writers before him, Edwards here uses the language of sense perception in a dynamic balance with abstraction to attempt a specific representation of heavenly existence or, more literally, a realization of the fulfillment of human aspiration.

The exegesis of the sermon's text begins almost pedantically for something that is supposedly an exalted vision, and the exposition of the doctrine is also highly schematic—even for an Edwards sermon—with several major numbered heads. However, the example of *God Glorified in the Work of Redemption* has made it apparent that one of the chief preoccupations of Edwards (and other metaphysical authors) is creating a specific, tangible presence for the spiritual, and his method is one of enumeration and iteration: striving to structure the concept presented through many precisely defined relationships until the sense of a structured presence is apparent. It is this sense of structure, anchored by just a few archetypal images like light or the fountain, that gives *Heaven Is a World of Love* its concreteness and immediacy. Without it, such evanescent, virtually "unreal" concepts as those represented by the three nouns of the title might well vaporize in the mouth of the preacher. But the tight rational structuring of the discovery of this world dramatizes Edwards' chief theme, that heaven endlessly multiplies harmonious relationships in the prototypical city upon a hill, truly a living of love. The exalted meditation concludes with one of the most precise and just warnings, as well as one of the most poetically appropriate endings, in all of Edwards' sermons.

Illustrated most notably in the above pieces but evident in varying degrees in all of Edwards' sermons, the metaphysical technique of representing the divine in vital human terms was required by what Edwards identified as contemporary "sensuality," a materialistic literalism or empiricism that shut people off from the realities of the spiritual life. However, the new eighteenth-century Enlightenment sophistication prevented a mere recapitulation of the mannerisms of the seventeenth-century metaphysicals and emblematic poets. In his response to this challenge, Edwards advanced his technique in unique ways that are still appreciated by such discerning modern readers as the poet Robert Lowell, who incorporated lines by Edwards in more than one of his poems.

Although the metaphysical concept is useful in considering Edwards as a literary artist, it by no means explains all, and there are remarkable sermons in this collection that are valuable, even from a strictly literary perspective, for other things. The greatest literary influence upon Edwards was of course the distinctive language of the Authorized Version or King James translation of the Bible. Edwards has been recognized as a master interpreter of the Bible, and his many scripture proofs of doctrinal points give evidence of his vast knowledge and ingenuity in the use of the sacred Christian texts. However, his response to the power of scriptural rhetoric is also evident, and some of his best sermons offer evidence of direct scriptural inspiration. There are certain patterns evident in his corpus of manuscript sermons indicating, for instance, that the language of Isaiah and Revelation inspired him. In this selection of sermons, *I Know My Redeemer Lives* (1740) best exemplifies Edwards' response to the powerful excitation of Scripture, the textual inspiration of which becomes an organizing force around which Edwards masses some of his most brilliant images and language, not only from the Scripture itself but from some of his own most powerful sermons, such as *Sinners*, and sermons of personal significance, such as the early *Christian Happiness*.[4] Intense personal feeling seems to illuminate the rhetoric of *I Know My Redeemer Lives*, but this quality is often found in those of Edwards' sermons that take their inception from the more poetical books of the Bible like Psalms and Job.

A talk, a complex and subtle theological expression, a work of literature: the Edwards sermon is all these things, preserving the bold and compelling thought of one of America's most creative theological thinkers within an oracular medium which contains the nuances of his voice as well as the brilliant images he employed in striving to make religion a reality in an age that, he believed, had begun to lose the *sense* of religion even while insisting upon its truth.

Edwards' Life and Times

The sermons in this volume begin when Jonathan Edwards was nineteen, a newly licensed preacher and pastor. Though he was young and inexperienced, Edwards' upbringing and education boded well. He was born

4. *Works of Jonathan Edwards, 10, Sermons and Discourses, 1720–1723*, ed. Wilson H. Kimnach (New Haven, Yale Univ. Press, 1992), 296–307.

on October 5, 1703, the only son of the eleven children of the Reverend Timothy and Esther Stoddard Edwards. From birth he was groomed for the ministry through a rigorous preparatory curriculum and revivalist preaching. In the family parlor, which was fitted with benches, Edwards' father ran a small school to prepare local boys for college. Here, aided by his mother and sisters, Jonathan learned Latin, Greek, Hebrew, natural philosophy, and church history. He excelled in natural sciences and had keen powers of observation. One of his favorite objects of study was the "flying spider" that inhabited the area, but he also observed other phenomena, such as rainbows, which formed the basis for college essays. These exercises also provided him with materials for the many sermons he would preach during his career.

In 1716, Edwards enrolled in collegiate studies. So new, and in such disarray, was Connecticut's college that it did not yet have the name (Yale) by which it would become famous, nor did it have a central location. Much of Edwards' undergraduate life centered at Wethersfield under the tutorship of his uncle Elisha Williams. Only in 1719 did Edwards and his fellow classmates take up residence in the newly built college hall in New Haven, where they completed their studies under the guidance of the new rector, Timothy Cutler.

After graduating as the valedictorian of the Yale College class of 1720, Edwards began his graduate studies. To be qualified for a settled ministry, a gentleman had to possess the Master's degree, which meant three years of study beyond the B.A. However, advanced students were freer to pursue their own interests, and Edwards plunged hungrily into the library. Here he discovered newly acquired volumes containing what was known as the New Learning, featuring the great thinkers of the age—Newton, Berkeley, and particularly Locke, whose works Edwards consumed like a "most greedy miser."[5] In the writings of these intellectual giants he found ideas on the nature of mechanical laws, matter, perception, and knowledge that he would fuse to his Reformed theology.

While laboring on his graduate degree, Edwards secured his first preaching post at a small Presbyterian church in New York City. This

5. Samuel Hopkins, *The Life and Character of the Late Reverend Mr. Jonathan Edwards* (Boston, 1765), 4.

post, which he filled during 1722 and 1723, had great advantages for a student-preacher. The smallness of the congregation provided an intimate, familial setting in which Edwards was supported and encouraged. The unofficial ecclesial standing of the church meant that Edwards did not have to spend much time in formal duties. But there would be plenty of time and opportunity for that later. For now, Edwards, recording his efforts to assess his spiritual state in such personal writings as his "Resolutions" and "Diary," could focus on his personal religion. He also incorporated his discoveries freely, in a marvelously self-revelatory fashion, into his sermons. As Edwards himself noted in his "Diary," he did not have any abiding conviction of his sinfulness or of God's wrath. His sermons during this period reflected his lack of a sense of God's "terribleness." As exemplified in *The Way of Holiness*, they are warm, earnest, and optimistic, emphasizing the beauty of God and the godly life. So gratifying was this sermon's description of the holy life to Edwards, and so close was this theme to his heart at the time, that a portion of it became the first entry of a new private notebook, which he called the "Miscellanies." Unfortunately, Edwards' nearly ideal situation in New York made it difficult for the congregations he would serve later in life to measure up to this first, formative experience. Decades later, he would still remember fondly the friends he had made there and the grand, panoramic view of the Hudson River from the highlands north of New York City.

In the spring of 1723 he returned home, melancholy with the realization that his life was to change dramatically in the near future. Over the summer he finished his Master's disquisition, or *Quaestio* (a response, in Latin, to a theological question) to be delivered in September at the college commencement as the final requirement of his education.[6] However, the conditions under which Edwards had to stand before the assembled townspeople, faculty, dignitaries, and fellow students were electrically charged. At the previous year's commencement, Cutler, the man in whom the colony had so willingly placed its trust to preserve its Puritan heritage, had shocked his audience when he closed the proceedings with the traditional phrase from the Anglican Book of Common Prayer, "And

6. *The Works of Jonathan Edwards, 14, Sermons and Discourses, 1723–1729*, ed. Kenneth P. Minkema (New Haven: Yale University Press, 1997), 47–66.

let the people say, Amen." In today's climate of easy liturgical borrowing, such a statement would go almost unnoticed, but in a colony founded by Puritans as a haven from Anglican oppression, those few words signaled heresy. Along with one of the tutors and several area ministers, Cutler afterward announced his decision to join the Church of England. This Great Apostasy, as it came to be known, was not to be borne. Cutler and the tutor were forced to resign, leaving Yale College leaderless and in turmoil.

The persecutions under Archbishop Laud in the early seventeenth century were still fresh in the New England memory. Yet this was only one reason for the third- and fourth-generation descendants of the original founders of the New England Puritan colonies to hate and fear the Church of England. After nearly a century of relative religious and political autonomy, rumors of the establishment of an American episcopate were rampant. To the people of New England, this represented immediate royal control and with it, conformity to the national church. Even more, the Church of England was viewed by the colonists as theologically liberal at best, having largely abandoned its original Calvinism. At its worst, the Church of England, with its "popish" rituals, was an arm of Rome and a servant of Antichrist.

Such was the climate of local and transatlantic controversy in which Edwards, as a student at the very western rim of the British Empire, delivered his Master's oration on the centrality of justification by faith alone through Christ's righteousness. Any who think that God's anger is appeased simply by the sinner's "sincere repentance" rather than by the free bestowal of divine grace, Edwards asserted, is guilty of making a "new law." While the doctrine may seem conventional enough, it signaled Edwards' embarkment on a personal campaign to defend New England Calvinism from Anglican corruption and oppression. A half-century before the outbreak of the American Revolution, Edwards had declared theological and ideological war against the mother country.

With his diploma in hand and his mission clear, Edwards temporarily ministered at Bolton, a town in eastern Connecticut, during late 1723 and early 1724. He migrated from position to position over the next few years; nonetheless, the period was one of intense intellectual growth for him. A central concept he developed during the Bolton pastorate was that of excellency, as first enunciated in a series of notes on "The Mind." The excellency of something, Edwards argued, consisted in its similarity or relation to something else. Thus the excellency of believers consists in their conformity to God and divine commands. But excellency can also be found in the harmony, peace, and order that reside in the faculties of regenerate human beings, a point he pursues in *The Pleasantness of Religion*. The good and the beautiful, he argued there, are the same thing.

In May 1724 Edwards accepted an appointment as a tutor at Yale College. The college was still in disarray and without a rector. To the trustees, it must have seemed a natural step to call on their newly minted graduate, who had so bravely defended the central Reformation tenet the year before. But his responsibilities were many. From the outset, Edwards wrote in his "Diary" that he faced "despondencies, fears, perplexities, multitudes of cares, and distraction of mind. . . . I have now, abundant reason to be convinced, of the troublesomeness and vexation of the world, and that it never will be another kind of world."[7] With the other tutor, his uncle Daniel Edwards, Jonathan Edwards kept the college going and restored public confidence in it. After one and a half hectic and exhausting years, Edwards was left emotionally and physically debilitated and spent the last months of 1725 recuperating from a breakdown at a relative's house outside New Haven.

Edwards ended his tutorship—no doubt with much relief—in August 1726, when he was called to Northampton to assist his aging and revered grandfather Solomon Stoddard. There he completed his training under Stoddard's watchful eye, composing sermons for many different occasions, including lectures, sacraments, and civic holidays (such as an annual day of thanksgiving, which Americans still celebrate every November). In early 1729 his grandfather died, leaving Edwards as the sole pastor of the large congregation.

After Stoddard's death, Edwards worked at establishing his own agenda for Northampton. He preached on the means and nature of grace and on the sovereignty of God, among other things. He also continued his

7. *Works, 16*, 786.

criticisms of liberal theology that were begun with his Master's *Quaestio. God Glorified in Man's Dependence* is a frontal attack on the notion that sinners can be saved by the merit of their good works. Though *God Glorified* was first preached in Northampton in the fall of 1730, Edwards subsequently delivered it in Boston at the prestigious Thursday lecture on July 8, 1731. Before the assembled clergy of Boston—to Edwards' mind New England's liberal stronghold—he affirmed the sovereignty of God in the work of redemption. The publication of *A Divine and Supernatural Light* three years later, one of Edwards' best efforts to describe the effect of God's renovating grace on the soul, raised and broadened the scope of his critique.

Edwards' preaching soon began to fall on sympathetic ears. In 1734 and 1735, Northampton experienced an unprecedentedly fervent revival. Edwards published a description of the awakening in *A Faithful Narrative of the Surprising Work of God*, a work that made him an international figure and the town a model for evangelism. A sterling memorial of the revival, and a key piece for understanding Edwards' christology, *The Excellency of Christ* was preached for a sacrament day in August 1736. Here he not only utilizes the concept of excellency developed earlier in such sermons as *The Pleasantness of Religion*, he joins the topic with the celebration of the Lord's Supper. In a religious culture heavily dependent on the sermon, the sacraments of baptism and the Lord's Supper nonetheless provided crucial focal points for piety in early New England, as the sacramental meditations of the Westfield, Massachusetts, pastor and poet Edward Taylor so beautifully demonstrate. Like his grandfather Stoddard, who had taught that the Lord's Supper was a "converting ordinance," Edwards made the sacrament a powerful means of revival.

The period from 1736 to 1739 in many ways represented the apex of Edwards' preaching. During this time he delivered a brilliant, ambitious sermon series on the parable of the ten virgins (Matt. 25) and *The History of the Work of Redemption* (published posthumously). Another lengthy sermon series he delivered in 1738 was later published as *Charity and Its Fruits*. In the final sermon from this series, *Heaven Is a World of Love*, Edwards paints an ideal picture of heaven as characterized by social harmony, dynamic progress in knowledge of things divine, and eternal praise. This sermon also reveals how many of Edwards' public statements arose from personal reflections. In his "Personal Narrative" (Edwards' own summary of his spiritual experience written only a year after the *Charity* sermons), he noted that as a young man his "sense of divine things" had increased dramatically. One special object of contemplation was the afterlife. He wrote, "The heaven I desired was a heaven of holiness; to be with God, and to spend my eternity in divine love, and holy communion with Christ. . . . Heaven appeared to me exceeding delightful as a world of love."[8]

During the late 1730s, however, the town of Northampton was hardly a world of love. These years were marked by strained relations between Edwards and his congregation. A new meetinghouse, for example, completed in 1737, gave preferential seating to the wealthiest in town. Edwards unsuccessfully resisted this departure from tradition, which gave the oldest and most "useful" church members the best seats. Even as Edwards rhapsodized on the excellencies of Christ and the glories of heaven, he repeatedly vented his frustration with his people for their failure to sustain the godly behavior and concern for religion that he had seen during 1734 and 1735. It was clear to Edwards that many of the so-called conversions had been false. Whenever he could, he compared the present contentiousness, greed, and worldliness of his parishioners with their harmony and selflessness during the earlier revival.

In 1739 Edwards began to work strenuously for a new revival. *The Importance and Advantage of a Thorough Knowledge of Divine Truth*, preached in that year, shows him trying to establish a new foundation for his listeners. Here he exhorted them to a love of learning about divine things and gave them practical advice on how to obtain it. In addition, he sought to make a philosophical distinction between mere rational knowledge and spiritual knowledge, a sort of perception and understanding to which only the regenerate were entitled. Practically speaking, Edwards was telling his congregation that in their efforts to acquire knowledge of the ways of God, they should seek this higher, spiritual knowledge.

Through the first half of 1740, Edwards continued his efforts to reignite

8. Ibid., 795–96.

the awakening spirit among his congregation. Edwards' optimism was fed by reports he had heard of the success of the Reverend George Whitefield, an English itinerant who would become one of the most significant Christian evangelists of modern history. In February, Edwards wrote to Whitefield requesting that he stop at Northampton during his upcoming tour of New England. Writing as one expert on revivalism to another, Edwards stated, "I believe I may venture to say that what has been heard of your labors and success has not been taken notice of more in any place in New England than here, or received with fuller credit." In a letter to a fellow New England minister, Eleazar Wheelock, Edwards expressed his hope that Whitefield's visit would be for "good to my soul, and the souls of my people."[9] *The Reality of Conversion*, preached in July, builds on past revivalistic experience while anticipating Whitefield's response.

Edwards' wish was fulfilled. Whitefield did indeed come to Northampton in October 1740 and preached there several times to a packed meetinghouse and weeping audiences who hung on his every word. Edwards reported that "the congregation was extraordinarily melted by every sermon; almost the whole assembly being in tears for a great part of sermon time."[10] In his published journals, Whitefield reported that even Edwards wept openly. The Great Awakening, as the revivals of the 1740s came to be known, had swept up Northampton and its pastor in its seemingly irresistible tide. It would forever change the nature of religion in America by democratizing religious experience and spawning new movements. Ironically, it would also propel Edwards and his congregation into a downward spiral that would end in his dismissal.

Now that the revival spark had been rekindled, Edwards sought to fan the flames. *Sinners in the Hands of an Angry God* is possibly one of the most affecting sermons ever preached in the English language. In it, Edwards collected the familiar biblical and natural images that had filled his sermons for years, but now developed with unprecedented intensity. The people of Northampton, already accustomed to these themes, did not respond to the sermon when Edwards first preached it. But when Edwards repreached it at Enfield (then a part of Massachusetts but later

9. Ibid., 81, 86.
10. Ibid., 116.

transferred to Connecticut) on July 8, 1741, the reaction was extraordinary. The Reverend Stephen Williams, pastor of Longmeadow, Massachusetts, and Edwards' cousin, was one of the ministers seated by the pulpit when Edwards preached. In his diary, Williams recorded the reaction of the congregation:

> before ye Sermon — was done there was a great moaning — & crying out throught ye whole House — what shall I do to be Sav^{d} — oh I am going to Hell — oh what shall I do for a christ &c &c — So y^{t} ye minister — was oblig^{d} to desist — shreiks & crys — were piercing & Amazing — after Some time of waiting — the congregation were still So y^{t} a prayr was made . . . & after that we descend^{d} from the pulpitt and discours^{d} — with the people — Some in one place & Some in another — and Amazing & Astonishing — ye powr — God was Seen — & Severall Souls were hopfully — wrought upon y^{t} — night & oh ye pleas^{nt}ness of their countenances — y^{t} receiv^{d} comfort.[11]

The people of Enfield on that day were treated to nothing short of a spiritual revolution. Edwards had gathered powerful images, which he had infused with a new starkness modeled on the extemporaneous, emotional preaching of itinerants like Whitefield and Gilbert Tennent of Pennsylvania. Yet *Sinners* shows Edwards going far beyond Whitefield, Tennent, and their like in his appreciation of how words convey to the mind and heart certain ideas and associations. His grafting of Locke and Newton onto Calvin and William Ames had yielded its choicest sermonic fruit.

After Enfield, Edwards became a chief apologist for the revivals against critics who claimed that the revivals were false and even demonic and feared the activities of such radicals as James Davenport of New London, who had instigated the public burning of irreligious books. In treatises like *The Distinguishing Marks of a Work of the Spirit of God* (1741), *Some Thoughts Concerning the Present Revival of Religion in New England* (1742), and *Religious Affections* (1746)—still consulted to this day by revivalists worldwide—Edwards sought to vindicate the divine origins of the

11. Stephen Williams, Diary, typescript, Storrs Library, Longmeadow, Massachusetts, 375–76.

revival and to formulate criteria for determining true conversion from counterfeit. In *Religious Affections*, particularly, he stresses persevering in holy behavior—the "fruits" of faith—as a sign of grace.

The emphasis on behavior would become a hallmark of Edwards' conversion theology, refined and tempered in the crucible of two awakenings. *I Know My Redeemer Lives* was preached in October 1740, immediately after Whitefield's departure. A frequent itinerant himself, Edwards deemed this sermon worthy of repreaching at least three times after giving it at Northampton. While the sermon seems to repeat Whitefield's assertion that believers can attain complete assurance of salvation, Edwards' focus in the sermon shows his departure from Whitefield on at least this issue. In the Application, for example, Edwards emphasizes that it is only through long-term manifestation and practice of "holy fruits" that the believer can achieve assurance—but never any absolute certainty—of salvation.

For Edwards, one of the key fruits of faith was almsgiving. Whatever misgivings Edwards had about Whitefield as a theologian, he recognized the "Grand Itinerant" as a true instrument of God and an effective organizer of charitable projects. Many of the proceeds from Whitefield's ministry went to support the orphanage he had established at Bethesda, Georgia. *Much in Deeds of Charity* is a "contribution" lecture that may well have had as its goal raising money for Whitefield's orphanage or for some other benevolent purpose. An affluent congregation, the church of Northampton was regularly called upon to make donations to various causes, such as support for indigent and needy individuals in town (as required by Massachusetts law) or for the establishment of an Indian mission at Stockbridge in the 1730s. In this sermon, Edwards not only mentions Whitefield's orphanage but also its model, the charitable center established in 1704 at Halle in Saxony by the German Pietist clergyman August Hermann Francke, which included an orphanage, a dispensary, teacher-training schools, a Bible institute, and a printing house.

Sermons like *Much in Deeds of Charity* clearly demonstrate the international perspective Edwards had achieved. He actively sought out information regarding the progress of religion throughout the world. His curiosity led him to correspond with English and Scottish ministers and to participate in the international Concert of Prayer, a movement that organized quarterly days of prayer for revival.

But as with the earlier awakening of 1734–35, the new revivals did not last. After 1742 Edwards and his congregation became more and more alienated from each other. In an effort to recapture the revival spirit and promote godly behavior, Edwards forced the congregation in March 1742 to adopt an expanded version of its church covenant (one that proved critical of many of the town's business practices); many thought it unnecessary and resented their pastor for it. From there, things grew worse. In humiliating fashion, Edwards was compelled to give an accounting of his expenditures when his family was accused of being extravagant. In 1744, long convinced that immorality among the young people of the town was rampant, Edwards launched a counter offensive by investigating reports that several young men were distributing an illustrated midwifery book and harassing young women. Unfortunately, his heavy-handedness only caused more resentment, and the accused got off with light punishments. A few years later, when a young woman of the town had twins by the son of a prominent family (related to Edwards), Edwards insisted on making the case public in order to force the two to marry. As it turned out, neither family wanted that, and the mother was content with the sum of money the father's family had given her.

Then, in 1748, the bubble burst. Edwards announced that he could no longer follow the church's traditional method of bringing applicants into full membership. His decision was in theory the result of a long process of study and contemplation that took into account the lessons learned during the revivals. In practice, it was also fueled by a failed relationship. Shepherding hundreds of souls, and seeing many fall away after supposed conversions and admission to the church, led Edwards to the conclusion that the requirements for entering the church needed to be stricter. Rather than reciting a short formulaic statement that had been used since Stoddard's time, Edwards wished applicants to give a profession "of the things wherein godliness consists." The townspeople, as well as his opponents in surrounding towns, interpreted his change of position to mean that he required proof of conversion and that he, as minister, was the only person qualified to judge.

The rancorous debate that ensued over the qualifications for communion stretched out over a two-year period. The details of Edwards' position were never fully discussed. Instead, the arguments consisted of procedural questions: whether to call an advisory council, who should be on the council, and what questions the council should address. The town leaders wanted Edwards gone. As a weary Edwards wrote to his disciple and friend, the Reverend Joseph Bellamy, "There have been abundance of meetings about our affairs since you was here: society meetings, and church meetings, and meetings of committees; of committees of the parish and committees of the church; conferences, debates, reports, and proposals drawn up, and replies and remonstrances."[12]

The bitter dispute culminated in Edwards' dismissal in June 1750. On June 22, Edwards delivered his *Farewell Sermon*, at once an awe-inspiring portrayal of the Day of Judgment and an indication of Edwards' wounded pride. He drew in vivid detail a picture of Christ sitting in judgment, separating saints on his right from sinners on his left. At that time, Edwards and his congregation would have to appear together before the Judge, and the members would have to give an account of their treatment of God's minister and of his message. Only then would all misrepresentations be cleared up; only then would Edwards, Christ's long-suffering messenger, be vindicated. He was intent on making his opponents think on their ways and repent. Several years later, one of the church leaders—Joseph Hawley, Edwards' cousin—did just that. In a letter published in a newspaper, he acknowledged that the church had behaved wrongly and asked for forgiveness. He also wrote separately to Edwards, which led to a mending of their broken friendship.

However much gratification Edwards may have garnered from his *Farewell Sermon*, he and his large family were nonetheless "thrown on the wide world." But he was not without recourse. Friends in Virginia and Scotland offered him pulpits, but he turned them down. In 1751 Edwards assumed his new position at the mission in Stockbridge. Here he ministered to Mahican (or Stockbridge) and Mohawk Indians as well as to a small English congregation. Though opposed at nearly every step by

12. Ibid., 308.

some of the English landowners—many of them members of the Williams clan, relatives of Edwards' who had been instrumental in his departure from Northampton—Edwards proved a tireless advocate for the Indians. Determined not to be run out of another position, he also tenaciously defended his own prerogatives. For his first few years at Stockbridge, he spent much of his time shoring up support for the mission and rectifying long-standing abuses. Between keeping tabs on his opponents in town, meeting with Indian and English leaders, writing innumerable reports—to the Boston overseers of the mission, to provincial officials, and to English benefactors—preaching to diverse congregations, and educating Indian children, Edwards hardly found Stockbridge a sylvan retreat. The circumstances under which Edwards composed some of the most important theological treatises in the history of American thought make his accomplishments all the more impressive.

Two sermons from early in the Stockbridge period represent Edwards the missionary. That Edwards has been under appreciated in this role is reflected in the fact that none of his Indian sermons has ever been published. The sermons printed here, one to the Mahicans and the other to the Mohawks, are the first such texts to be made available.

These sermons are distinctive in several respects. The first thing that one notices about them is that they *look* different from Edwards' sermons to English audiences. Gone are the divisions between sections and a formal statement of doctrine. Gone, too, are lengthy developments of heads and subheads. Instead, Edwards speaks concisely. The form and style of the Indian sermon was dictated by the necessity of preaching through a translator, John Wauwaumppequunnaunt, a Mahican Christian who had formerly worked with the missionary David Brainerd, whose *Life* Edwards published in 1749. To be effective in his preaching to the Indians, Edwards realized that he had to keep his statements brief and to the point.

Edwards' attitude toward the Indians was, for the most part, that of a typical eighteenth-century European: paternalistic and superior. For example, he refers to the Indians as "infants," an indication of how he viewed them both spiritually and culturally. Yet he was influenced by his interactions with the Indians and came to identify with them. When addressing them he spoke candidly about competition for Indian allegiance among European settlers. He explicitly referred to, and criticized, French, Dutch, and even other English efforts to acculturate and Christianize the Indians. Indeed, the occasion for his August 16, 1751, sermon to the Mohawks was the signing of a treaty between the tribe and English representatives, as Edwards' prologue, mentioning "these honorable gentlemen" (meaning the provincial representatives), makes clear. This treaty provided for members of the tribe to live at Stockbridge and for the education of their children in the mission school. Implicit in its provisions was a political and military alliance with the English. And Edwards was keenly aware of the relationship of the political and religious spheres in his work with the Indians. So astute, in fact, were his analyses that one of his reports made its way to the archbishop of Canterbury.

After seven years at Stockbridge, Edwards received an invitation to become the president of the College of New Jersey in Princeton, as the successor of his late son-in-law Aaron Burr. Edwards had been a strong supporter of the college's founding and had functioned as an advisor through its early years. Now the trustees looked to him for leadership, and, after being released from his duties at Stockbridge, he took up the task. Soon after his arrival, a smallpox epidemic in the area made it necessary for Edwards to take an inoculation, but the serum was infected, and he died on March 22, 1758, after an illness of several weeks. The attending physician, William Shippen, wrote: "Never did any Person expire with more perfect freedom from pain, not so much as one distorted hair but in ye most proper sense of the Words, he really fell asleep—for Death had certainly lost its Sting, as to him."[13] Edwards was gone, but his voluminous writings, including his many sermons, remained to influence generations of Americans.

The Theological Aims of Edwards' Preaching

By twentieth-century standards, Edwards was a very theological preacher. Few pastors today would spend an hour delivering a sermon that focuses

13. William Shippen to Sarah Pierpont Edwards, Mar. 22, 1758, Edwards Papers, f. 1756–1759.C.1, Franklin Trask Library, Andover Newton Theological School.

closely on a single religious doctrine. But Edwards did this regularly, usually two or three times a week, over the years providing his people with a well-rounded theological system. Edwards was also much more of a traditional Calvinist than is common today. He drank deeply at the well of early modern "Reformed" Protestantism and committed himself wholeheartedly to its leading theological principles: he viewed the sovereignty of God as the most basic fact of human existence and sought to submit his life and work to the perfect will of his heavenly Father; he believed in the deep-seated depravity of every wayward human heart and lamented that sin had separated humanity from its Creator; he trusted that God had become incarnate in the person of Jesus Christ, whose life, death, and resurrection had provided an atonement for human sin; and he believed in the power of the Holy Spirit to renovate human lives (both individually and collectively), restoring them to fellowship with their God and empowering them for charitable service.

Whereas Edwards was well-acquainted and adept with the entire range of Reformed theology, however, his primary interest as a pastor was in shepherding souls to heaven. Thus as one reads through Edwards' sermons, one discovers a special interest in the theology of human salvation (soteriology, as it is technically known). In the sermon *The Importance and Advantage of a Thorough Knowledge of Divine Truth*, Edwards declares that "the knowledge of no truth in divinity is of any significance to us, any otherwise than as it some way or other belongs to the gospel scheme, or as it relates to a Mediator." In Edwards' view, God's work in redeeming humanity through the mediatorial suffering and death of Christ provided the key to understanding not just divinity but all life. He believed that "the great work of redemption by Jesus Christ" was "the grand design of God," that God actually "intended the world for his Son's use" in this great, redemptive affair.[14]

Edwards also believed that God worked in redemption in a fairly regular manner, and he often preached in a way that reflected the stages of God's dealings with sinful souls. (Edwards' Calvinist predecessors referred to these stages as the "order of salvation," or *ordo salutis.*) He did

14. *The Works of Jonathan Edwards, 9, A History of the Work of Redemption*, ed. John F. Wilson (New Haven: Yale Univ. Press, 1989), 62, 518.

confess to his "Diary" in an anxious moment of insecurity that his own religious experience had not proceeded "in those particular steps" that had become so normative to the majority of his Puritan ancestors.[15] He insists in *Religious Affections*, moreover, that "no order or method of operations and experiences" in religion "is any certain sign of their divinity."[16] As mentioned above, this reflected his own personal religious experience. But Edwards believed utterly in the trustworthiness of God's covenant promises regarding redemption, and he worked assiduously to discern a reliable pattern or typical "morphology of conversion."[17] Though it was inconceivable to him that God should be bound by such a pattern, and while Edwards' God proved less predictable than that of many of his contemporaries, his respect for God's sovereignty in the matter of saving souls never undermined his commitment to prepare parishioners for divine grace.

Although it may seem obvious to general readers that sermons lie at the center of a preacher's vocation, most scholars have somehow failed to notice this fact as it applies to Edwards. Somewhat surprisingly, they have most often looked to Edwards' major treatises as the supreme sources of his most deeply held ideas. But sermons above all stood as Edwards' favored literary form and his most time-consuming activity. As one whose paramount concern was with God's gracious work of redemption, his ideas—even at their most profound—were evangelical. Thus week in and week out for nearly thirty-five years Edwards preached his way through the problems that troubled him most. Although his treatises provide more extensive coverage of particular theological issues than could be achieved in even the lengthy sermons of colonial New England clergy, virtually all of Edwards' thought was worked out first from the local pulpit (or "desk," as it was called by most sober-minded colonial Calvinists), and the sermons in this volume reflect the range of his most important intellectual concerns.

15. *Works, 16*, 779.

16. *The Works of Jonathan Edwards, 2, Religious Affections*, ed. John E. Smith (New Haven: Yale University Press, 1959), 159.

17. The notion of a Puritan "morphology of conversion" was first developed by Edmund S. Morgan in *Visible Saints: The History of a Puritan Idea* (New York, New York Univ. Press, 1963). On Edwards' appropriation (and truncation) of the traditional morphology, see *Works, 4*, 25–32.

The texts below also reflect Edwards' understanding of the order of salvation and reveal his efforts to speak to people at every stage along the way. In fact, we have chosen to arrange the contents at hand in a manner that represents Edwards' view of God's "usual" method of saving souls rather than chronologically. Beginning with *The Way of Holiness* and *The Pleasantness of Religion*, and through sermons like *Sinners in the Hands of an Angry God*, we see the logic of God's various efforts to convert the wayward from lives of sin. By the time we reach the sublimity of Edwards' *Heaven Is a World of Love*, we discover the wonderful end toward which, in Edwards' view, his hearers' conversions had been directed.

In between, we hope readers will realize that there is a method to Edwards' seeming madness, and that even his most frightening sermons were part of his larger effort to open what he took to be hard and calloused hearts to the love of his gracious and merciful God. Indeed, while the horrifying hellfire of *Sinners* has become by far the best-known element of the entire Edwards corpus, it is important to note that Edwards employed many other measures by which to motivate his listeners to attend to religion. To drive this home, we begin *The Sermons of Jonathan Edwards* with what modern audiences might call "upbeat" sermons. For the young Edwards, these sermons were attempts to describe the truth and beauty of religion as he experienced it.

In the first of these, *The Way of Holiness*, Edwards is not the fatalistic Calvinist many have come to expect. Rather, he calls on his listeners to be warriors of faith, counseling evangelical zeal and unceasing personal striving as ways to force open heaven's door. Although it is true that God sovereignly bestows grace, and we cannot predict who will be saved, it is safe to say that the lazy and lackadaisical will not be among them. Edwards tells his listeners, "The kingdom of heaven must suffer violence; it must be taken by force, or else it never will be taken at all." He argues that "many"—he might have said, especially those in his own Calvinist New England—"are not sensible enough of the necessity of holiness in order to salvation." They stand idly by, rather, and wait passively for the Lord to grant them salvation, failing to recognize that God usually grants grace to those trying to reform their sinful ways. Sinners should not dare "be so foolish as to entertain hopes of heaven," he warns, "except they intend forthwith to set about repentance and reformation of heart and life." Conversion requires exertion. It does not come to the faint of heart. Indeed, sinners "will never reach heaven to eternity except they alter their course, turn about, and steer [toward] another point; for the way is a way of holiness, and the unclean shall not pass over it." What awaits the faithful seeker who finds grace? *The Pleasantness of Religion* evinces Edwards' attempt to allure his audience with the sensuous delights of faith. "It would be worth the while to be religious," he contends, "if it were only for the pleasantness of it." Contrary to the assumptions of the worldly, Christianity actually "sweetens temporal delights." It intensifies earthly pleasures "beyond what wicked and sensual men can find in them."

What are good Calvinists supposed to do, then, who believe that true holiness comes only from God, that sinful humans can do nothing good without first receiving the aid of supernatural grace? With the Puritans, Edwards replies that they are to get "in the way" of grace, taking advantage of the appointed means that God has provided for salvation. The means include practices such as Bible reading, family devotions, listening to sermons, meditation, prayer, and the sacraments (though, significantly, later in his life Edwards would restrict the sacrament of communion to people who had already been converted). But for Edwards, the most important means of grace was theological knowledge (or the knowledge of God).

As he preaches in *The Importance and Advantage of a Thorough Knowledge of Divine Truth*, "there is no other way by which any means of grace whatsoever can be of any benefit, but by knowledge." An intellectually inclined pastor, Edwards regaled his parishioners regularly with the pleasures of the knowledge of "the things of divinity." He taught that these "are the things to know [for] which we had the faculty of reason given us. They are the things which appertain to the end of our being, and to the great business for which we are made." And in a statement that places Edwards in continuity with many of his premodern forebears, particularly those who taught that the field of theology was the "queen of the sciences," he claims that "there are no things so worthy to be known as these things. They are as much above those things which are treated of in other sciences, as heaven is above the earth."

Sinners in the Hands of an Angry God, without which no Edwards anthology would be complete, rhetorically stands in stark contrast to these sermons. Yet it is similar in that it represents a well-meaning warning preached by a man genuinely concerned for his neighbors' souls. This sermon, and many others like it, *were* intended almost literally to scare the hell out of Edwards' listeners, many of whom had grown up under gospel light but had not responded. But these sermons were not sadistic attempts to leave his parishioners in abject fear. Rather, as we hope readers will see in the other types of sermons included here, Edwards' goal was to raise people up from their fears and doubts to a higher reality, and to everlasting peace.

God Glorified in the Work of Redemption was Edwards' first published sermon and, as such, it helped to define the shape of his increasingly public reputation. By 1731, when Edwards preached this famous sermon, he feared that Arminianism had made dangerous inroads into the traditionally Calvinist New England churches, especially in and around Boston. A somewhat slippery term that he often used to designate an attitude of spiritual self-sufficiency, Arminianism represented a significant threat to conservative Calvinists like Edwards himself. So when invited to deliver a public lecture to the Boston-area clergy, he decided to herald the Calvinist doctrine of the absolute sovereignty of almighty God. Arguing that humans stand utterly dependent on their God for eternal salvation, he proclaims in *God Glorified* that the work of redemption is entirely *of* God, *through* God, and *in* God.

Once Edwards had established God's absolute sovereignty in the matter of redemption, however, he pressed equally hard to persuade his hearers to strive toward conversion. "There is such a thing as conversion," he preaches in *The Reality of Conversion*, and "'tis the most important thing in the world." Though no one can earn this experience by meriting God's favor with moral effort, God has called all of us to seek it by applying ourselves with all of our might. In short, though Edwards believed in theory that salvation depended on God's free act of "electing" certain sinners out of the slough of human corruption, in practice he knew that lives did not change without a great deal of moral effort. Although in the abstract, religious conversions took place because God had willed them from eternity, in practice they almost never occurred for those who failed to seek them. Thus Edwards implores, "Labor to be so thorough in the use of means for your conversion that your conscience mayn't hereafter accuse [you] of any willful negligence." And further, "Don't perplex your mind with the secret decrees of God, and particularly about the eternal decrees of God with respect to yourself." Just do your duty, he says, and pray that God will save you in spite of your sins.

Edwards reiterated the importance of means over and over again in Stockbridge, while instructing the Indians there in Christianity and the way of salvation. In *To the Mohawks at the Treaty, August 16, 1751*, he asserts that "religion is the greatest concern of mankind," arguing that "the temporal concerns that they [the English political leaders] treat with you about at Albany from year to year are mere childish trifles in comparison of this." Thus Edwards pleaded with the Indians often to "seek to know the Word of God" and, in *He That Believeth Shall Be Saved*, highlighted the importance of biblical preaching throughout the centuries of salvation history. He steered the Stockbridge Indians away from what he considered their idolatrous heathen animism toward a Protestant Christian monotheism that was mediated by God's Word. Just as in the earliest years of Christianity when many thousands converted from paganism, "Christ was the light of the world" that continued to shine on what Edwards deemed heathen superstition. Then and now, he declares, "the preaching of the gospel was like the rising of the sun in the morning that drove away all darkness and filled the world with light."

The theme of light takes center stage in what is probably Edwards' most beloved sermon, his illustrious exposition on spiritual new birth, *A Divine and Supernatural Light.* To those elected by God from eternity who have prepared themselves for grace, God imparts a wondrously luminous heavenly light, he explains. The Holy Spirit indwells their souls, illuminating their minds with divine truth and instilling "a true sense of the divine excellency of the things revealed in the Word of God." God's Spirit begins to "[act] in the mind of a saint as an indwelling vital principle." As Edwards describes it, "he unites himself with the mind of a saint, takes him for his temple, actuates and influences him as a new, supernatural principle of life and action." When this happens, one is born again and begins to see everything anew. For the first time, the convert is convinced in an "experimental" (many today would say "personal") way of the view of reality revealed in the Bible, for the Holy Spirit infuses within the believer what Edwards liked to call a new sense, a "sense of the heart," by which Christians apprehend God's truth existentially. Just as "there is a difference," Edwards claims (in what has become a classic passage), "between having a rational judgment that honey is sweet, and having a sense of its sweetness," so "there is a difference between having an opinion that God is holy and gracious, and having a sense of the loveliness and beauty of that holiness and grace." Many nominal Christians, according to Edwards, have only a "head knowledge" of the things of religion. But the illumination of the Holy Spirit persuades the heart.

In spite of the conviction that Edwards believed should pervade the heart of a born-again Christian, however, there were plenty of people in his own parish who remained quite worried about the state of their souls. As one can imagine, Edwards' tendency to insist simultaneously on divine sovereignty *and* human responsibility bred anxiety in spiritual seekers who believed in the hellfire Edwards preached. If the minister was right that God redeemed only those predestined to this honor, then how was one to know whether one's moral effort would prove efficacious? Further, what grounds did practicing Christians have to believe that their heartfelt faith had not been misplaced in something other than the utterly transcendent God of the Bible? In *I Know My Redeemer Lives*, Edwards attempts a workable answer, suggesting that a reasonable—though never total—assurance of one's salvation was not only possible but should be sought. As a sensitive and experienced pastor, he knows that "as long as the saints are at a loss whether Christ is their Redeemer or no, it tends to make 'em afraid to take comfort." But in response to this fear, Edwards pledges that God wishes to give us peace of mind. With Job of old, then, Christians should "seek that assurance of faith" they so desperately need. "'Tis not a privilege attainable only by a few," Edwards claims, "but that which in the use of proper means might ordinarily be obtained by the saints." In fact, for people to enjoy "this glorious privilege," only "four things are ordinarily requisite": first, "that troublers [hidden or secret sins] be cast out and kept out"; second, "that grace be not in low degrees"; third, "an abounding in holy fruits"; and fourth, "frequent and strict self-examination." Those who meet these requirements need not worry about their salvation; for though he is inscrutable and sovereign, God is not trying to play tricks with human souls. Those sincere about their faith who truly believe that God has redeemed them can and should proclaim with Job, "'I know that my Redeemer lives.'"

For Edwards, the most reliable signs that one has been redeemed always revolve around the practice of living a new life in Jesus Christ, the resurrected Savior of the world with whom Christians dwell in mystical union. Significantly, Edwards became the first major Reformed thinker since the Reformation era to place such a high premium on the doctrine of what scholastic (or academic) theologians called in Latin the *unio Christi.* And while his best-known christological sermon, *The Excellency of Christ*, was intended primarily as a beautiful portrait that would attract his hearers to its subject, it also presents a compelling view of the benefits of union with Christ. "Christ will give himself to you," Edwards promises, "with all those various excellencies that meet in him." You "shall behold his glory, and shall dwell with him, in most free and intimate communion." Christians will continue to sin and thus, here on earth, their union with Christ will remain imperfect. Nevertheless, they will enjoy "an immensely higher, more intimate, and full enjoyment of God, than otherwise could have been."

The most important earthly benefit of the believers' union with Christ is that it empowers them for works of charity or Christian love. In his widely read treatise on the *Religious Affections*, Edwards became famous for stressing this benefit, employing it as a barometer for gauging the spirituality of religious seekers. But he also developed this theme in a substantial number of weekly sermons, one of which we have published for the first time here. In *Much in Deeds of Charity*, Edwards focuses on the relation between works of charity and what he calls "spiritual discoveries." He shows that not only are deeds of charity a natural outgrowth of union with Christ, and not only are they the best "way to obtain assurance" of one's salvation, but they are also the most likely way to enhance an ongoing relationship with Christ and to facilitate the process of further discovery in one's spiritual life. "If we would obtain any great benefits at the hand of God for what we do in deeds of charity," he writes, "we must not only do something but we must be liberal and bountiful, free-hearted and open-handed." Edwards makes clear, then, that he is not talking about the hypocritical or half-hearted charity of comfortable Christians but the earnest efforts of those who feel enormous gratitude for God's saving grace. "Though we can't now be charitable to Christ in person," he exclaims, "yet we may be charitable to Christ now, . . . for, though Christ is not here, he has left others in his room to be his receivers, and they are the poor, and has told us that he shall look upon what is done to them as done to him." Edwards promises that "if we will feed Christ with the food of our houses, even outward food, Christ will reward us by feeding us with the food of his house, which is spiritual food. He will feed us with the angels' food . . . of spiritual discoveries and divine comforts." To those who sought the Spirit's presence in that age of fervent revival, then, Edwards advised a very concrete life of love.

If we do not perform those acts of charity that stem from our union with Christ, however; if we fail to heed the warnings of our clergy to turn to God, the same Savior in whose glorious excellencies the regenerate dwell with joy will become an awesome and fearful judge who renders a verdict of everlasting punishment. It took great courage (indeed, great gall) for Edwards to preach in his *Farewell Sermon* to the people of Northampton—the very people who had recently fired him—that on Judgment Day the clergy would assist the Lord in judging their flocks. But he proclaimed this theme in a parting shot at his ex-parishioners, enclosing it in the provocative thesis that "Ministers and the people that have been under their care, must meet one another, before Christ's tribunal." Up to this point, Edwards' entire career might be said to have centered on his longing to steer lost souls away from the course that he believed would lead to their destruction. And he did persist in this endeavor in his *Farewell Sermon*. But the painful wounds his flock had inflicted in the months before this sermon proved too tender for Edwards to preach with his usual charity and equanimity. Instead, striking fear into the hearts of those who have dared to question his authority, he announces that whereas Judgment Day will prove glorious for those who have lived their lives in Christ, it will be nothing short of horrific for those who have not.

Edwards was never one to give the final word to the forces of evil, however, and we have decided accordingly to end this volume with his most vivid depiction of heaven. Even on Judgment Day, he thought, there would be much joy among the redeemed, and in heaven that joy would reach its culmination. Edwards was always wont to advise that the saints need not fear the fires of hell, for their Redeemer had prepared them a place of eternal bliss and undying love. Indeed, for Edwards, heaven itself was best described as "a world of love," a world where the charity that had been practiced by those united to Christ while here on earth would become the rule and would be experienced with an unfathomable degree of intensity. In heaven, he explained, "love is always mutual, and the returns are always in due proportion." Heavenly love is never "damped or interrupted by jealousy." In short, in heaven everyone "shall enjoy each other's love in perfect and undisturbed prosperity." Everything "in that world shall conspire to promote their love, and give advantage for mutual enjoyment." In a compelling conclusion to this remarkable sermon, entitled *Heaven Is a World of Love*, Edwards epitomizes the major themes of his theology: "by living a life of love . . . you will be in the way to heaven. As heaven is a world of love, so the way to heaven is the way of love. This will best prepare you for heaven, and make you meet for an inheritance with the saints in that land of light and love. And if ever you arrive at heaven, faith and love must be the wings which must carry you there."

Editing the Texts

The text of Edwards' sermons is reproduced here as originally written in manuscript, without later emendations; or, if Edwards published a sermon himself, as it was printed in the first edition; or as it appears in the earliest posthumous edition. Dates of the selections are provided in parentheses after the titles. In order to present this text to modern readers, several technical adjustments have been made, including the regularization of spelling, punctuation, and capitalization. Lacunae caused by manuscript damage as well as by Edwards' omissions are filled by insertions in square brackets. Textual intervention to regularize Edwards' citation of Scripture includes the correction of erroneous citations, the regularizing of citation form, and the completion of quotations that Edwards' textual markings indicate should be completed. In the latter case, the supplied text is in curly brackets.

Acknowledgements

The editors would like to express their appreciation to George M. Marsden, Harry S. Stout, Kyle P. Farley, and Carole S. Kimnach for commenting on drafts of the introduction, as well as to Otto Bohlmann and Susan Laity of Yale University Press for guiding the volume through production.

Five of the following sermons (*The Reality of Conversion, To the Mohawks at the Treaty, August 16, 1751, He That Believeth Shall Be Saved, I Know My Redeemer Lives*, and *Much in Deeds of Charity*) have never been published before. The manuscripts of these sermons are printed courtesy of the Beinecke Rare Book and Manuscript Library, Yale University.

Chronology of Edwards' Life

1703	October 5, born at East Windsor, Connecticut
1716–20	Undergraduate student at Yale College
1720–22	M.A. student at Yale College
	Begins "Of Being"
1722–23	Minister to Presbyterian church in New York City
	Begins "Resolutions," "Diary," "The Mind," and "The Miscellanies"
1723	October, writes the Spider Letter
	Begins "Notes on the Apocalypse"
	November, agrees to settle as pastor of Bolton, Connecticut
1724	May, begins two-year tutorship at Yale College
1725	Begins "Beauty of the World"
1726	Moves to Northampton, Massachusetts, as colleague of his grandfather Solomon Stoddard
1727	July, marries Sarah Pierpont
1729	February, becomes full pastor of Northampton upon death of Solomon Stoddard
1731	Preaches and publishes Boston lecture, *God Glorified in the Work of Redemption*
1734	Local Connecticut Valley revivals begin
	Preaches and publishes *A Divine and Supernatural Light*
1737	Publishes *A Faithful Narrative of the Surprising Work of God*
1738	Publishes *Discourses on Various Important Subjects* (sermons from the 1734–35 awakening)
	Preaches *Charity and Its Fruits* (pub. 1852)
1739	Preaches *History of the Work of Redemption* (pub. 1774)
	Probable composition of "Personal Narrative"
1740	George Whitefield's first tour of New England
1741	Preaches and publishes *Sinners in the Hands of an Angry God*
	Preaches and publishes *Distinguishing Marks of the Work of the Spirit of God*
1742	Publishes *Some Thoughts Concerning the Present Revival of Religion in New England*

1744	Bad Book Case
1746	Publishes *A Treatise Concerning Religious Affections*
1747	Publishes *An Humble Attempt to Promote Explicit Agreement and Visible Union of God's People in Extraordinary Prayer*
1749	Publishes *An Account of the Life of the Late Reverend David Brainerd*
	Publishes *An Humble Inquiry into the Rules of the Word of God*
1750	June, council of churches votes to dismiss Edwards as pastor of Northampton
	July, preaches *Farewell Sermon*
1751	Settles in Stockbridge, Massachusetts, as local pastor and missionary to Indians
1754	Publishes *Freedom of the Will*
1755	Writes *Concerning the End for Which God Created the World* and *The Nature of True Virtue* (pub. 1765)
1758	Publishes *Original Sin*
	January, assumes office as president of the College of New Jersey
	March 22, dies of smallpox inoculation

Further Reading

Cherry, Conrad. *The Theology of Jonathan Edwards: A Reappraisal.* Garden City, N.Y., Doubleday, 1966; rep. Bloomington, Indiana Univ. Press, 1990.

Daniel, Stephen H. *The Philosophy of Jonathan Edwards: A Study in Divine Semiotics.* Bloomington, Indiana Univ. Press, 1994.

Delattre, Roland A. *Beauty and Sensibility in the Thought of Jonathan Edwards.* New Haven, Yale Univ. Press, 1968.

Fiering, Norman. *Jonathan Edwards's Moral Thought and Its British Context.* Chapel Hill, Univ. of North Carolina Press, 1981.

Gerstner, John H. *Steps to Salvation: The Evangelistic Message of Jonathan Edwards.* Philadelphia, Westminster Press, 1960.

Guelzo, Allen C. *Edwards on the Will: A Century of American Theological Debate.* Middletown, Conn., Wesleyan Univ. Press, 1989.

Hatch, Nathan O., and Harry S. Stout, eds. *Jonathan Edwards and the American Experience.* New York, Oxford Univ. Press, 1988.

Howe, Daniel Walker. *Making the American Self: From Jonathan Edwards to Abraham Lincoln.* Cambridge, Mass., Harvard Univ. Press, 1997.

Jenson, Robert. *America's Theologian: A Recommendation of Jonathan Edwards.* New York, Oxford Univ. Press, 1988.

Kuklick, Bruce. *Churchmen and Philosophers: From Jonathan Edwards to John Dewey.* New Haven, Yale Univ. Press, 1985.

Lee, Sang Hyun. *The Philosophical Theology of Jonathan Edwards.* Princeton, Princeton Univ. Press, 1988.

Lesser, M. X. *Jonathan Edwards: An Annotated Bibliography, 1979–1993.* Westport, Conn., Greenwood Press, 1994.

Lesser, M. X. *Jonathan Edwards: A Reference Guide.* Boston, G. K. Hall, 1981.

Lowance, Mason I., Jr. *The Language of Canaan: Metaphor and Symbol in New England from the Puritans to the Transcendentalists.* Cambridge, Harvard Univ. Press, 1980.

McClymond, Michael J. *Encounters with God: An Approach to the Theology of Jonathan Edwards.* New York, Oxford Univ. Press, 1998.

McDermott, Gerald R. *One Holy and Happy Society: The Public Theology of Jonathan Edwards.* University Park, Pa., Pennsylvania State Univ. Press, 1992.

Miller, Perry. *Jonathan Edwards*. New York, Sloane, 1949; rep. Amherst, Univ. of Massachusetts Press, 1981.

Morimoto, Anri. *Jonathan Edwards and the Catholic Vision of Salvation*. University Park, Pa., Pennsylvania State Univ. Press, 1995.

Murray, Iain H. *Jonathan Edwards: A New Biography*. Carlisle, Pa., Banner of Truth, 1987.

Oberg, Barbara B., and Harry S. Stout, eds. *Benjamin Franklin, Jonathan Edwards, and the Representation of American Culture*. New York, Oxford Univ. Press, 1993.

Smith, John E. *Jonathan Edwards: Puritan, Preacher, Philosopher*. Notre Dame, Ind., Univ. of Notre Dame Press, 1992.

Tracy, Patricia. *Jonathan Edwards, Pastor: Religion and Society in Eighteenth-Century Northampton*. New York, Hill and Wang, 1980.

Westra, Helen P. *The Minister's Task and Calling in the Sermons of Jonathan Edwards*. Lewiston, N.Y., Edwin Mellen Press, 1986.

Winslow, Ola E. *Jonathan Edwards, 1703–1758*. New York, Macmillan, 1940.

The Sermons of Jonathan Edwards

The Way of Holiness (1722)

Isaiah 35:8.
And an highway shall be there, and a way,
and it shall be called the way of holiness;
the unclean shall not pass over it.

This book of Isaiah speaks so much of Christ, gives such a particular account of the birth, life, miracles and passion, and of the gospel state, that it has been called a fifth Gospel. In this chapter is contained a glorious prophecy of the evangelical state:

1. We have a description of the flourishing state of Christ's kingdom in the two first verses, in the conversion and enlightening of the heathen, here compared to a wilderness, and a desert, solitary place: "The wilderness and the solitary place shall be glad for them; and the desert shall rejoice, and blossom as the rose. It shall blossom abundantly and rejoice, even with joy and singing; the glory of Lebanon shall be given unto it, the excellency of Carmel and Sharon, they shall see the glory of the Lord, and the excellency of our God."

2. The great privileges and precious advantages of the gospel, in the five following verses wherein the strength, the courage, the reward, the salvation, the light and understanding, comforts and joys, that are conferred thereby, are very aptly described and set forth: "Strengthen ye the weak hands and confirm the feeble knees. Say to them that are of a fearful heart, Be strong, fear not; behold, your God will come with vengeance, even God with a recompense; he will come and save you. Then the eyes of the blind shall be opened, and the ears of the deaf shall be unstopped. Then shall the lame man leap as an hart, and the tongue of the dumb sing: for in the wilderness shall waters break out, and streams in the desert. And the parched ground shall become a pool, and the thirsty land springs of water: in the habitation of dragons, where each lay, shall be grass with reeds and rushes."

3. The nature of the gospel, and way of salvation therein brought to

light. First, the holy nature of it, in the eighth and ninth verses: "And an highway shall be there, and it shall be called the way of holiness; the unclean shall not pass over it, but it shall be for those: the wayfaring men, though fools, shall not err therein. No lion shall be there, nor any ravenous beast shall go up thereon, it shall not be found there; but the redeemed shall walk there." Second, the joyful nature of it, "And the ransomed of the Lord shall return, and come to Zion with songs and everlasting joy upon their heads: they shall obtain joy and gladness, and sorrow and sighing shall flee away" [v. 10].

Observation 1. Observe in our text the subject spoken, that is, the way to salvation: "An highway shall be there, and a way." This highway is the common and only way to heaven, for the way to heaven is but one. There is none ever get to heaven except they walk in this way: some men don't get to heaven one way and others another, but it is one highway that is always traveled by those that obtain heaven.

It is the same narrow way that Christ tells us of. Some don't go to heaven in a broad way, and others in a narrow; some in an easy and others in a difficult way; some in a way of self-denial and mortification, and others in a way of enjoyment of their lusts and sinful pleasures; some up hill and others down: but the way to heaven is the same, and it is the highway here spoken of. There is only one highway, or common road, and no by-paths that some few go to heaven in, as exceptions from the rest.

If we seek never so diligently, we shall never find out an easier way to heaven than that which Christ has revealed to us. We cannot find a broader way, but if we go to heaven, the way is so narrow that we must rub hard to get along and press forward. The kingdom of heaven must suffer violence; it must be taken by force, or else it never will be taken at all. If we don't go by the footsteps of the flock, we shall never find the place where Christ feeds, and where he makes his flock to rest at noon.

It appears that the way here spoken of is the way of salvation, by the last verse of the chapter. When speaking of this way, it is said, "the ransomed of the Lord shall return and come to Zion," etc. "Zion" is the common appellation by which, in the Old Testament, the church both militant and triumphant is signified.

Obs. 2. In the words observe the holy nature of this way described: first, by the name by which it is called, "the way of holiness"; "and it shall be called the way of holiness." Secondly, the holiness of those that travel in it, and its purity from those that are unclean, or unholy; "the unclean shall not pass over it." No wicked person shall ever travel in this way of holiness. To the same purpose is the next verse, "No lion shall be there, nor any ravenous beast shall go up thereon, it shall not be found there." That is, none of the wicked men of this world, which are like lions or ravenous beasts more than like men: in their eager raging and lustful appetites and evil affections, or by their insatiable covetousness, are like hungry wolves, are violently set upon the world and will have it, whether by right or by wrong. Or make themselves like ravenous beasts by their proud, invidious, malicious dispositions, which is directly contrary to a Christian spirit and temper. They are more like wild beasts than Christians, that are wrongful and injurious, are all for themselves and the satisfying their own appetites, and care nothing for the welfare of others, their fellow-men that are of the same blood, make a god of their bellies, and therein resemble tigers and wolves.

"Now," says the Prophet, "none such shall go upon this highway to Zion; such unclean and ravenous beasts shall not be found there. No, but the redeemed shall walk there, and the ransomed of the Lord shall return and come to Zion." This way is a way of holiness and not to be defiled by wicked persons. That in Rev. 21:27 will serve well for an explication of these words; "And there shall in no wise enter into it anything that defileth, neither whatsoever worketh abomination or maketh a lie, but they which are written in the Lamb's book of life."

DOCTRINE.

Those only that are holy are in the way to heaven.

Many are not sensible enough of the necessity of holiness in order to salvation. Everyone hopes for heaven, but if everyone that hoped for heaven ever got there, heaven by this time would have been full of murderers, adulterers, common swearers, drunkards, thieves, robbers, and licentious debauchers. It would have been full of all manner of wickedness and wicked men, such as the earth abounds with at this day. There would have been those there that are no better than wild beasts, howling wolves, and poisonous serpents; yea, devils incarnate, as Judas was.

What a wretched place would the highest heavens have been by this time if it were so: that pure, undefiled, light and glorious place, the heavenly temple, would be as the temple of Jerusalem was in Christ's time, a den of thieves; and the royal palace of the Most High, the holy metropolis of the creation, would be turned into a mere hell. There would be no happiness there for those that are holy. What a horrible, dreadful confusion would there be if the glorious presence of God the Father; the glorified Lamb of God; and the Heavenly Dove, spirit of all grace and original of all holiness; the spotless, glorified saints; the holy angels; and wicked men, beasts and devils [were] all mixed up together!

Therefore, it behooves us all to be sensible of the necessity of holiness in order to salvation; of the necessity of real, hearty and sincere, inward and spiritual holiness, such as will stand by us forever and will not leave us at death, that sinners may not be so foolish as to entertain hopes of heaven, except they intend forthwith to set about repentance and reformation of heart and life. Wherefore, this is what we are now upon: to show the necessity of holiness, and this we shall do in these three things.

I. Show what holiness is.

II. That those that have it not are not in the way to heaven.

III. The reasons why it must needs be so.

I. What is holiness? I shall answer to this question in three things which fully comprehend the nature of holiness, which are not in themselves distinct as so many parts of holiness, but the same thing in three different lights, to give us the fuller understanding of it.

First. Holiness is a conformity of the heart and the life unto God. Whatever outward appearance men may make by their external actions, as if they were holy, yet if it proceeds not from a most inward, hearty and sincere holiness within, it is nothing. Amaziah did that which was right in the sight of the Lord, but not with a perfect heart [II Kgs. 14:1–20]; all that he did was not acceptable to God, who searcheth the hearts and trieth the reins of the children of men, and must be worshipped in spirit and in truth.

And whatever holiness they may pretend to have in their hearts, whatever hypocritical pangs of affection they may have had, it is all to no purpose except it manifest itself in the holiness of their lives and conversations: Jas. 1:26–27, "If any man among you seem to be religious, and bridleth not his tongue but deceiveth his own heart, this man's religion is vain. Pure religion and undefiled before God and the Father is this, to visit the fatherless and widows in their affliction, and to keep himself unspotted from the world." And in the second chapter, eighteenth verse: "Yea, a man may say, Thou hast faith, and I have works: show me thy faith without thy works, and I will show thee my faith by my works." And in the nineteenth [and] twentieth verses, "Thou believest that there is one God; thou doest well: the devils also believe and tremble. But wilt thou know, O vain man, that faith without works is dead?" So that there must be a conformity of both heart and life to God, in order to true holiness.

Holiness is the image of God, his likeness, in him that is holy. By being conformed unto God is not meant a conformity to him in his eternity, or infinity, or infinite power. These are God's inimitable and incommunicable attributes; but a conformity to his will, whereby he wills things that are just, right, and truly excellent and lovely; whereby he wills real perfection, and goodness; and perfectly abhors everything that is really evil, unjust, and unreasonable. And it is not only a willing as God wills, but also a doing as he doth: in acting holily and justly and wisely and mercifully, like him. It must become natural thus to be, and thus to act; it must be the constant inclination and new nature of the soul, and then the man is holy, and not before.

Second. It is a conformity to Jesus Christ. Christ Jesus is perfectly conformed unto God, for he is God. He is his express image. Now Christ is nearer to us in some respects than God the Father, for he is our Mediator and is more immediately conversant with us; John 1:18, "No man hath seen God at any time; the only begotten Son, who is in the bosom of the Father, he hath declared him." Jesus Christ, he has been with us in the flesh and as one of us he appeared in the form of a servant, and we have seen his holiness brightly shining forth in all his actions. We have seen his holy life; we have a copy drawn, and an example set for us.

Now holiness is a conformity unto this copy: he that copies after Jesus Christ, after that copy which he has set us and which is delivered to us by the evangelists, is holy. He that diligently observes the life of Christ in the

New Testament need not be at a loss to know what holiness is. Christ commands us to follow his example: Matt. 11:29, "Take my yoke upon you and learn of me, for I am meek and lowly in heart, and ye shall find rest unto your souls."

Have you ever read the four Gospels, and did you not observe in the life of Christ wonderful instances of humility, love to God, love to religion; wonderful instances of zeal for God's glory, steadfastness in resisting temptations, entire trust and reliance on God, strict adherence to all his commands; astonishing instances of condescension, humility, meekness, lowliness, love to men, love to his enemies, charity and patience? Why, this is holiness. When we imitate Christ in these things, then are we holy, and not till then.

Third. Holiness is a conformity to God's laws and commands. When all God's laws without exception are written in our hearts, then are we holy. If you can go along with David in Psalm 119, where he speaks of his love and delight in God's law, in your own experience; when a man feels in some good measure what David declares concerning himself towards the law of God, then may God's law be said to be written in his heart. By God's law I mean all his precepts and commands, especially as they are delivered to us in the gospel, which is the fulfillment of the law of God. If you feel Christ's Sermon upon the Mount engraven on the fleshly tables of your hearts, you are truly sanctified.

The new covenant is written in the hearts of those that are sanctified, of which the prophet Jeremiah speaks, 31:31,33, "Behold, the days come, saith the Lord, that I will make a new covenant with the house of Israel, and with the house of Judah. This shall be my covenant, that I will make with the house of Israel; after those days, saith the Lord, I will put my law in their inward parts, and write it in their hearts; and will be their God, and they shall be my people."

The commands and precepts which God has given us are all pure, perfect, and holy. They are the holiness of God in writing, and, when the soul is conformed to them, they have holiness of God upon their hearts; II Cor. 3:3, "Forasmuch as ye are manifestly declared to be the epistle of Christ ministered by us, written not with ink, but with the spirit of the living God; not in tables of stone, but in the fleshly tables of the heart."

When the soul is molded and fashioned according to the image of God, the example of Christ, and the rules of the gospel, then it is holy, and not else.

II. Those that have not this holiness are not in the way to heaven. Those that are not thus conformed to God, to Christ, and God's commands, are not in the way to heaven and happiness; they are not traveling that road; the road they are in will never bring them there. Whatever hopes and expectations they may have, they will never reach heaven to eternity except they alter their course, turn about, and steer [towards] another point; for the way is a way of holiness, and the unclean shall not pass over it. Christ said that it was easier for a camel to go through the eye of a needle, than for a rich man to enter into heaven, but yet he left it absolutely possible with God that it might be; but he said positively and without exception that except a man be born again, he cannot see the kingdom of God. None but those that are holy are in the way to heaven, whatever profession they may make, whatever church they may be in: for in Christ Jesus neither circumcision availeth anything nor uncircumcision, but a new creature.

Whatever external acts of religion they may perform, however they may be constant attendants on the public [or] family worship, and live outwardly moral lives; yea, what is more, if they speak with the tongues of men and angels, though they could prophesy and understand all mysteries and all knowledge, and though they have faith that they can remove mountains; though they bestow all their goods to feed the poor, and though they give their very bodies to be burnt: yet if they have not charity or holiness—which is the same thing, for by charity is intended love to God as well as man—though they have and do all those things, yet they are nothing; they are as a sounding brass or a tinkling cymbal (see I Cor. 13). It is good that we should be thoroughly convinced of the most absolute and indispensable necessity of a real, spiritual, active and vital—yea, immortal—holiness.

III. We shall now, in the third place, give the reasons why none that are not holy can be in the way to heaven, and why those who never are so can never obtain the happiness thereof.

First. 'Tis contrary to God's justice, to make a wicked man eternally happy. God is a God of infinite justice, and his justice (to speak after the manner of men) "obliges" him to punish sin eternally; sin must be punished, the sins of all men must be punished. If the sinner retains his sin, and it is not washed off by the blood of Christ, and he purified and sanctified and made holy, it must be punished upon him. If he is sanctified, his sin has been already punished in the passion of Christ, but if not, it still remains to be punished in his eternal ruin and misery; for God has said that he is a holy and jealous God, and will by no means clear the guilty. It is reckoned amongst the rest of God's attributes which he proclaims in Ex. 34:7 and Num. 14:18.

Second. 'Tis impossible by reason of God's holiness, that anything should be united to God and brought to the enjoyment of him which is not holy. Now is it possible that a God of infinite holiness, that is perfect and hates sin with perfect hatred, that is infinitely lovely and excellent, should embrace in his arms a filthy, abominable creature, a hideous, detestable monster, more hateful than a toad and more poisonous than a viper? But so hateful, base, and abominable is every unsanctified man, even the best hypocrite and most painted sepulchers of them all.

How impossible is it that this should be, that such loathsome beings, the picture of the devil, should be united to God: should be a member of Christ, a child of God, be made happy in the enjoyment of his love and the smiles of his countenance, should be in God and God in them? It is therefore as impossible for an unholy thing to be admitted unto the happiness of heaven as it is for God not to be, or be turned to nothing. For it is as impossible that God should love sin as it is for him to cease to be, and it is as impossible for him to love a wicked man that has not his sin purified, and it is as impossible for him to enjoy the happiness of heaven except God love him, for the happiness of heaven consists in the enjoyment of God's love.

Third. It would defile heaven and interrupt the happiness of the saints and angels. It would defile that holy place, the Holy of Holies, and would fright and terrify the sanctified spirits, and obstruct them in their delightful ecstasies of devotion, and [his] praise would quite confound the heavenly society. How would one unsanctified person interrupt their happiness, and fill those regions all over with the loathsome stench of his sin and filthiness!

Fourth. The nature of sin necessarily implies misery. That soul that remains sinful must of a necessity of nature remain miserable, for it is impossible there should be any happiness where such a hateful thing as sin reigns and bears rule. Sin is the most cruel tyrant that ever ruled, seeks nothing but the misery of his subjects; as in the very keeping [of] God's commands there is great reward, so in the very breaking of them there is great punishment.

Sin is a woeful confusion and dreadful disorder in the soul, whereby everything is put out of place, reason trampled under foot and passion advanced in the room of it, conscience dethroned and abominable lusts reigning. As long as it is so, there will unavoidably be a dreadful confusion and perturbation in the mind; the soul will be full of worry, perplexities, uneasiness, storms and frights, and thus it must necessarily be to all eternity, except the Spirit of God puts all to rights. So that if it were possible that God should desire to make a wicked [man] happy while he is wicked, the nature of the thing would not allow of it, but it would be simply and absolutely impossible.

Thus I have given some reasons of the doctrine, why it must needs be that those that are not holy cannot be in the way to heaven. Many more reasons might be offered, which the time will not allow to take notice of at this time; but these alone would have been enough to certify us that none but those who are holy ever attain to a crown of glory, if God had not expressly said that without holiness no man should see the Lord.

Wherefore, the

APPLICATION.

We shall apply this doctrine in three uses: first, of inference; second, of trial or self-examination; third, of exhortation.

I. [*Use*] of *Inference.* If it be so that none but those that are holy are in the way to heaven, how many poor creatures are there that think they are in the way to heaven who are not? There are many that think that they are undoubtedly in the way to heaven, and without question shall enter there at last, that have not the least grain of true holiness, that manifest none in their lives and conversations, of whom we may be certain that either they have no holiness at all, or that which they have is a dormant, inactive sort—which is in effect to be certain that there is none. There are a great many others that are not so distinctly and plainly perceived, that have nothing but what is external, the shell without the kernel. Vast multitude are of these two kinds.

What a pitiable, miserable condition are they in: to step out of this world into an uncertain eternity, with an expectation of finding themselves exceeding happy and blessed in the highest heaven, and all at once find themselves deceived, and are undeceived, finding themselves sinking in the bottomless pit!

II. [*Use*] of *Trial.* If none are in the way to heaven but those that are holy, let us try and examine ourselves by this doctrine to see whereabouts we are, and see whether or no we are in the way to heaven. To know which way we are going, whether towards Canaan or Egypt, whether towards heaven or hell; for if we think ourselves in the road to heaven, and are going to the place of torment all the while, and continue deceived, without doubt fire and brimstone will undeceive us. If we find ourselves in the broad way to destruction, how dare we stir a step further? If we would know whether we are holy or no, let us try ourselves by these five following things:

First. Meditate on the holiness of God, and see if you cannot see a conformity, a *likeness* in your mind. There is no likeness or comparison in degree—we speak not of that—but yet there is a likeness in *nature* between God and the soul of the believer. The holy soul, when it thinks and meditates upon God's nature, finds a pleasure and delight, because there is an agreeableness in his new nature to the divine perfections. If those that think themselves in the way to heaven, that are unholy in the meantime in their hearts, would compare themselves and their nature to the holy nature of God, such a glorious light as the holiness of God would quickly discover their rottenness and unsoundness.

Second. See if you can see any resemblance in your life to the life of Christ. It is not supposed that ever any copy comes near to this original, nor ever will; but yet they may perceive whether the same spirit, the same temper and disposition, in a lesser degree be in them, that was manifested by the life and conversation of Jesus Christ.

Third. Is there an agreeableness between your souls and the Word of God? The Bible is the epistle of Christ that he has written to us; now, if the same epistle is also written in our hearts that is written in the Scriptures, it may be found out by comparing. Have you love to all God's commands and a respect to them in your actions? Is it your delight to obey and hearken to the will of God? Do you obey them of choice? Is it what you would choose to do if God had not threatened to punish the breach of them?

Fourth. Do you find by a comparison a likeness and agreeableness between your hearts and lives, and the hearts and lives of those holy men that we [are] assured were such by the Word of God? Do you walk with God as Enoch did, [or] distinguish yourselves by your piety in the midst of wicked examples as Noah did? And when you read the lives of Abraham, Isaac, Jacob, Moses, and the prophets, wherein holiness is drawn to the life, you may viewing so exact a picture discover whether you have not the root of the matter in you, though it be much obscurer in you than in them. When we read the Psalms of David, we may clearly see what David's holiness was by that spirit that is breathed there; when we read the Epistles of the apostles, we may know what is a truly evangelical spirit, and whether such a spirit reigns in our souls.

Fifth. Do you in a measure imitate the saints and angels in heaven? They spend their duration to the glory of God; they love him above all things, are delighted with the beauties of Jesus Christ, entirely love one another, and hate sin. And those that are holy on earth have also a resemblance and imitation of them: they are of an heavenly temper, of heavenly lives and conversions.

III. [*Use* of] *Exhortation.* Exhort all to holiness. You have heard what holiness is and of the necessity of it, the absolute necessity in order to escaping hell; what we must have or die forever, must be forever forsaken. Now, nothing is so necessary to us as holiness; other things may be necessary to discover this life, and things that are necessary men will strive for with all their might, if there is a probability of obtaining of them. How much more is that to be sought after, without which we shall [fare] infinitely worse than die ten thousand deaths!

This is motive enough without any other; for what can be a greater motive than necessity? But besides that, if it were not necessary, the amiable and excellent nature of it is enough to make it worthy the most earnest seeking after.

Holiness is a most beautiful, lovely thing. Men are apt to drink in strange notions of holiness from their childhood, as if it were a melancholy, morose, sour, and unpleasant thing: but there is nothing in it but what is sweet and ravishingly lovely. 'Tis the highest beauty and amiableness, vastly above all other beauties; 'tis a divine beauty, makes the soul heavenly and far purer than anything here on earth—this world is like mire and filth and defilement [compared] to that soul which is sanctified—'tis of a sweet, lovely, delightful, serene, calm, and still nature. 'Tis almost too high a beauty for any creature to be adorned with; it makes the soul a little, amiable, and delightful image of the blessed Jehovah. How may angels stand with pleased, delighted, and charmed eyes, and look and look with smiles of pleasure upon that soul that is holy!

Christian holiness is above all the heathen virtue, of a more bright and pure nature, more serene, calm, peaceful, and delightsome. What a sweet calmness, what a calm ecstasy, doth it bring to the soul! Of what a meek and humble nature is true holiness; how peaceful and quiet. How doth it change the soul, and make it more pure, more bright, and more excellent than other beings.

The Pleasantness of Religion (1723)

Proverbs 24:13–14.
My son, eat thou honey, because it is good;
and the honeycomb, which is sweet to thy taste:
so shall the knowledge of wisdom be unto thy soul:
when thou hast found it, then there shall be a reward,
and thy expectation shall not be cut off.

'Tis very probable that Solomon wrote these Proverbs more especially for the use of his children, and particularly of his son that was to be the heir of the kingdom and of the chief of his riches and honors, to give him wisdom that he might be prudent and righteous in all his life. And therefore he so frequently says in this book, "My son do thus," or "Thus, my son, hear the instruction of thy father," "My son, forget not my law," and the like. And so in our text: "My son, eat thou honey, because it is good; and the honeycomb, which is sweet to thy taste: so shall the knowledge of wisdom be unto thy soul: when thou hast found it, then there shall be a reward, and thy expectation shall not be cut off."

Or, [second], he says, "My son," because in teaching these Proverbs he does the part of a father to all those who will be instructed by him, to every reader or hearer of them, because it appertains to fathers more especially to instruct their children and tell them how they shall live and act. He does the part of a tutor to children in writing of these excellent instructions. He is in the room of a father to us, and we who receive instruction from him are in the room of children.

Or, third, because he speaks by the inspiration of the [Holy] Ghost and in the name of God, who is our heavenly Father. And so God is dealing with us as with children in giving of us those blessed instructions, and so says according to his goodness, "My son," that he may thereby draw [us] to hearken to him.

And here we are argued with from our own actions, and God makes use of what we ourselves grant and the principles we in ordinary things act according to. "Eat thou honey, because it is good"; that is, you do eat honey, because it is good. "So shall the knowledge of wisdom be unto thy soul: when thou hast found it, then there shall be a reward, and thy expectation shall not be cut off."

We may take notice in the words of

1. The drift and design of the wise man in these words, that is, to exhort us to seek wisdom. Wisdom in the book of Proverbs, for the most part, is put either for Jesus Christ, the Word, the power and wisdom of God, as in the eighth chapter and other places; or for grace and spiritual wisdom, taking in also a moral prudence, a measure of which is always given to those who have true grace. Both these may be resolved into the same, for true wisdom and grace in the heart is nothing else but Christ dwelling in the wise, the Spirit of Christ in the godly, for they are the temples of Jesus. So in which sense soever we shall take it in these words, it comes to the same thing: for if by wisdom we understand Christ, then the meaning is that Christ is pleasant to the soul when we find him and get an interest in him; or if we understand it of grace in the heart, that grace is sweet and raises pleasure when we obtain it. Grace is obtained at the same moment that Christ is obtained, and the sweetness of grace is little different from the pleasantness of Jesus Christ.

2. Observe the argument that is made use of to persuade us to seek wisdom, that is, the pleasantness of it.

3. The comparison here made use of to enforce this argument upon us, that is, the eating of honey for the sake of its sweetness. "Eat thou honey, because it is good; and the honeycomb, which is sweet to thy taste." We are not to take this as a command but a concession, that is, you do eat honey for the sake of the sweetness of [it]. And there is the same reason why you should seek wisdom and get grace: for however that may seem an insipid thing to you before you have tried it, yet when you have found it, you will find it to be as sweet as honey to you. "So shall the knowledge of wisdom be unto thy soul: when thou hast found it, then there shall be a reward, and thy expectation shall not be cut off."

DOCTRINE.

It would be worth the while to be religious,
if it were only for the pleasantness of it.

You will eat honey, says Solomon, only for the pleasantness of it and because it is sweet to your taste. And there is the same reason it is well worth your while to seek wisdom and grace: for this is as sweet as honey when you have found it.

This I hope to clear up beyond contradiction, and demonstrate beyond objection, by five reasons.

I. Religion does not deny a man the pleasures of sense, only taken moderately and with temperance and a right manner.

II. Religion sweetens temporal delights and pleasures.

III. Because there is no pleasure but what brings more of sorrow than of pleasure, but what the religious man either does or may enjoy.

IV. Religion brings no new trouble upon a man but what brings more of pleasure than of trouble.

V. The religious man enjoys spiritual pleasures that are much better and sweeter than any others.

If all these are true, certain I am that it cannot be denied that there is much the most delight in a religious life, and that 'tis as we say therefore worth the while to be religious, if it were only for the delight and pleasantness of it.

I. Religion does not deny a man the pleasures of sense, only taken moderately and with temperance and in a reasonable manner. God has given us of his redundant bounty many things for the delight of our senses, for our pleasure and gratification. Religion is not a thing that makes these things useless to us, does not cut us off from the enjoyment of them. The sensual man cannot boast of the enjoyment of any kind of gratifications but what the religious man may enjoy as well as he. There are none of the senses but God allows of the gratification of; yea, he has made much provision for their gratification. Religion allows us to take the full comfort of our meat and drink, all reasonable pleasures that are to be enjoyed in conversation or recreation; allows of the gratification of all our natural appetites. And there are none of the five senses but what we are allowed to please and gratify.

Indeed, religion does forbid the wicked man's unreasonable and brutish manner of enjoying sensitive pleasure, which a godly [man] does not desire and no reasonable man would choose. Religion teaches us to use temporal comforts like men and not like brutes, like reasonable creatures and not as if we had nothing else but sense and no understanding.

Religion allows of the enjoyment of sensitive delights temperately, moderately and with reason, but the wicked man gluts himself with them. Any of the delights of this world are abundantly sweeter when taken temperately than when taken immoderately, as he that at a feast feeds with temperance has much greater pleasure of what he eats and drinks than he that gluts himself and vomits it up again. The godly have the prudence to take of earthly delights moderately, but the wicked man, he is unreasonable in it by being so greedy and violent, he presently loses the relish of his pleasure; but the godly takes those things so that the sweet relish of them remains all his lifetime. Prov. 25:16, "Hast thou found honey? eat so much as is sufficient for thee, lest thou be filled therewith, and vomit it." The righteous man has the prudence to eat no more honey than he can digest, and that the relish of it may remain.

II. Religion sweetens temporal delights and pleasures. Religion does not only allow us to enjoy temporal comforts, but adds a new sweetness to them beyond what wicked and sensual men can find in them. When the wicked man pursues sensual delights in a wicked manner, he doth it against his reason and conscience; his flesh drives him on against his mind, his understanding consents not but opposes him in it. So that he enjoys his pleasures with war with himself, his own reason and conscience opposing him, which takes away the sweetness of the pleasure, and his body only is partaker of the pleasure and not his mind. He enjoys pleasures, but there is a sting in them, and conscience roars the while and will not give him peace. His own reason will not let him alone to enjoy them peaceably.

But the godly, taking those delights according to reason and conscience, his internal man consents to his external in the enjoyment of them and partakes with him therein, and it is a pleasant feast that the body and soul enjoy together. His reason, the highest faculty of the man, gives him leave and his conscience commends him in it, and there is no such perplexing disturbance in his breast as the wicked have; but all is done with peace and without the sting of conscience. The reasonable creature never feels better and more easy than when he acts reasonably and like according to the nature of a man, and like consistent with himself.

And as we have already said, the temporal delights of the Christian are much sweeter than the earthly pleasures of the wicked, because they are taken with moderation; so also because they are taken in their own season and, in other respects, right manner. Every[thing] is most beautiful and most pleasant in its season. Snow is not beautiful in summer, or rain in harvest. Eccles. 3:11, "He hath made everything beautiful in his time."

The Christian partakes of the comforts of this life with an honest mind and with singleness of heart. Those things that are enjoyed with an honest mind are much sweeter and pleasanter than the enjoyments of a wicked heart. We read in the second [chapter] of Acts, at the last verse, that the primitive Christians "did eat their meat with gladness and singleness of heart." Prov. 16:8, "Better is a little with righteousness than great revenues without right."

The wicked man, though he has the pleasures of this life, yet he partakes of them with fear. He lives in a slavish fear, all his days, of death and hell. He eats and drinks with fear, in fear, and this takes away much of the delight of what he enjoys. Though a man be rich and fares sumptuously, yet if he eats and drinks in fear of his life, this takes away all the comfort of his riches. If one lives in the enjoyment of many good things, yet if he lives so that he is exposed to an enemy continually, a man that dwells in a cottage lives better than he. Feed a malefactor condemned to the gallows with the richest fare, he will not have so much comfort of it as one that eats only bread and water without fear. The wicked man, he takes these things as a thief that is afraid of the shaking of a leaf. Prov. 28:1, "The wicked fleeth when no man pursueth." Also Job 24:17. But the Christian, he partakes of his delights in safety and without fear, can eat and drink without terrors, with boldness and confidence.

The earthly comforts of the Christian are also very much sweetened by the consideration of the love of God, that God is their Father and friend and gives them these blessings from love to them, and because he delights in them. But the wicked can have no assurance that his enjoyments are not given to him in anger and in judgment.

The temporal delights of the godly are also very much sweetened because they are enjoyed in love and peace. He eats and drinks in love to God and Jesus Christ, and in peace with his neighbors and charity towards the whole world. Prov. 15:17, "Better is a dinner of herbs where love is, than a stalled ox and hatred therewith"; and 17:1, "Better is a dry morsel, and quietness, than a house full of sacrifices with strife." Eccles. 4:6, "Better is an handful with quietness, than both the hands full with travail and vexation of spirit."

III. There is no pleasure but what brings more of sorrow than of pleasure, but what the godly man either does or may enjoy. The sinful, unreasonable and beastly pleasures of the wicked, they bring more of sorrow with them. The wicked may feel some pleasure for a moment; it turns to sorrow and bitterness in a little time. And then even in this life it is but a little pleasure that is enjoyed in the time of it, and that is speedily over and turns to bitterness in the reflection, and makes such a disorder in the mind and uproar in the soul that the lasting uneasiness far more than compensates the short-lived pleasure.

All the pleasures of sin for the most part do bring more of sorrow than of pleasure in this life, whether the pleasures of sloth, of luxury, or drunkenness, or rioting, or fornication. If these things were let alone, a man's life in the general would be much more pleasant to him. They bring a great deal of trouble on their minds and quite destroy all peace there by fear, or accusation of conscience, or shame and disgrace in the world, the ruin of their children and the like, and also upon their bodies—sensuality being a spring of all manner of diseases—[and the] ruin of their estates. And many other ways do vices ruin the comfort of a man's life. And it is only those pleasures that do so that religion forbids. Prov. 23:32, "At last it will bite like a serpent, and sting like an adder."

IV. Religion brings no new troubles upon man but what have more of pleasure than of trouble. There is repentance of sin: though it be a deep sorrow for sin that God requires as necessary to salvation, yet the very nature of it necessarily implies delight. Repentance of sin is a sorrow arising from the sight of God's excellency and mercy, but the apprehension of excellency or mercy must necessarily and unavoidably beget pleasure in the mind of the beholder. 'Tis impossible that anyone should see anything that appears to him excellent and not behold it with pleasure, and it's impossible to be affected with the mercy and love of God, and his willingness to be merciful to us and love us, and not be affected with pleasure at the thoughts of [it]; but this is the very affection that begets true repentance. How much soever of a paradox it may seem, it is true that repentance is a sweet sorrow, so that the more of this sorrow, the more pleasure.

Especially do great delights ensue and follow it. Repentance, it clears up the mind and makes it easy and serene, and brings the good of comfort into the soul.

There is self-denial will also be reckoned amongst the troubles of the godly, and their laboriousness and diligence in their Christian course, and mortification in their warfare. But whoever has tried self-denial can give in his testimony that they never experience greater pleasures and joys than after great acts of self-denial. Self-denial destroys the very root and foundation of sorrow, and is nothing else but the lancing of a grievous and painful sore that effects a cure and brings abundance of health as a recompense for the pain of the operation.

Reproaches and the malice and envy of the wicked may also be reckoned as some of the chief troubles of the godly. But the true Christian is of such a magnanimous mind that he ordinarily can contemn this and return into the arms of Jesus, his best friend, with the more delight. The world hates them, but they can be of good cheer because Christ has overcome the world. And although they themselves don't perceive in the time how those reproaches conduce to their comfort afterwards, yet God in his wise providence brings it about for their joy and greater enlightening. Reproaches are ordered by God for this end, that they may destroy sin, which is the chief root of the troubles of the godly man, and the destruction of it a foundation for delight. And when the godly patiently bear them, God commonly requites for their reproaches. II Sam. 16:12, "It may be the Lord will look on mine affliction, and that the Lord will requite me good for his cursing this day."

And so the other persecutions that Christians may meet with from the wicked. See what Christ commands concerning revilings and persecutions, Matt. 5:11–12, "Blessed are ye, when men shall revile you, and persecute you, and shall say all manner of evil against you falsely for my sake. Rejoice, and be exceeding glad." And Jas. 1:2, "My brethren, count it all joy when ye fall into diverse temptations." And we find that the apostles acted accordingly, Acts 5:41, "And they departed from the presence of the council, rejoicing that they were counted worthy to suffer shame for his name." And this was the practice of other Christians in those times. Heb. 10:34, "Ye took joyfully the spoiling of your goods."

V. The fifth reason why it would be worth the while to be religious if it were only for the pleasantness of it, is that the religious man enjoys spiritual pleasures that are much better than any others. He has pleasures of mind as well as pleasure of body. The wicked man cuts himself off from all pleasures in his noble and more excellent part, even his soul. We must needs conclude that the pleasures of the soul are far better than of the body, for that that is most excellent and has the highest faculties must needs be capable of the greatest delights and most excellent gratifications.

First. Religion sets all to rights in the soul, so that there is no opposition between one faculty and another. Wickedness disorders the mind and casts things over of their most natural and excellent order, which must needs cause trouble and uneasiness. But religion places all in its true and natural order. When things are in their natural order, they are at rest and quiet, and there is no disturbance; so religion causes a calmness and quietness in the mind. The wicked man's passions are always at war with his reason, his inclination with his light and understanding; but in the religious man, all the powers are of one consent, and there is peace among them, and they all concur in the same thing.

Second. 'Tis a great pleasure for an intelligent and rational being to be excellent. Happiness and delight of soul arise always from the sight or apprehension of something that appears excellent. Thus even God himself has infinite delight in beholding his own infinite excellency, and for an excellent being there necessarily arises pleasure. Not the godly are pleased with proud and haughty thoughts of their own excellency, for they know they have nothing but what they received and that their excellency is wholly communicated to them by God. But the believer may rejoice, and does rejoice, to see the image of God upon their souls, to see the likeness of his dear Jesus. The saints in heaven, who have all remainders of pride taken away, do yet rejoice to see themselves made excellent by God and appearing beautiful with holiness. And if it be a great pleasure to see excellent things, it must be a sweet consideration to think that God of his grace has made me excellent and lovely. If they delight to see the loveliness of Jesus Christ, it must needs be matter of delight to see that Christ has communicated of his loveliness to their souls.

Third. The pleasures of doing well are very sweet to the godly. We must take heed that we do not confound the pleasure of the proud man, who is lifted up because he thinks he of his own ability does better than others, and of the Christian, who rejoices in the grace of God that enables him to obey him and do good works. 'Tis essential to a Christian that it be his delight and pleasure to obey God and do well. The wicked loves to act basely, but the Christian loves to act rationally and excellently. 'Tis their delight to imitate God and live [like] Jesus, and act like a rational creature.

Fourth. The Christian enjoys the pleasure of the most excellent knowledge. 'Tis natural to the reasonable creature to love knowledge of one kind or other and to delight in the attainment of knowledge. Some seek the knowledge of earthly things and some of heavenly, but the believer has the most excellent kind of knowledge: he has the pleasure of knowing the most glorious truths, the most excellent verities. What a delight do some men take in human learning: how much greater delight does the Christian take in divine. Great part of the happiness of the angels and saints in heaven is their knowledge; their understandings are enlarged, and their knowledge, we may conclude, is immensely larger than of the wisest men in this world.

Fifth. There is very great delight the Christian enjoys in the sight he has of the glory and excellency of God. How many arts and contrivances have men to delight the eye of the body. Men take delight in the beholding of great cities, splendid buildings and stately palaces. And what delight is often taken in the beholding of a beautiful face. May we not well conclude that great delights may also be taken in pleasing the eye of the mind in seeing the most beautiful, the most glorious, the most wonderful Being in the world?

Sixth. The godly man takes unspeakable delight in thinking that God, the governor of the world and the most excellent Being, loves him and is his friend. What delight do men take sometimes in the love of their fellow creatures, that they think ['em excellent]. And can we be so foolish as to think that there is any comparison between this and the delight that the godly take in thinking that God is their friend, yea, that he loves them with a very great love, has given himself to them, and the like?

Seventh. 'Tis most sweet to the godly to behold the beauty and enjoy the love of Christ the Mediator. He appears the most beautiful to them of anything in the world; he is to them as the rose and lily, as a bundle of myrrh; his love is a sweet fragrancy. None can tell the power of that joy that they feel from the consideration that so lovely a person loves them so as to lay down his life for them.

Eighth. Religion helps a man to enjoy much more pleasure in the society and conversation of men. It begets love and peace, good will one towards another, brotherly kindness, mutual benevolence, bounty and a feeling of each other's welfare. And this sweetens their conversation and fellowship, makes men to delight in each other.

Ninth. There are the great pleasures of hope, of glory of a resurrection, of an enjoyment of Christ forever. These are pleasures too big to be expressed. The righteous may meditate what glory, what happiness they can desire, and may be assured at the same time that they shall enjoy it all, and abundantly more.

Against this particular, it may be objected that these refer to the pleasures of another life, whereas the doctrine speaks of the pleasures of religion in this life. I answer, although the things hoped for are in another life, yet the pleasure of the hope of them is enjoyed in this life.

Thus I have gone through those five particulars by which I proposed to prove the doctrine, and believe none will deny but that 'tis most certain, that if religion does not deny us pleasures of sense taken with temperance, but rather sweetens them; and if it denies no pleasures at all but those that have more of sorrow than of pleasure, and brings no new sorrow but what has more of pleasure than of sorrow; and besides, gives spiritual delights that are better than all others: I think it cannot be questioned in any measure, but that 'tis well worth the while to be religious, if it were only for the pleasantness of it.

USE.

[*Use*] I. Hence we learn that, seeing it is so, that 'tis worth the while to be religious if it were only for the delight and pleasantness of it, then hence we may learn that sinners are left without any manner of objection against religion. They cannot [object] against the excellency {of religion}, nor profitableness {of it}. Their last objection that they commonly fly to is the unpleasantness of it. And I am satisfied, if there be any person in this congregation that does not determine immediately after God, that this is the objection that he makes: the unpleasantness of being religious and seeking God, the contrariety to his own inclinations, the opposition to the bent of his heart. But this objection we have fully answered. Can any deny but that the doctrine must needs be true, and has been evidenced so to be from the proofs that have been brought for it? If you object that you must deny yourself pleasures of sense, we have shown that {religion does not deny us outward delights and pleasures}; yea, that it sweetens {temporal delights and pleasures}. We have shown that there is no pleasure but what brings more of sorrow that religion denies, {but what the godly man does or may enjoy}. You cannot object the troubles that you must meet with in a religious course of life, as the troubles of {a religious life bring no new troubles but what bring more of pleasure than of trouble}. We have also told what great spiritual pleasures the godly meet with besides; and they must needs be great. 'Tis impossible but that pleasures of that kind should be exceeding great, for it is necessary in nature that spiritual pleasures, when enjoyed, should be the greatest to a spirit. 'Tis so in all cases: the things that are most becoming the nature of the soul, will certainly cause the greatest pleasure in it. I know 'tis impossible to convince men of this {spiritual pleasure}. But however this [may be], they may consider that by this doctrine they will be left without excuse before God.

[*Use*] II. [Second,] then, we come with double forces against the wicked, to persuade them to a godly life. The most common argument that is used to urge men to godliness is the pleasures of the life to come;

but this has not its effect for the sinner [who] is in pursuit of the pleasures of this life. Now, therefore, we urge to you the pleasures of this [life]: therefore you can have nothing to say. The common argument is the profitableness of religion, but alas, the wicked man is not in pursuit of profit; 'tis pleasure he seeks. Now, then, we will fight with them with their own weapons, {for religion does not deny us outward delights and pleasures}.

[*Use*] III. If it be so, that 'tis worth the while to be religious if it were only for the pleasantness of it, then how exceeding great is the reward of the godly. What a reward have they in the world to come; what joys {in another life}. But yet this is not all; no, they have a reward in this life. In the very keeping of God's commands, there is great reward (Ps. 19:11). The reward they have in hand, besides that which is promised, is well worth all the pains they take, all the troubles they endure. God has not only promised them a great reward, and exceeding great beyond conception; but he has given them a foretaste in this world. And this taste is better than all the pleasures and riches of the wicked. Ps. 119:14, "I have rejoiced in the way of thy commandments, as much as in all riches." Ps. 84:10, "A day in thy courts is better than a thousand elsewhere." The Christian spends every day as it were in the courts of God. The very pledge that God has given to the godly as an earnest of the reward, is such that it's well worth the while to deny all the pleasures of sin and to take all the troubles of religion for it. Rev. 2:17, "To him that overcometh will I give to eat of the hidden manna, and will give him a white stone, and in the stone a new name written, which no man knoweth saving he that receiveth it." What pure delights have the godly in {this life}. How great, then, is the reward of the righteous, if they have such a great reward in the life to come, and so great a reward in this life into the bargain.

But it may be objected, Did not the Apostle say, I Cor. 15:19, "If in this life only we have hope in Christ, we are of all men most miserable"? But I answer, the Christian has hope in another life, even while in this life. Indeed, if he expected to be turned to nothing when he died, and that he should never after enjoy God whom he so earnestly loved, nor enjoy Christ which he so exceedingly desired, it would be such a dreadful consideration that, together with his persecutions and troubles, would quite sink his heart and render him most miserable. But the Christian has the pleasure and joy of hope in this life, and this made the Apostle, even in this life, though sorrowful, yet always rejoicing (II Cor. 6:10).

Use IV of *Trial.* Is it so, {that 'tis worth the while to be religious if only for the pleasure of it}? Then from this we may have an excellent characteristic of a godly man. It is briefly thus: every man that is convinced by his own experience, what he has found of the pleasantness of religion, that 'tis well worth the while to be religious if it were only for the sake of the sweetness of religion. Is religion so sweet to him? If so, he may conclude that 'tis he has tasted the real sweetness of it.

The Importance and Advantage of a Thorough Knowledge of Divine Truth (1739)

Hebrews 5:12.

For when for the time ye ought to be teachers, ye have need that one teach you again which be the first principles of the oracles of God; and are become such as have need of milk, and not of strong meat.

These words are a complaint, which the Apostle makes of a certain defect in the Christian Hebrews, to whom he wrote. Wherein we may observe,

1. What the defect complained of is, viz. a want of such a proficiency in the knowledge of the doctrines and mysteries of religion, as might have been expected of them. The Apostle complains of them, that they had not made that progress in their acquaintance with the things of divinity, or things taught in the oracles of God, which they ought to have made. And he means to reprove them, not merely for their deficiency in *spiritual* and *experimental* knowledge of divine things, but for their deficiency in a *doctrinal* acquaintance with the principles of religion, and the truths of Christian divinity; as is evident by several things.

It appears by the manner in which the Apostle introduces this complaint or reproof. The occasion of his introducing it is this: in the next verse but one preceding, he mentions Christ's being an high priest after the order of Melchizedek: "Called of God a high priest after the order of Melchizedek." This Melchizedek being in the Old Testament, which was the oracles of God, held forth as an eminent type of Christ, and the account we there have of Melchizedek containing many gospel mysteries, these the Apostle was willing to point out to the Christian Hebrews. But he apprehended, that through their weakness in knowledge, and little acquaintance in mysteries of that nature, they would not understand him; and therefore breaks off for the present from saying anything about

Melchizedek. Thus, in v. 11, "Of whom we have many things to say, and hard to be uttered; seeing ye are dull of hearing"; i.e. "There are many things concerning Melchizedek, which contain wonderful gospel-mysteries, and which I would take notice of to you, were it not that I am afraid, that through your dullness and backwardness in understanding these things, you would only be puzzled and confounded by my discourse, and so receive no benefit; and that it would be too hard for you, as meat that is too strong."

Then come in the words of the text: "For when for the time ye ought to be teachers, ye have need that one teach you again which be the first principles of the oracles of God; and are become such as have need of milk, and not of strong meat." As much as to say, "Indeed it might have been expected of you, that you should have known enough of divinity, and the holy Scriptures, to be able to understand and digest such mysteries: but it is not so with you."

Again, the Apostle speaks of their proficiency in such knowledge as is conveyed and received by *human* teaching; as appears by that expression, "When for the time ye ought to be teachers"; which includes not only a practical and experimental, but also a doctrinal knowledge of the truths and mysteries of religion.

Again, the Apostle speaks of such a knowledge, whereby Christians are enabled to digest strong meat; i.e. to understand those things in divinity which are more abstruse and difficult to be understood, and which require great skill in things of this nature. This is more fully expressed in the two next verses: "For every one that useth milk, is unskillful in the word of righteousness: for he is a babe. But strong meat belongeth to them that are of full age, even those who, by reason of use, have their senses exercised to discern both good and evil."

Again, it is such a knowledge, that proficiency in it shall carry persons beyond the first principles of religion. As here: "Ye have need that one teach you again which be the first principles of the oracles of God." Therefore the Apostle, in the beginning of the next chapter, advises them "to leave the first principles of the doctrine of Christ, and to go on unto perfection."

2. We may observe wherein the fault of this defect appears, viz. in that

they had not made proficiency according to their time. For the time, they ought to have been teachers. As they were Christians, their business was to learn and gain Christian knowledge. They were scholars in the school of Christ; and if they had improved their time in learning, as they ought to have done, they might, by the time when the Apostle wrote, have been fit to be teachers in this school. To whatever business anyone is devoted, it may be expected that his perfection in it shall be answerable to the time he has had to learn and perfect himself. Christians should not always remain babes, but should grow in Christian knowledge; and leaving the food of babes, which is milk, should learn to digest strong meat.

DOCTRINE.

Every Christian should make a business of endeavoring to grow in knowledge in divinity.

This is indeed esteemed the business of divines and ministers: it is commonly thought to be their work, by the study of the Scriptures, and other instructive books, to gain knowledge; and most seem to think that it may be left to them, as what belongeth not to others. But if the Apostle had entertained this notion, he would never have blamed the Christian Hebrews for not having acquired knowledge enough to be teachers: or if he had thought that this concerned Christians in general only as a thing by the by, and that their time should not in a considerable measure be taken up with this business, he never would have so much blamed them, that their proficiency in knowledge had not been answerable to the time which they had had to learn.

In handling this subject, I shall show,

I. What divinity is.

II. What kind of knowledge in divinity is intended in the doctrine.

III. Why knowledge in divinity is necessary.

IV. Why all Christians should make a business of endeavoring to grow in this knowledge.

I. I shall very briefly show what divinity is.

Various definitions have been given of it by those who have treated on the subject. I shall not now stand to inquire which, according to the rules of art, is the most accurate definition; but shall so define or describe it, as I think has the greatest tendency to convey a notion of it to this auditory.

By divinity is meant, that science or doctrine which comprehends all those truths and rules which concern the great business of religion. There are various kinds of arts and sciences taught and learned in the schools, which are conversant about various objects; about the works of nature in general, as philosophy; or the visible heavens, as astronomy; or the sea, as navigation; or the earth, as geography; or the body of man, as physic and anatomy; or the soul of man, with regard to its natural powers and qualities, as logic and pneumatology; or about human government, as politics and jurisprudence. But there is one science, or one certain kind of knowledge and doctrine, which is above all the rest, as it is concerning God and the great business of religion: *this is divinity*; which is not learned, as other sciences, merely by the improvement of man's natural reason, but is taught by God himself in a certain book that he hath given for that end, full of instruction. This is the rule which God hath given to the world to be their guide in searching after this kind of knowledge, and is a summary of all things of this nature needful for us to know. Upon this account divinity is rather called a doctrine, than an art or science.

Indeed there is what is called *natural religion* or *divinity*. There are many truths concerning God, and our duty to him, which are evident by the light of nature. But Christian divinity, properly so called, is not evident by the light of nature; it depends on revelation. Such are our circumstances now in our fallen state, that nothing which it is needful for us to know concerning God, is manifest by the light of nature in the manner in which it is necessary for us to know it. For the knowledge of no truth in divinity is of any significance to us, any otherwise than as it some way or other belongs to the gospel scheme, or as it relates to a Mediator. But the light of nature teaches us no truth of divinity in this manner. Therefore it cannot be said, that we come to the knowledge of any part of Christian divinity by the light of nature. The light of nature teaches no truth as it is in Jesus. It is only the Word of God, contained in the Old and New Testament, which teaches us Christian divinity.

Divinity comprehends all that is taught in the Scriptures, and so all that we need know, or is to be known, concerning God and Jesus Christ, concerning our duty to God, and our happiness in God. Divinity is commonly defined, *the doctrine of living to God;* and by some who seem to be more accurate, *the doctrine of living to God by Christ.* It comprehends all Christian doctrines as they are in Jesus, and all Christian rules directing us in living to God by Christ. There is nothing in divinity, no one doctrine, no promise, no rule, but what some way or other relates to the Christian and divine life, or our living to God by Christ. They all relate to this, in two respects, viz. as they tend to promote our living to God here in this world, in a life of faith and holiness, and also as they tend to bring us to a life of perfect holiness and happiness, in the full enjoyment of God hereafter. But I hasten to the

II. [Second] thing proposed, viz. to show what kind of knowledge in divinity is intended in the doctrine.

Here I would observe,

First. That there are two kinds of knowledge of the things of divinity, viz. *speculative* and *practical*, or in other terms, *natural* and *spiritual.* The former remains only in the head. No other faculty but the understanding is concerned in it. It consists in having a natural or rational knowledge of the things of religion, or such a knowledge as is to be obtained by the natural exercise of our own faculties, without any special illumination of the Spirit of God. The latter rests not entirely in the head, or in the speculative ideas of things; but the heart is concerned in it: it principally consists in the sense of the heart. The mere intellect, without the heart, the will or the inclination, is not the seat of it. And it may not only be called seeing, but feeling or tasting. Thus there is a difference between having a right speculative notion of the doctrines contained in the Word of God, and having a due sense of them in the heart. In the former consists speculative or natural knowledge of the things of divinity; in the latter consists the spiritual or practical knowledge of them.

Second. Neither of these is intended in the doctrine exclusively of the other: but it is intended that we should seek the former in order to the latter. The latter, even a spiritual and practical knowledge of divinity, is of the greatest importance; for a speculative knowledge of it, without a spiritual knowledge, is in vain and to no purpose, but to make our condemnation the greater. Yet a speculative knowledge is also of infinite importance in this respect, that without it we can have no spiritual or practical knowledge; as may be shown by and by.

I have already shown, that the Apostle speaks not only of a spiritual knowledge, but of such knowledge as can be acquired, and communicated from one to another. Yet it is not to be thought, that he means this exclusively of the other. But he would have the Christian Hebrews seek the one, in order to the other. Therefore the former is first and most directly intended; it is intended that Christians should, by reading and other proper means, seek a good rational knowledge of the things of divinity. The latter is more indirectly intended, since it is to be sought by the other, as its end. But I proceed to the

III. [Third] thing proposed, viz. to show the usefulness and necessity of knowledge in divinity.

First. There is no other way by which any means of grace whatsoever can be of any benefit, but by knowledge. All teaching is in vain, without learning. Therefore the preaching of the gospel would be wholly to no purpose, if it conveyed no knowledge to the mind. There is an order of men which Christ has appointed on purpose to be teachers in his church. They are to teach the things of divinity. But they teach in vain, if no knowledge in these things is gained by their teaching. It is impossible that their teaching and preaching should be a means of grace, or of any good in the hearts of their hearers, any otherwise than by knowledge imparted to the understanding. Otherwise it would be of as much benefit to the auditory, if the minister should preach in some unknown tongue. All the difference is, that preaching in a known tongue conveys something to the understanding, which preaching in an unknown tongue doth not. On this account, such preaching must be unprofitable. Men in such things receive nothing, when they understand nothing; and are not at all edified, unless some knowledge be conveyed; agreeably to the Apostle's arguing in I Cor. 14:2–6.

No speech can be any means of grace, but by conveying knowledge. Otherwise the speech is as much lost as if there had been no man there, and he that spoke, had spoken only into the air; as it follows in the passage just quoted, vv. 6–10. He that doth not understand, can receive no faith, nor any other grace; for God deals with man as with a rational creature;

and when faith is in exercise, it is not about something he knows not what. Therefore hearing is absolutely necessary to faith; because hearing is necessary to understanding, Rom. 10:14. "How shall they believe in him of whom they have not heard?"

So there can be no love without knowledge. It is not according to the nature of the human soul, to love an object which is entirely unknown. The heart cannot be set upon an object of which there is no idea in the understanding. The reasons which induce the soul to love, must first be understood, before they can have a reasonable influence on the heart.

God hath given us the Bible, which is a book of instructions. But this book can be of no manner of profit to us, any otherwise than as it conveys some knowledge to the mind: it can profit us no more than if it were written in the Chinese or Tartarian language, of which we know not one word.

So the sacraments of the gospel can have a proper effect no other way, than by conveying some knowledge. They represent certain things by visible signs. And what is the end of signs, but to convey some knowledge of the things signified? Such is the nature of man, that nothing can come at the heart but through the door of the understanding: and there can be no spiritual knowledge of that of which there is not first a rational knowledge. It is impossible that anyone should see the truth or excellency of any doctrine of the gospel, who knows not what that doctrine is. A man cannot see the wonderful excellency and love of Christ in doing such and such things for sinners, unless his understanding be first informed how those things were done. He cannot have a taste of the sweetness and divine excellency of such and such things contained in divinity, unless he first have a notion that there are such and such things.

Second. Without knowledge in divinity, none would differ from the most ignorant and barbarous heathens. The heathens remain in gross heathenish darkness, because they are not instructed, and have not obtained the knowledge of the truths of divinity. So if we live under the preaching of the gospel, this will make us to differ from them, only by conveying to us more knowledge of the things of divinity.

Third. If men have no knowledge of these things, the faculty of reason in him will be wholly in vain. The faculty of reason and understanding was given for *actual* understanding and knowledge. If a man have no actual knowledge, the faculty or capacity of knowing is of no use to him. And if he have actual knowledge, yet if he be destitute of the knowledge of those things which are the last end of his being, and for the sake of the knowledge of which he had more understanding given him than the beasts; then still his faculty of reason is in vain; he might as well have been a beast, as a man with this knowledge. But the things of divinity are the things to know [for] which we had the faculty of reason given us. They are the things which appertain to the end of our being, and to the great business for which we are made. Therefore a man cannot have his faculty of understanding to any purpose, any further than he hath knowledge of the things of divinity.

So that this kind of knowledge is absolutely necessary. Other kinds of knowledge may be very useful. Some other sciences, such as astronomy, and natural philosophy, and geography, may be very excellent in their kind. But the knowledge of this divine science is infinitely more useful and important than that of all other sciences whatever.

IV. I come now to the fourth, and principal thing proposed under the doctrine, viz. to give the reasons why all Christians should make a business of endeavoring to grow in the knowledge of divinity. This implies two things.

First. That Christians ought not to content themselves with such degrees of knowledge in divinity as they have already obtained. It should not satisfy them, that they know as much as is absolutely necessary to salvation, but should seek to make progress.

Second. That this endeavoring to make progress in such knowledge ought not to be attended to as a thing by the by, but all Christians should make a business of it; they should look upon it as a part of their daily business, and no small part of it neither. It should be attended to as a considerable part of the work of their high calling. The reason of both these may appear in the following things.

1. Our business should doubtless much consist in employing those faculties, by which we are distinguished from the beasts, about those things which are the main end of those faculties. The reason why we have faculties superior to those of the brutes given us, is, that we are indeed

designed for a superior employment. That which the Creator intended should be our main employment, is something above what he intended the beasts for, and therefore hath given us superior powers. Therefore, without doubt, it should be a considerable part of our business to improve those superior faculties. But the faculty by which we are chiefly distinguished from the brutes, is the faculty of understanding. It follows then, that we should make it our chief business to improve this faculty, and should by no means prosecute it as a business by the by. For us to make the improvement of this faculty a business by the by, is in effect for us to make the faculty of understanding itself a by-faculty, if I may so speak, a faculty of less importance than others: whereas indeed it is the highest faculty we have.

But we cannot make a business of the improvement of our intellectual faculty, any otherwise than by making a business of improving ourselves in actual understanding and knowledge. So that those who make not this very much their business; but instead of improving their understanding to acquire knowledge, are chiefly devoted to their inferior powers, to provide wherewithal to please their senses, and gratify their animal appetites, and so rather make their understanding a servant to their inferior powers, than their inferior powers servants to their understanding; not only behave themselves in a manner not becoming Christians, but also act as if they had forgotten that they are men, and that God hath set them above the brutes, by giving them understanding.

God hath given to man some things in common with the brutes, as his outward senses, his bodily appetites, a capacity of bodily pleasure and pain, and other animal faculties: and some things he hath given him superior to the brutes, the chief of which is a faculty of understanding and reason. Now God never gave man those faculties whereby he is above the brutes, to be subject to those which he hath in common with the brutes. This would be great confusion, and equivalent to making man to be a servant to the beasts. On the contrary, he has given those inferior powers to be employed in subserviency to man's understanding; and therefore it must be a great part of man's principal business, to improve his understanding by acquiring knowledge. If so, then it will follow, that it should be a main part of his business to improve his understanding in acquiring divine knowledge, or the knowledge of the things of divinity: for the knowledge of these things is the principal end of this faculty. God gave man the faculty of understanding, chiefly, that he might understand divine things.

The wiser heathens were sensible that the main business of man was the improvement and exercise of his understanding. But they were in the dark, as they knew not the object about which the understanding should chiefly be employed. That science which many of them thought should chiefly employ the understanding, was philosophy; and accordingly they made it their chief business to study it. But we who enjoy the light of the gospel are more happy; we are not left, as to this particular, in the dark. God hath told us about what things we should chiefly employ our understandings, having given us a book full of divine instructions, holding forth many glorious objects about which all rational creatures should chiefly employ their understandings. These instructions are accommodated to persons of all capacities and conditions, and proper to be studied, not only by men of learning, but by persons of every character, learned and unlearned, young and old, men and women. Therefore the acquisition of knowledge in these things should be a main business of all those who have the advantage of enjoying the holy Scriptures.

2. The things of divinity are things of superlative excellency, and are worthy that all should make a business of endeavoring to grow in the knowledge of them. There are no things so worthy to be known as these things. They are as much above those things which are treated of in other sciences, as heaven is above the earth. God himself, the eternal Three in One, is the chief object of this science; in the next place, Jesus Christ, as God-man and Mediator, and the glorious work of redemption, the most glorious work that ever was wrought; then the great things of the heavenly world, the glorious and eternal inheritance purchased by Christ, and promised in the gospel; the work of the Holy Spirit of God on the hearts of men; our duty to God, and the way in which we ourselves may become like angels, and like God himself in our measure: all these are objects of this science.

Such things as these have been the main subject of the study of the holy patriarchs, prophets, and apostles, and the most excellent men that ever were in the world, and are also the subject of the study of the angels in heaven; I Pet. 1:10–12.

These things are so excellent and worthy to be known, that the knowledge of them will richly pay for all the pains and labor of an earnest seeking of it. If there were a great treasure of gold and pearls hid in the earth but should accidentally be found, and should be opened among us with such circumstances that all might have as much as they could gather of it; would not every one think it worth his while to make a business of gathering it while it should last? But that treasure of divine knowledge, which is contained in the Scriptures, and is provided for everyone to gather to himself as much of it as he can, is a far more rich treasure than any one of gold and pearls. How busy are all sorts of men, all over the world, in getting riches? But this knowledge is a far better kind of riches, than that after which they so diligently and laboriously pursue.

3. The things of divinity not only concern ministers, but are of infinite importance to all Christians. It is not with the doctrines of divinity as it is with the doctrines of philosophy and other sciences. These last are generally speculative points, which are of little concern in human life; and it very little alters the case as to our temporal or spiritual interests, whether we know them or not. Philosophers differ about them, some being of one opinion, and others of another. And while they are engaged in warm disputes about them, others may well leave them to dispute among themselves, without troubling their heads much about them; it being of little concern to them whether the one or the other be in the right.

But it is not thus in matters of divinity. The doctrines of this nearly concern everyone. They are about those things which relate to every man's eternal salvation and happiness. The common people cannot say, "Let us leave these matters to ministers and divines; let them dispute them out among themselves as they can; they concern not us," for they are of infinite importance to every man. Those doctrines which relate to the essence, attributes, and subsistencies of God, concern all; as it is of infinite importance to common people, as well as to ministers, to know what kind of being God is. For he is the Being who hath made us all, "in whom we live, and move, and have our being"; who is the Lord of all; the Being to whom we are all accountable; is the last end of our being, and the only fountain of our happiness.

The doctrines also which relate to Jesus Christ, and his mediation, his incarnation, his life and death, his resurrection and ascension, his sitting at the right hand of the Father, his satisfaction and intercession, infinitely concern common people as well as divines. They stand in as much need of this Savior, and of an interest in his person and offices, and the things which he hath done and suffered, as ministers and divines.

The same may be said of the doctrines which relate to the manner of a sinner's justification, or the way in which he becomes interested in the mediation of Christ. They equally concern all; for all stand in equal necessity of justification before God. That eternal condemnation, to which we are all naturally exposed, is equally dreadful. So with respect to those doctrines of divinity, which relate to the work of the Spirit of God on the heart, in the application of redemption in our effectual calling and sanctification, all are equally concerned in them. There is no doctrine of divinity whatever, which doth not some way or other concern the eternal interest of every Christian. None of the things which God hath taught us in his Word are needless speculations, or trivial matters; all of them are indeed important points.

4. We may argue from the great things which God hath done in order to give us instruction in these things. As to other sciences, he hath left us to ourselves, to the light of our own reason. But the things of divinity being of infinitely greater importance to us, he hath not left us to an uncertain guide; but hath himself given us a revelation of the truth in these matters, and hath done very great things to convey and confirm to us this revelation; raising up many prophets in different ages, immediately inspiring them with his Holy Spirit, and confirming their doctrine with innumerable miracles or wonderful works out of the established course of nature. Yea, he raised up a succession of prophets, which was upheld for several ages.

It was very much for this end that God separated the people of Israel, in so wonderful a manner, from all other people, and kept them separate; that to them he might commit the oracles of God, and that from them they might be communicated to the world. He hath also often sent angels to bring divine instructions to men; and hath often himself appeared in miraculous symbols or representations of his presence; and now in these last days hath sent his own Son into the world, to be his great prophet, to teach us divine truth, Heb. 1, at the beginning. By means of all, God hath given a book of divine instructions, which contains the sum of divinity. Now, these things hath God done, not only for the instruction of ministers and men of learning; but for the instruction of all men, of all sorts, learned and unlearned men, women, and children. And certainly if God doth such great things to *teach* us, we ought not to do little to *learn*.

God hath not made giving instructions to men in things of divinity a business by the by; but a business which he hath undertaken and prosecuted in a course of great and wonderful dispensations, as an affair in which his heart hath been greatly engaged: which is sometimes in Scripture signified by the expression of God's rising early to teach us, and to send prophets and teachers to us. Jer. 7:25, "Since that day that your fathers came forth out of the land of Egypt unto this day I have even sent unto you all my servants the prophets, daily rising up early, and sending them." And so, v. 13, "I spake unto you, rising up early and speaking." This is a figurative speech, signifying that God hath not done this as a by-business, but as a business of great importance, in which he took great care, and had his heart much engaged; because persons are wont to rise early to prosecute such business as they are earnestly engaged in. If God hath been so engaged in teaching, certainly we should not be negligent in learning; nor should we make growing in knowledge a by-business, but a great part of the business of our lives.

5. It may be argued from the abundance of the instructions which God hath given us, from the largeness of that book which God hath given to teach us divinity, and from the great variety that is therein contained. Much was taught by Moses of old, which we have transmitted down to us; after that, other books were from time to time added; much is taught us by David and Solomon; and many and excellent are the instructions communicated by the prophets: yet God did not think all this enough, but after this sent Christ and his apostles, by whom there is added a great and

excellent treasure to that holy book, which is to be our rule in the study of this important subject.

This book was written for the use of all; all are directed to search the Scriptures. John 5:39, "Search the scriptures; for in them ye think ye have eternal life: and they are they that testify of me"; and Is. 34:16, "Seek ye out of the book of the Lord, and read." They that read and understand are pronounced blessed. Rev. 1:3, "Blessed is he that readeth, and they that understand the words of this prophecy." If this be true of that particular book of the Revelation, much more is it true of the Bible in general. Nor is it to be believed that God would have given instructions in such abundance, if he had intended that receiving instruction should be only a by-concernment with us.

It is to be considered, that all those abundant instructions which are contained in the Scriptures were written that they might be understood; otherwise they are not instructions. That which is not given that the learner may understand it, is not given for the learner's instruction; and unless we endeavor to grow in the knowledge of divinity, a very great part of those instructions will to us be in vain; for we can receive benefit by no more of the Scriptures than we understand, no more than if they were locked up in an unknown tongue. We have reason to bless God that he hath given us such various and plentiful instruction in his Word; but we shall be hypocritical in so doing, if we, after all, content ourselves with but little of this instruction.

When God hath opened a very large treasure before us, for the supply of our wants, and we thank him that he hath given us so much; if at the same time we be willing to remain destitute of the greatest part of it, because we are too lazy to gather it, this will not show the sincerity of our thankfulness. We are now under much greater advantages to acquire knowledge in divinity, than the people of God were of old; because since that time, the canon of Scripture is much increased. But if we be negligent of our advantages, we may be never the better for them, and may remain with as little knowledge as they.

6. However diligently we apply ourselves, there is room enough to increase our knowledge in divine truth, without coming to an end. None

have this excuse to make for not diligently applying themselves to gain knowledge in divinity, that they know all already; nor can they make this excuse, that they have no need diligently to apply themselves, in order to know all that is to be known. None can excuse themselves for want of business in which to employ themselves. There is room enough to employ ourselves forever in this divine science, with the utmost application. Those who have applied themselves most closely, have studied the longest, and have made the greatest attainments in this knowledge, know but little of what is to be known. The subject is inexhaustible. That Divine Being, who is the main subject of this science, is infinite, and there is no end to the glory of his perfections. His works at the same time are wonderful, and cannot be found out to perfection; especially the work of redemption, which is that work of God about which the science of divinity is chiefly conversant, is full of unsearchable wonders.

The Word of God, which is given for our instruction in divinity, contains enough in it to employ us to the end of our lives, and then we shall leave enough uninvestigated to employ the heads of the ablest divines to the end of the world. The Psalmist found an end to the things that are human; but he could never find an end to what is contained in the Word of God. Ps. 119:96, "I have seen an end to all perfection: but thy command is exceeding broad." There is enough in this divine science to employ the understandings of saints and angels to all eternity.

7. It doubtless concerns everyone to endeavor to excel in the knowledge of things which pertain to his profession or principal calling. If it concerns men to excel in anything, or in any wisdom or knowledge at all, it certainly concerns them to excel in the affairs of their main profession and work. But the calling and work of every Christian is to live to God. This is said to be his *high calling*, Phil. 3:14. This is the business, and, if I may so speak, the *trade* of a Christian, his main work, and indeed should be his only work. No business should be done by a Christian, but as it is some way or other a part of this. Therefore certainly the Christian should endeavor to be well acquainted with those things which belong to this work, that he may fulfill it, and be thoroughly furnished to it.

It becomes one who is called to be a soldier, and to go a warfare, to endeavor to excel in the art of war. It becomes one who is called to be a mariner, and to spend his life in sailing the ocean, to endeavor to excel in the art of navigation. It becomes one who professes to be a physician, and devotes himself to that work, to endeavor to excel in the knowledge of those things which pertain to the art of physic. So it becomes all such as profess to be Christians, and to devote themselves to the practice of Christianity, to endeavor to excel in the knowledge of divinity.

8. It may be argued from this, that God hath appointed an order of men for this end, to assist persons in gaining knowledge in these things. He hath appointed them to be teachers. I Cor. 12:28, "And God hath set some in the church, first apostles, secondarily prophets, thirdly teachers." Eph. 4:11–12, "He gave some, apostles; some, prophets; some, evangelists; some, pastors and teachers; for the perfecting of the saints, for the work of the ministry, for the edifying of the body of Christ." If God hath set them to be teachers, making that their business, then he hath made it their business to impart knowledge. But what kind of knowledge? Not the knowledge of philosophy, or of human laws, or of mechanical arts, but of divinity.

If God hath made it the business of some to be teachers, it will follow, that he hath made it the business of others to be learners; for teachers and learners are correlates, one of which was never intended to be without the other. God hath never made it the duty of some to take pains to teach those who are not obliged to take pains to learn. He hath not commanded ministers to spend themselves, in order to impart knowledge to those who are not obliged to apply themselves to receive it.

The name by which Christians are commonly called in the New Testament is *disciples*, the signification of which word is *scholars* or *learners*. All Christians are put into the school of Christ, where their business is to learn, or receive knowledge from Christ, their common master and teacher, and from those inferior teachers appointed by him to instruct in his name.

9. God hath in the Scriptures plainly revealed it to be his will, that all Christians should diligently endeavor to excel in the knowledge of divine things. It is the revealed will of God, that Christians should not only have some knowledge of things of this nature, but that they should be *enriched with all knowledge*. I Cor. 1:4–5, "I thank my God always on your behalf,

for the grace of God that is given you by Jesus Christ; that in every thing ye are enriched by him, in all utterance, and in *all knowledge*." So the Apostle earnestly prayed, that the Christian Philippians might abound more and more, not only in love, but in Christian knowledge. Phil. 1:9, "And this I pray, that your love may abound yet more and more in knowledge, and in all judgment." So the apostle Peter advises to "give all diligence to add to faith virtue, and to virtue knowledge" (II Pet. 1:5). And the apostle Paul, in the next chapter to that wherein is the text, counsels the Christian Hebrews, leaving the first principles of the doctrine of Christ, to go on to perfection. He would by no means have them always to rest only in those fundamental doctrines of repentance, and faith, and the resurrection from the dead, and the eternal judgment, in which they were indoctrinated when they were first baptized, and had the Apostle's hands laid on them, at their first initiation in Christianity. See Heb. 6, at the beginning.

APPLICATION.

The *Use* that I would make of this doctrine, is to exhort all diligently to endeavor to gain this kind of knowledge.

Consider yourselves as scholars or disciples, put into the school of Christ; and therefore be diligent to make proficiency in Christian knowledge. Content not yourselves with this, that you have been taught your catechism in your childhood, and that you know as much of the principles of religion as is necessary to salvation. So you will be guilty of what the Apostle warns against, viz. going no further than "laying the foundation of repentance from dead works," etc. [Heb. 6:1].

You are all called to be Christians, and this is your profession. Endeavor, therefore, to acquire knowledge in things which pertain to your profession. Let not your teachers have cause to complain, that while they spend and are spent, to impart knowledge to you, you take little pains to learn. It is a great encouragement to an instructor, to have such to teach as make a business of learning, bending their minds to it. This makes teaching a pleasure, when otherwise it will be a very heavy and burdensome task.

You all have by you a large treasure of divine knowledge, in that you have the Bible in your hands; therefore be not contented in possessing but little of this treasure. God hath spoken much to you in the Scripture; labor to understand as much of what he saith as you can. God hath made you all reasonable creatures; therefore let not the noble faculty of reason or understanding lie neglected. Content not yourselves with having so much knowledge as is thrown in your way, and as you receive in some sense unavoidably by the frequent inculcation of divine truth in the preaching of the word, of which you are obliged to be hearers, or as you accidentally gain in conversation; but let it be very much your business to search for it, and that with the same diligence and labor with which men are wont to dig in mines of silver and gold.

Especially I would advise those that are young to employ themselves in this way. Men are never too old to learn; but the time of youth is especially the time for learning; it is peculiarly proper for gaining and storing up knowledge. Further, to stir up all, both old and young, to this duty, let me entreat you to consider,

First. If you apply yourselves diligently to this work, you will not want employment, when you are at leisure from your common secular business. In this way, you may find something in which you may profitably employ yourselves these long winter evenings. You will find something else to do, besides going about from house to house, spending one hour after another in unprofitable conversation, or, at best, to no other purpose but to amuse yourselves, to fill up and wear away your time. And it is to be feared that very much of the time that is spent in our winter evening visits, is spent to a much worse purpose than that which I have now mentioned. Solomon tells us, Prov. 10:19, that "in the multitude of words there wanteth not sin." And is not this verified in those who find little else to do for so great a part of the winter, but to go to one another's houses, and spend the time in such talk as comes next, or such as anyone's present disposition happens to suggest?

Some diversion is doubtless lawful; but for Christians to spend so much of their time, so many long evenings, in no other conversation than that which tends to divert and amuse, if nothing worse, is a sinful way of spending time, and tends to poverty of soul at least, if not to outward poverty. Prov. 14:23, "In all labor there is profit: but the talk of the lips tendeth only to *penury*." Besides, when persons for so much of their time have nothing else to do but to sit, and talk, and chat in one another's chimney corners, there is great danger of falling into foolish and sinful conversation, venting their corrupt dispositions in talking against others, expressing their jealousies and evil surmises concerning their neighbors; not considering what Christ hath said, Matt. 12:36, "Of every idle word that men shall speak, shall they give account in the day of judgment."

If you would comply with what you have heard from this doctrine, you would find something else to spend your winters in, one winter after another, besides contention, or talking about those public affairs which tend to contention. Young people might find something else to do, besides spending their time in vain company; something that would be much more profitable to themselves, as it would really turn to some good account; something, in doing which, they would both be more out of the devil's way, the way of temptation, and be more in the way of duty, and of a divine blessing. And even aged people would have something to employ themselves in, after they are become incapable of bodily labor. Their time, as is now often the case, would not lie heavy upon their hands, as they would with both profit and pleasure, be engaged in searching the Scriptures, and in comparing and meditating upon the various truths which they should find there.

Second. This would be a noble way of spending your time. The Holy Spirit gives the Bereans this epithet, because they diligently employed themselves in this business. Acts 17:11, "These were more *noble* than those of Thessalonica, in that they received the word with all readiness of mind, and searched the scriptures daily, whether those things were so." This is very much the employment of heaven. The inhabitants of that world spend much of their time in searching into the great things of divinity, and endeavoring to acquire knowledge in them, as we are told of the angels, I Pet. 1:12, "which things the angels desire to look into." This will be very agreeable to what you hope will be your business to all eternity, as you doubtless hope to join in the same employment with the angels of light. Solomon says, Prov. 25:2, it is the honor of kings "to search out a matter"; and certainly, above all others, to search out divine matters. Now, if this be the honor even of kings, is it not equally, if not much more, your honor?

Third. This is a pleasant way of improving time. Knowledge is pleasant and delightful to intelligent creatures, and above all the knowledge of divine things; for in them are the most excellent truths, and the most beautiful and amiable objects held forth to view. However tedious the labor necessarily attending this business may be, yet the knowledge once obtained will richly requite the pains taken to obtain it. "When wisdom entereth the heart, [and] knowledge is pleasant to the soul" (Prov. 2:10).

Fourth. This knowledge is exceeding useful in Christian practice. Such as have much knowledge in divinity have great means and advantages for spiritual and saving knowledge; for no means of grace, as was said before, have their saving effect on the heart, otherwise than by the knowledge they impart. The more you have of a rational knowledge of the things of the gospel, the more opportunity will there be, when the Spirit shall be breathed into your heart, to see the excellency of these things, and to taste the sweetness of them. The heathens, who have no rational knowledge of the things of the gospel, have no opportunity to see the excellency of them; and therefore the more rational knowledge of these things you have, the more opportunity and advantage you have to see the divine excellency and glory of them.

Again, the more knowledge you have of divine things, the better will you know your duty; your knowledge will be of great use to direct you as to your duty in particular cases. You will also be the better furnished against the temptations of the devil. For the devil often takes the advantage of persons' ignorance to ply them with temptations, which otherwise would have no hold of them.

By having much knowledge, you will be under greater advantages to conduct yourselves with prudence and discretion in your Christian course, and so to live much more to the honor of God and religion. Many who mean well, and are full of a good spirit, yet, for want of prudence, conduct themselves so as to wound religion. Many have a zeal of God, which does more hurt than good, because it is "not according to knowledge" (Rom. 10:2). The reason why many good men behave no better in many instances, is not so much that they want grace, as that they want knowledge.

Beside, an increase of knowledge would be a great help to profitable conversation. It would supply you with matter for conversation when you come together, or when you visit your neighbors: and so you would have less temptation to spend the time in such conversation as tends to your own and others' hurt.

Fifth. Consider the advantages you are under to grow in the knowledge of divinity. We are under far greater advantages to gain much knowledge in divinity now, than God's people under the Old Testament, both because the canon of Scripture is much enlarged since that time, and also, because evangelical truths are now so much more plainly revealed. So that common men are now in some respects under advantages to know more of divinity, than the greatest prophets were then. Thus that saying of Christ is in a sense applicable to us, Luke 10:23–24. "Blessed are the eyes which see the things which ye see: for I tell you, that many prophets and kings have desired to see those things which ye see, and have not seen them; and to hear those things which ye hear, and have not heard them." We are in some respects under far greater advantages for gaining knowledge, now in these latter ages of the church, than Christians were formerly; especially by reason of the art of printing, of which God hath given us the benefit, whereby Bibles and other books of divinity are exceedingly multiplied, and persons may now be furnished with helps for the obtaining of Christian knowledge, at a much easier and cheaper rate than they formerly could.

Sixth. We know not what opposition we may meet with in the principles which we hold in divinity. We know that there are many adversaries to the gospel and its truths. If therefore we embrace those truths, we must expect to be attacked by the said adversaries; and unless we be well informed concerning divine things, how shall we be able to defend ourselves? Besides, the apostle Peter enjoins it upon us, always to be ready to give an answer to every man who asketh us a reason of the hope that is in us [I Pet. 3:15]. But this we cannot expect to do without considerable knowledge in divine things.

I shall now conclude my discourse with some *Directions* for the acquisition of this knowledge.

First. Be assiduous in reading the holy Scriptures. This is the fountain whence all knowledge in divinity must be derived. Therefore let not this treasure lie by you neglected. Every man of common understanding who can read, may, if he please, become well acquainted with the Scriptures. And what an excellent attainment would this be!

Second. Content not yourselves with only a cursory reading, without regarding the sense. This is an ill way of reading, to which, however, many accustom themselves all their days. When you read, observe what you read. Observe how things come in. Take notice of the drift of the discourse, and compare one scripture with another. For the Scripture, by the harmony of the different parts of it, casts great light upon itself. We are expressly directed by Christ, to "*search* the scriptures," which evidently intends something more than a mere cursory reading. And use means to find out the meaning of the Scripture. When you have it explained in the preaching of the word, take notice of it; and if at any time a scripture that you did not understand be cleared up to your satisfaction, mark it, lay it up, and if possible remember it.

Third. Procure, and diligently use other books which may help you to grow in this knowledge. There are many excellent books extant, which might greatly forward you in this knowledge, and afford you a very profitable and pleasant entertainment in your leisure hours. There is doubtless a great defect in many, that through a loathness to be at a little expense, they furnish themselves with no more helps of this nature. They have a few books indeed, which now and then on sabbath days they read; but they have had them so long, and read them so often, that they are weary of them, and it is now become a dull story, a mere task to read them.

Fourth. Improve conversation with others to this end. How much might persons promote each other's knowledge in divine things, if they would improve conversation as they might; if men that are ignorant were not ashamed to show their ignorance, and were willing to learn of others; if those that have knowledge would communicate it, without pride and ostentation; and if all were more disposed to enter on such conversation as would be for their mutual edification and instruction.

Fifth. Seek not to grow in knowledge chiefly for the sake of applause, and to enable you to dispute with others; but seek it for the benefit of your souls, and in order to practice. If applause be your end, you will not be so likely to be led to the knowledge of the truth, but may justly, as often is the case of those who are proud of their knowledge, be led into error to your own perdition. This being your end, if you should obtain much rational knowledge, it would not be likely to be of any benefit to you, but would puff you up with pride. I Cor. 8:1, "Knowledge puffeth up."

Sixth. Seek to God, that he would direct you, and bless you, in this pursuit after knowledge. This is the Apostle's direction. Jas. 1:5, "If any man lack wisdom, let him ask it of God, who giveth to all liberally, and upbraideth not." God is the fountain of all divine knowledge. Prov. 2:6, "The Lord giveth wisdom; out of his mouth cometh knowledge and understanding." Labor to be sensible of your own blindness and ignorance, and your need of the help of God, lest you be led into error, instead of true knowledge. I Cor. 3:18, "If any man" would be wise, "let him become a fool, that he may be wise."

Seventh. Practice according to what knowledge you have. This will be the way to know more. The Psalmist warmly recommends this way of seeking knowledge in divine truth, from his own experience. Ps. 119:100, "I understand more than the ancients, because I keep thy precepts." Christ also recommends the same. John 7:17, "If any man will do his will, he shall know of the doctrine, whether it be of God, or whether I speak of myself."

Sinners in the Hands of an Angry God (1741)

Deuteronomy 32:35.
Their foot shall slide in due time.

In this verse is threatened the vengeance of God on the wicked unbelieving Israelites, that were God's visible people, and lived under means of grace; and that, notwithstanding all God's wonderful works that he had wrought towards that people, yet remained, as is expressed, v. 28, void of counsel, having no understanding in them; and that, under all the cultivations of heaven, brought forth bitter and poisonous fruit; as in the two verses next preceding the text.

The expression that I have chosen for my text, "Their foot shall slide in due time," seems to imply the following things, relating to the punishment and destruction that these wicked Israelites were exposed to.

1. That they were *always* exposed to destruction, as one that stands or walks in slippery places is always exposed to fall. This is implied in the manner of their destruction's coming upon them, being represented by their foot's sliding. The same is expressed, Ps. 73:18, "Surely thou didst set them in slippery places; thou castedst them down into destruction."

2. It implies that they were always exposed to *sudden* unexpected destruction. As he that walks in slippery places is every moment liable to fall; he can't foresee one moment whether he shall stand or fall the next; and when he does fall, he falls at once, without warning. Which is also expressed in that, Ps. 73:18–19, "Surely thou didst set them in slippery places; thou castedst them down into destruction. How are they brought into desolation as in a moment?"

3. Another thing implied is that they are liable to fall *of themselves*, without being thrown down by the hand of another. As he that stands or walks on slippery ground, needs nothing but his own weight to throw him down.

4. That the reason why they are not fallen already, and don't fall now, is only that God's appointed time is not come. For it is said, that when that due time, or appointed time comes, "their foot shall slide." Then they shall be left to fall as they are inclined by their own weight. God won't hold them up in these slippery places any longer, but will let them go; and then, at that very instant, they shall fall into destruction; as he that stands in such slippery declining ground on the edge of a pit that he can't stand alone, when he is let go he immediately falls and is lost.

The observation from the words that I would now insist upon is this,

[DOCTRINE.]

There is nothing that keeps wicked men, at any one moment, out of hell, but the mere pleasure of God.

By the mere pleasure of God, I mean his sovereign pleasure, his arbitrary will, restrained by no obligation, hindered by no manner of difficulty, any more than if nothing else but God's mere will had in the least degree, or in any respect whatsoever, any hand in the preservation of wicked men one moment.

The truth of this observation may appear by the following considerations.

I. There is no want of *power* in God to cast wicked men into hell at any moment. Men's hands can't be strong when God rises up: the strongest have no power to resist him, nor can any deliver out of his hands.

He is not only able to cast wicked men into hell, but he can most *easily* do it. Sometimes an earthly prince meets with a great deal of difficulty to subdue a rebel, that has found means to fortify himself, and has made himself strong by the numbers of his followers. But it is not so with God. There is no fortress that is any defense from the power of God. Though hand join in hand, and vast multitudes of God's enemies combine and associate themselves, they are easily broken in pieces: they are as great heaps of light chaff before the whirlwind; or large quantities of dry stubble before devouring flames. We find it easy to tread on and crush a worm that we see crawling on the earth; so 'tis easy for us to cut or singe a slender thread that anything hangs by; thus easy is it for God when he pleases to cast his enemies down to hell. What are we, that we should think to stand before him, at whose rebuke the earth trembles, and before whom the rocks are thrown down?

II. They *deserve* to be cast into hell; so that divine justice never stands in the way, it makes no objection against God's using his power at any moment to destroy them. Yea, on the contrary, justice calls aloud for an infinite punishment of their sins. Divine justice says of the tree that brings forth such grapes of Sodom, "Cut it down, why cumbreth it the ground," Luke 13:7. The sword of divine justice is every moment brandished over their heads, and 'tis nothing but the hand of arbitrary mercy, and God's mere will, that holds it back.

III. They are *already* under a sentence of condemnation to hell. They don't only justly deserve to be cast down thither; but the sentence of the law of God, that eternal and immutable rule of righteousness that God has fixed between him and mankind, is gone out against them, and stands against them; so that they are bound over already to hell. John 3:18, "He that believeth not is condemned already." So that every unconverted man properly belongs to hell; that is his place; from thence he is. John 8:23, "Ye are from beneath." And thither he is bound; 'tis the place that justice, and God's Word, and the sentence of his unchangeable law assigns to him.

IV. They are now the objects of that very *same* anger and wrath of God that is expressed in the torments of hell: and the reason why they don't go down to hell at each moment, is not because God, in whose power they are, is not then very angry with them; as angry as he is with many of those miserable creatures that he is now tormenting in hell, and do there feel and bear the fierceness of his wrath. Yea, God is a great deal more angry with great numbers that are now on earth, yea, doubtless with many that are now in this congregation, that it may be are at ease and quiet, than he is with many of those that are now in the flames of hell.

So that it is not because God is unmindful of their wickedness, and don't resent it, that he don't let loose his hand and cut them off. God is not altogether such an one as themselves, though they may imagine him to be so. The wrath of God burns against them, their damnation don't slumber, the pit is prepared, the fire is made ready, the furnace is now hot, ready to receive them, the flames do now rage and glow. The glittering sword is whet, and held over them, and the pit hath opened her mouth under them.

V. The *devil* stands ready to fall upon them and seize them as his own, at what moment God shall permit him. They belong to him; he has their souls in his possession, and under his dominion. The Scripture represents them as his "goods," Luke 11:21. The devils watch them; they are ever by them, at their right hand; they stand waiting for them, like greedy hungry lions that see their prey, and expect to have it, but are for the present kept back; if God should withdraw his hand, by which they are restrained, they would in one moment fly upon their poor souls. The old serpent is gaping for them; hell opens its mouth wide to receive them; and if God should permit it, they would be hastily swallowed up and lost.

VI. There are in the souls of wicked men those hellish *principles* reigning, that would presently kindle and flame out into hellfire, if it were not for God's restraints. There is laid in the very nature of carnal men a foundation for the torments of hell: there are those corrupt principles, in reigning power in them, and in full possession of them, that are seeds of hellfire. These principles are active and powerful, and exceeding violent in their nature, and if it were not for the restraining hand of God upon them, they would soon break out, they would flame out after the same manner as the same corruptions, the same enmity does in the hearts of damned souls, and would beget the same torments in 'em as they do in them. The souls of the wicked are in Scripture compared to the troubled sea, Is. 57:20. For the present God restrains their wickedness by his mighty power, as he does the raging waves of the troubled sea, saying, "Hitherto shalt thou come, and no further"; but if God should withdraw that restraining power, it would soon carry all afore it. Sin is the ruin and misery of the soul; it is destructive in its nature; and if God should leave it without restraint, there would need nothing else to make the soul perfectly miserable. The corruption of the heart of man is a thing that is immoderate and boundless in its fury; and while wicked men live here, it is like fire pent up by God's restraints, whenas if it were let loose it would set on fire the course of nature; and as the heart is now a sink of sin, so, if sin was not restrained, it would immediately turn the soul into a fiery oven, or a furnace of fire and brimstone.

VII. It is no security to wicked men for one moment, that there are no *visible means of death* at hand. 'Tis no security to a natural man, that he is now in health, and that he don't see which way he should now immediately go out of the world by any accident, and that there is no visible danger in any respect in his circumstances. The manifold and continual experience of the world in all ages, shows that this is no evidence that a man is not on the very brink of eternity, and that the next step won't be into another world. The unseen, unthought of ways and means of persons going suddenly out of the world are innumerable and inconceivable. Unconverted men walk over the pit of hell on a rotten covering, and there are innumerable places in this covering so weak that they won't bear their weight, and these places are not seen. The arrows of death fly unseen at noonday; the sharpest sight can't discern them. God has so many different unsearchable ways of taking wicked men out of the world and sending 'em to hell, that there is nothing to make it appear that God had need to be at the expense of a miracle, or go out of the ordinary course of his providence, to destroy any wicked man, at any moment. All the means that there are of sinners going out of the world, are so in God's hands, and so universally absolutely subject to his power and determination, that it don't depend at all less on the mere will of God, whether sinners shall at any moment go to hell, than if means were never made use of, or at all concerned in the case.

VIII. Natural men's prudence and care to preserve their own lives, or the care of others to preserve them, don't secure 'em a moment. This divine providence and universal experience does also bear testimony to. There is this clear evidence that men's own wisdom is no security to them from death; that if it were otherwise we should see some difference between the wise and politic men of the world, and others, with regard to their liableness to early and unexpected death; but how is it in fact? Eccles. 2:16, "How dieth the wise man? as the fool."

IX. All wicked men's pains and contrivance they use to escape hell, while they continue to reject Christ, and so remain wicked men, don't secure 'em from hell one moment. Almost every natural man that hears of hell, flatters himself that he shall escape it; he depends upon himself for his own security; he flatters himself in what he has done, in what he is now doing, or what he intends to do; everyone lays out matters in his own mind how he shall avoid damnation, and flatters himself that he contrives well for himself, and that his schemes won't fail. They hear indeed that there are but few saved, and that the bigger part of men that have died heretofore are gone to hell; but each one imagines that he lays out matters better for his own escape than others have done: he don't intend to come to that place of torment; he says within himself, that he intends to take care that shall be effectual, and to order matters so for himself as not to fail.

But the foolish children of men do miserably delude themselves in their own schemes, and in their confidence in their own strength and wisdom; they trust to nothing but a shadow. The bigger part of those that heretofore have lived under the same means of grace, and are now dead, are undoubtedly gone to hell: and it was not because they were not as wise as those that are now alive: it was not because they did not lay out matters as well for themselves to secure their own escape. If it were so, that we could come to speak with them, and could inquire of them, one by one, whether they expected when alive, and when they used to hear about hell, ever to be the subjects of that misery, we doubtless should hear one and another reply, "No, I never intended to come here; I had laid out matters otherwise in my mind; I thought I should contrive well for myself; I thought my scheme good; I intended to take effectual care; but it came upon me unexpected; I did not look for it at that time, and in that manner; it came as a thief; death outwitted me; God's wrath was too quick for me. O my cursed foolishness! I was flattering myself, and pleasing myself with vain dreams of what I would do hereafter, and when I was saying peace and safety, then sudden destruction came upon me."

X. God has laid himself under *no obligation* by any promise to keep any natural man out of hell one moment. God certainly has made no promises either of eternal life, or of any deliverance or preservation from eternal death, but what are contained in the covenant of grace, the promises that are given in Christ, in whom all the promises are yea and amen. But surely they have no interest in the promises of the covenant of grace that are not the children of the covenant, and that don't believe in any of the promises of the covenant, and have no interest in the *mediator* of the covenant.

So that whatever some have imagined and pretended about promises made to natural men's earnest seeking and knocking, 'tis plain and manifest that whatever pains a natural man takes in religion, whatever prayers he makes, till he believes in Christ, God is under no manner of obligation to keep him a *moment* from eternal destruction.

So that thus it is, that natural men are held in the hand of God over the pit of hell; they have deserved the fiery pit, and are already sentenced to it; and God is dreadfully provoked, his anger is as great towards them as to those that are actually suffering the executions of the fierceness of his wrath in hell, and they have done nothing in the least to appease or abate that anger, neither is God in the least bound by any promise to hold 'em up one moment; the devil is waiting for them, hell is gaping for them, the flames gather and flash about them, and would fain lay hold on them, and swallow them up; the fire pent up in their own hearts is struggling to break out; and they have no interest in any mediator, there are no means within reach that can be any security to them. In short, they have no refuge, nothing to take hold of, all that preserves them every moment is the mere arbitrary will, and uncovenanted unobliged forbearance of an incensed God.

APPLICATION.

The *Use* may be of *Awakening* to unconverted persons in this congregation. This that you have heard is the case of every one of you that are out of Christ. That world of misery, that lake of burning brimstone is extended abroad under you. *There* is the dreadful pit of the glowing flames of the wrath of God; there is hell's wide gaping mouth open; and you have nothing to stand upon, nor anything to take hold of: there is nothing between you and hell but the air; 'tis only the power and mere pleasure of God that holds you up.

You probably are not sensible of this; you find you are kept out of hell, but don't see the hand of God in it, but look at other things, as the good state of your bodily constitution, your care of your own life, and the means you use for your own preservation. But indeed these things are nothing; if God should withdraw his hand, they would avail no more to keep you from falling, than the thin air to hold up a person that is suspended in it.

Your wickedness makes you as it were heavy as lead, and to tend downwards with great weight and pressure towards hell; and if God should let you go, you would immediately sink and swiftly descend and plunge into the bottomless gulf, and your healthy constitution, and your own care and prudence, and best contrivance, and all your righteousness, would have no more influence to uphold you and keep you out of hell, than a spider's web would have to stop a falling rock. Were it not that so is the sovereign pleasure of God, the earth would not bear you one moment; for you are a burden to it; the creation groans with you; the creature is made subject to the bondage of your corruption, not willingly; the sun don't willingly shine upon you to give you light to serve sin and Satan; the earth don't willingly yield her increase to satisfy your lusts; nor is it willingly a stage for your wickedness to be acted upon; the air don't willingly serve you for breath to maintain the flame of life in your vitals, while you spend your life in the service of God's enemies. God's creatures are good, and were made for men to serve God with, and don't willingly subserve to any other purpose, and groan when they are abused to purposes so directly contrary to their nature and end. And the world would spew you out, were it not for the sovereign hand of him who hath subjected it in hope. There are the black clouds of God's wrath now hanging directly over your heads, full of the dreadful storm, and big with thunder; and were it not for the restraining hand of God it would immediately burst forth upon you. The sovereign pleasure of God for the present stays his rough wind; otherwise it would come with fury, and your destruction would come like a whirlwind, and you would be like the chaff of the summer threshing floor.

The wrath of God is like great waters that are dammed for the present; they increase more and more, and rise higher and higher, till an outlet is given, and the longer the stream is stopped, the more rapid and mighty is its course, when once it is let loose. 'Tis true, that judgment against your evil works has not been executed hitherto; the floods of God's vengeance have been withheld; but your guilt in the meantime is constantly increasing, and you are every day treasuring up more wrath; the waters are continually rising and waxing more and more mighty; and there is nothing but the mere pleasure of God that holds the waters back that are unwilling to be stopped, and press hard to go forward; if God should only withdraw his hand from the floodgate, it would immediately fly open, and the fiery floods of the fierceness and wrath of God would rush forth with inconceivable fury, and would come upon you with omnipotent power; and if your strength were ten thousand times greater than it is, yea ten thousand times greater than the strength of the stoutest, sturdiest devil in hell, it would be nothing to withstand or endure it.

The bow of God's wrath is bent, and the arrow made ready on the string, and justice bends the arrow at your heart, and strains the bow, and it is nothing but the mere pleasure of God, and that of an angry God, without any promise or obligation at all, that keeps the arrow one moment from being made drunk with your blood.

Thus are all you that never passed under a great change of heart, by the mighty power of the Spirit of God upon your souls; all that were never born again, and made new creatures, and raised from being dead in sin, to a state of new, and before altogether unexperienced light and life (however you may have reformed your life in many things, and may have had religious affections, and may keep up a form of religion in your families and closets, and in the house of God, and may be strict in it), you are thus in the hands of an angry God; 'tis nothing but his mere pleasure that keeps you from being this moment swallowed up in everlasting destruction.

However unconvinced you may now be of the truth of what you hear, by and by you will be fully convinced of it. Those that are gone from being in the like circumstances with you, see that it was so with them; for destruction came suddenly upon most of them, when they expected nothing of it, and while they were saying, "Peace and safety": now they see, that those things that they depended on for peace and safety, were nothing but thin air and empty shadows.

The God that holds you over the pit of hell, much as one holds a spider, or some loathsome insect, over the fire, abhors you, and is dreadfully provoked; his wrath towards you burns like fire; he looks upon you as worthy of nothing else, but to be cast into the fire; he is of purer eyes than to bear to have you in his sight; you are ten thousand times so abominable in his eyes as the most hateful venomous serpent is in ours. You have offended him infinitely more than ever a stubborn rebel did his prince: and yet 'tis nothing but his hand that holds you from falling into the fire every moment: 'tis to be ascribed to nothing else, that you did not go to hell the last night; that you was suffered to awake again in this world, after you closed your eyes to sleep: and there is no other reason to be given why you have not dropped into hell since you arose in the morning, but that God's hand has held you up: there is no other reason to be given why you han't gone to hell since you have sat here in the house of God, provoking his pure eyes by your sinful wicked manner of attending his solemn worship: yea, there is nothing else that is to be given as a reason why you don't this very moment drop down into hell.

O sinner! Consider the fearful danger you are in: 'tis a great furnace of wrath, a wide and bottomless pit, full of the fire of wrath, that you are held over in the hand of that God, whose wrath is provoked and incensed as much against you as against many of the damned in hell: you hang by a slender thread, with the flames of divine wrath flashing about it, and ready every moment to singe it, and burn it asunder; and you have no interest in any mediator, and nothing to lay hold of to save yourself, nothing to keep off the flames of wrath, nothing of your own, nothing that you ever have done, nothing that you can do, to induce God to spare you one moment.

And consider here more particularly several things concerning that wrath that you are in such danger of.

First. Whose wrath it is: it is the wrath of the infinite God. If it were only the wrath of man, though it were of the most potent prince, it would be comparatively little to be regarded. The wrath of kings is very much dreaded, especially of absolute monarchs, that have the possessions and lives of their subjects wholly in their power, to be disposed of at their mere will. Prov. 20:2, "The fear of a king is as the roaring of a lion: whoso provoketh him to anger, sinneth against his own soul." The subject that very much enrages an arbitrary prince, is liable to suffer the most extreme torments, that human art can invent or human power can inflict. But the greatest earthly potentates, in their greatest majesty and strength, and when clothed in their greatest terrors, are but feeble despicable worms of the dust, in comparison of the great and almighty Creator and King of heaven and earth: it is but little that they can do, when most enraged, and when they have exerted the utmost of their fury. All the kings of the earth before God are as grasshoppers, they are nothing and less than nothing: both their love and their hatred is to be despised. The wrath of the great King of Kings is as much more terrible than theirs, as his majesty is greater. Luke 12:4–5, "And I say unto you my friends, be not afraid of them that kill the body, and after that have no more that they can do: but I will forewarn you whom ye shall fear; fear him, which after he hath killed, hath power to cast into hell; yea I say unto you, fear him."

Second. 'Tis the *fierceness* of his wrath that you are exposed to. We often read of the *fury* of God; as in Is. 59:18, "According to their deeds, accordingly he will repay fury to his adversaries." So Is. 66:15, "For behold, the Lord will come with fire, and with chariots like a whirlwind, to render his anger with fury, and his rebukes with flames of fire." And so in many other places. So we read of God's *fierceness.* Rev. 19:15, there we read of "the winepress of the fierceness and wrath of almighty God." The words are exceeding terrible: if it had only been said, "the wrath of God," the words would have implied that which is infinitely dreadful: but 'tis not only said so, but "the fierceness and wrath of God": the fury of God! the fierceness of Jehovah! Oh how dreadful must that be! Who can utter or conceive what such expressions carry in them! But it is not only said so, but "the fierceness and wrath of *almighty God.*" As though there would be a very great manifestation of his almighty power, in what the fierceness of his wrath should inflict, as though omnipotence should be as it were enraged, and exerted, as men are wont to exert their strength in the fierceness of their wrath. Oh! then what will be the consequence! What will become of the poor worm that shall suffer it! Whose hands can be strong? and whose heart endure? To what a dreadful, inexpressible, inconceivable depth of misery must the poor creature be sunk, who shall be the subject of this!

Consider this, you that are here present, that yet remain in an unregenerate state. That God will execute the fierceness of his anger, implies that he will inflict wrath without any pity: when God beholds the ineffable extremity of your case, and sees your torment to be so vastly disproportioned to your strength, and sees how your poor soul is crushed and sinks down, as it were into an infinite gloom, he will have no compassion upon you, he will not forbear the executions of his wrath, or in the least lighten his hand; there shall be no moderation or mercy, nor will God then at all stay his rough wind; he will have no regard to your welfare, nor be at all careful lest you should suffer too much, in any other sense than only that you shall not suffer beyond what strict justice requires: nothing shall be withheld, because it's so hard for you to bear. Ezek. 8:18, "Therefore will I also deal in fury; mine eye shall not spare, neither will I have pity; and though they cry in mine ears with a loud voice, yet I will not hear them." Now God stands ready to pity you; this is a day of mercy; you may cry now with some encouragement of obtaining mercy: but when once the day of mercy is past, your most lamentable and dolorous cries and shrieks will be in vain; you will be wholly lost and thrown away of God as to any regard to your welfare; God will have no other use to put you to but only to suffer misery; you shall be continued in being to no other end; for you will be a vessel of wrath fitted to destruction; and there will be no other use of this vessel but only to be filled full of wrath: God will be so far from pitying you when you cry to him, that 'tis said he will only laugh and mock, Prov. 1:25–32.

How awful are those words, Is. 63:3, which are the words of the great God, "I will tread them in mine anger, and will trample them in my fury, and their blood shall be sprinkled upon my garments, and I will stain all my raiment." 'Tis perhaps impossible to conceive of words that carry in them greater manifestations of these three things, viz. contempt, and hatred, and fierceness of indignation. If you cry to God to pity you, he will be so far from pitying you in your doleful case, or showing you the least regard or favor, that instead of that he'll only tread you under foot: and though he will know that you can't bear the weight of omnipotence treading upon you, yet he won't regard that, but he will crush you under his feet without mercy; he'll crush out your blood, and make it fly, and it shall be sprinkled on his garments, so as to stain all his raiment. He will not only hate you, but he will have you in the utmost contempt; no place shall be thought fit for you, but under his feet, to be trodden down as the mire of the streets.

Third. The misery you are exposed to is that which God will inflict to that end, that he might show what that wrath of Jehovah is. God hath had it on his heart to show to angels and men, both how excellent his love is, and also how terrible his wrath is. Sometimes earthly kings have a mind to show how terrible *their* wrath is, by the extreme punishments they would execute on those that provoke 'em. Nebuchadnezzar, that mighty and haughty monarch of the Chaldean empire, was willing to show *his* wrath, when enraged with Shadrach, Meshach, and Abednego; and accordingly gave order that the burning fiery furnace should be het seven times hotter than it was before; doubtless it was raised to the utmost degree of fierceness that human art could raise it: but the great God is also willing to show *his wrath*, and magnify his awful majesty and mighty power in the extreme sufferings of his enemies. Rom. 9:22, "What if God, willing to show *his* wrath, and to make his power known, endured with much long-suffering the vessels of wrath fitted to destruction?" And seeing this is his design, and what he has determined, to show how terrible the unmixed, unrestrained wrath, the fury and fierceness of Jehovah is, he will do it to effect. There will be something accomplished and brought to pass, that will be dreadful with a witness. When the great and angry God hath risen up and executed his awful vengeance on the poor sinner; and the wretch is actually suffering the infinite weight and power of his indignation, then will God call upon the whole universe to behold that awful majesty, and mighty power that is to be seen in it. Is. 33:12–14, "And the people shall be as the burning of lime, as thorns cut up shall they be burnt in the fire. Hear ye that are far off what I have done; and ye that are near acknowledge my might. The sinners in Zion are afraid, fearfulness hath surprised the hypocrites. Who among us shall dwell with the devouring fire? who among us shall dwell with everlasting burnings?"

Thus it will be with you that are in an unconverted state, if you continue in it; the infinite might, and majesty and terribleness of the omnipotent God shall be magnified upon you, in the ineffable strength of your torments: you shall be tormented in the presence of the holy angels, and in the presence of the Lamb; and when you shall be in this state of suffering, the glorious inhabitants of heaven shall go forth and look on the awful spectacle, that they may see what the wrath and fierceness of the Almighty is, and when they have seen it, they will fall down and adore that great power and majesty. Is. 66:23–24, "And it shall come to pass, that from one new moon to another, and from one sabbath to another, shall all flesh come to worship before me, saith the Lord; and they shall go forth and look upon the carcasses of the men that have transgressed against me; for their worm shall not die, neither shall their fire be quenched, and they shall be an abhorring unto all flesh."

Fourth. 'Tis *everlasting* wrath. It would be dreadful to suffer this fierceness and wrath of almighty God one moment; but you must suffer it to all eternity: there will be no end to this exquisite horrible misery: when you look forward, you shall see a long forever, a boundless duration before you, which will swallow up your thoughts, and amaze your soul; and you will absolutely despair of ever having any deliverance, any end, any mitigation, any rest at all; you will know certainly that you must wear out long ages, millions of millions of ages, in wrestling and conflicting with this almighty merciless vengeance; and then when you have so done, when so many ages have actually been spent by you in this manner, you will know that all is but a point to what remains. So that your punishment will indeed be infinite. Oh who can express what the state of a soul in such circumstances is! All that we can possibly say about it, gives but a very feeble faint representation of it; 'tis inexpressible and inconceivable: for "who knows the power of God's anger?" [Ps. 90:11].

How dreadful is the state of those that are daily and hourly in danger of this great wrath, and infinite misery! But this is the dismal case of every soul in this congregation, that has not been born again, however moral and strict, sober and religious they may otherwise be. Oh that you would consider it, whether you be young or old. There is reason to think, that there are many in this congregation now hearing this discourse, that will actually be the subjects of this very misery to all eternity. We know not who they are, or in what seats they sit, or what thoughts they now have: it may be they are now at ease, and hear all these things without much disturbance, and are now flattering themselves that they are not the persons, promising themselves that they shall escape. If we knew that there was one person, and but one, in the whole congregation that was to be the subject of this misery, what an awful thing would it be to think of! If we knew who it was, what an awful sight would it be to see such a person! How might all the rest of the congregation lift up a lamentable and bitter cry over him! But alas! instead of one, how many is it likely will remember this discourse in hell? And it would be a wonder if some that are now present, should not be in hell in a very short time, before this year is out. And it would be no wonder if some person that now sits here in some seat of this meeting house in health, and quiet and secure, should be there before tomorrow morning. Those of you that finally continue in a natural condition, that shall keep out of hell longest, will be there in a little time! your damnation don't slumber; it will come swiftly, and in all probability very suddenly upon many of you. You have reason to wonder, that you are not already in hell. 'Tis doubtless the case of some that heretofore you have seen and known, that never deserved hell more than you, and that heretofore appeared as likely to have been now alive as you: their case is past all hope; they are crying in extreme misery and perfect despair; but here you are in the land of the living, and in the house of God, and have an opportunity to obtain salvation. What would not those poor damned, hopeless souls give for one day's such opportunity as you now enjoy!

And now you have an extraordinary opportunity, a day wherein Christ has flung the door of mercy wide open, and stands in the door calling and crying with a loud voice to poor sinners; a day wherein many are flocking to him, and pressing into the kingdom of God; many are daily coming from the east, west, north and south; many that were very lately in the same miserable condition that you are in, are in now an happy state, with their hearts filled with love to him that has loved them and washed them from their sins in his own blood, and rejoicing in hope of the glory of God. How awful is it to be left behind at such a day! To see so many others feasting, while you are pining and perishing! To see so many rejoicing and singing for joy of heart, while you have cause to mourn for sorrow of heart, and howl for vexation of spirit! How can you rest one moment in such a condition? Are not your souls as precious as the souls of the people at Suffield,[1] where they are flocking from day to day to Christ?

Are there not many here that have lived *long* in the world, that are not to this day born again, and so are aliens from the commonwealth of Israel, and have done nothing ever since they have lived, but treasure up wrath against the day of wrath? Oh sirs, your case in an especial manner is extremely dangerous; your guilt and hardness of heart is extremely great. Don't you see how generally persons of your years are passed over and left,

1. The next neighboring town.—Edwards' note.

in the present remarkable and wonderful dispensation of God's mercy? You had need to consider yourselves, and wake thoroughly out of sleep; you cannot bear the fierceness and wrath of the infinite God.

And you that are *young men*, and *young women*, will you neglect this precious season that you now enjoy, when so many others of your age are renouncing all youthful vanities, and flocking to Christ? You especially have now an extraordinary opportunity; but if you neglect it, it will soon be with you as it is with those persons that spent away all the precious days of youth in sin, and are now come to such a dreadful pass in blindness and hardness.

And you *children* that are unconverted, don't you know that you are going down to hell, to bear the dreadful wrath of that God that is now angry with you every day, and every night? Will you be content to be the children of the devil, when so many other children in the land are converted, and are become the holy and happy children of the King of Kings?

And let everyone that is yet out of Christ, and hanging over the pit of hell, whether they be old men and women, or middle aged, or young people, or little children, now hearken to the loud calls of God's Word and providence. This acceptable year of the Lord, that is a day of such great favor to some, will doubtless be a day of as remarkable vengeance to others. Men's hearts harden, and their guilt increases apace at such a day as this, if they neglect their souls: and never was there so great danger of such persons being given up to hardness of heart, and blindness of mind. God seems now to be hastily gathering in his elect in all parts of the land; and probably the bigger part of adult persons that ever shall be saved, will be brought in now in a little time, and that it will be as it was on that great outpouring of the Spirit upon the Jews in the apostles' days, the election will obtain, and the rest will be blinded. If this should be the case with you, you will eternally curse this day, and will curse the day that ever you was born, to see such a season of the pouring out of God's Spirit; and will wish that you had died and gone to hell before you had seen it. Now undoubtedly it is, as it was in the days of John the Baptist: the ax is in an extraordinary manner laid at the root of the trees, that every tree that brings not forth good fruit, may be hewn down, and cast into the fire.

Therefore let everyone that is out of Christ, now awake and fly from the wrath to come. The wrath of almighty God is now undoubtedly hanging over great part of this congregation: let everyone fly out of Sodom: "Haste and escape for your lives, look not behind you, escape to the mountain, lest you be consumed" [Gen. 19:17].

God Glorified in the Work of Redemption, by the Greatness of Man's Dependence upon Him, in the Whole of It (1731)

I Corinthians 1:29–31.
That no flesh should glory in his presence. But of him are ye in Christ Jesus, who of God is made unto us wisdom, and righteousness, and sanctification, and redemption. That, according as it is written, He that glorieth, let him glory in the Lord.

Those Christians to whom the Apostle directed this epistle, dwelt in a part of the world where human wisdom was in great repute; as the Apostle observes in the twenty-second verse of this chapter, "The Greeks seek after wisdom." Corinth was not far from Athens, that had been for many ages the most famous seat of philosophy and learning in the world.

The Apostle therefore observes to them how that God by the gospel destroyed, and brought to naught, their human wisdom. The learned Grecians, and their great philosophers, by all their wisdom did not know God, they were not able to find out the truth in divine things. But after they had done their utmost to no effect, it pleased God at length, to reveal himself by the gospel which they accounted foolishness: he "chose the foolish things of the world to confound the wise, and the weak things of the world to confound the things which are mighty, and the base things of the world, and things that are despised, yea and things which are not, to bring to naught the things that are." And the Apostle informs them why he thus did, in the verse of the text, "That no flesh should glory in his presence," etc. In which words many be observed,

1. What God aims at in the disposition of things in the affair of redemption, viz. that man should not glory in himself, but alone in God;

"That no flesh should glory in his presence. . . . That according as it is written, He that glorieth, let him glory in the Lord."

2. How this end is attained in the work of redemption, viz. by that absolute and immediate dependence which men have upon God in that work, for all their good. Inasmuch as,

(1) All the good that they have is in and through Christ; he "is made unto us wisdom, righteousness, sanctification, and redemption." All the good of the fallen and redeemed creature is concerned in these four things, and can't be better distributed than into them; but Christ is each of them to us, and we have none of them any otherwise than in him. He "is made of God unto us wisdom": in him are all the proper good, and true excellency of the understanding. Wisdom was a thing that the Greeks admired; but Christ is the true light of the world, 'tis through him alone that true *wisdom* is imparted to the mind. 'Tis in and by Christ that we have *righteousness*: 'tis by being in him that we are justified, have our sins pardoned, and are received as righteous into God's favor. 'Tis by Christ that we have *sanctification*: we have in him true excellency of heart, as well as of understanding; and he is made unto us inherent as well as imputed righteousness. 'Tis by Christ that we have *redemption*, or the actual deliverance from all misery, and the bestowment of all happiness and glory. Thus we have all our good by Christ who is God.

(2) Another instance wherein our dependence on God for all our good appears, is this, that 'tis God that has given us Christ, that we might have these benefits through him; he "of God is made unto us wisdom, righteousness," etc.

(3) 'Tis of him that we are in Christ Jesus, and come to have an interest in him, and so do receive those blessings which he is made unto us. 'Tis God that gives us faith whereby we close with Christ.

So that in this verse is shown our dependence on each person in the Trinity for all our good. We are dependent on Christ the Son of God, as he is our wisdom, righteousness, sanctification, and redemption. We are dependent on the Father, who have given us Christ, and made him to be these things to us. We are dependent on the Holy Ghost, for 'tis "of him that we are in Christ Jesus"; 'tis the Spirit of God that gives faith in him, whereby we receive him, and close with him.

DOCTRINE.

God is glorified in the work of redemption in this, that there appears in it so absolute and universal a dependence of the redeemed on him.

Here I propose to show,

I. That there is an absolute and universal dependence of the redeemed on God for all their good. And,

II. That God hereby is exalted and glorified in the work of redemption.

I. There is an absolute and universal dependence of the redeemed on God. The nature and contrivance of our redemption is such, that the redeemed are in everything directly, immediately, and entirely dependent on God: they are dependent on him for all, and are dependent on him every way.

The several ways wherein the dependence of one being may be upon another for its good, and wherein the redeemed of Jesus Christ depend on God for all their good, are these, viz. that they have all their good *of* him, and that they have all *through* him, and that they have all *in* him: that he be the cause and original whence all their good comes, therein it is *of* him; and that he be the medium by which it is obtained and conveyed, therein they have it *through* him; and that he be that good itself that is given and conveyed, therein it is *in* him.

Now those that are redeemed by Jesus Christ do in all these respects very directly and entirely depend on God for their all.

First. The redeemed have all their good *of* God. God is the great Author of it; he is the first cause of it, and not only so but he is the only proper cause.

'Tis *of* God that we have our Redeemer. 'Tis God that has provided a Savior for us. Jesus Christ is not only of God in his person, as he is the only begotten Son of God; but he is from God as we are concerned in him, and in his office of mediator; he is the gift of God to us: God chose and anointed him, appointed him his work, and sent him into the world.

And as it is God that gives, so 'tis God that accepts the Savior. As it is God that provides and gives the Redeemer to buy salvation for us, so it is *of*

God that that salvation is bought: he gives the purchaser, and he affords the thing purchased.

'Tis of God that Christ becomes ours, that we are brought to him, and are united to him: 'tis of God that we receive faith to close with him, that we may have an interest in him. Eph. 2:8, "For by grace ye are saved, through faith; and that not of yourselves, it is the gift of God." 'Tis of God that we actually do receive all the benefits that Christ has purchased. 'Tis God that pardons and justifies, and delivers from going down to hell, and 'tis his favor that the redeemed are received into, and are made the objects of, when they are justified. So it is God that delivers from the dominion of sin, and cleanses us from our filthiness, and changes us from our deformity. 'Tis of God that the redeemed do receive all their true excellency, wisdom and holiness; and that two ways, viz. as the Holy Ghost by whom these things are immediately wrought is from God, proceeds from him, and is sent by him; and also as the Holy Ghost himself is God, by whose operation and indwelling, the knowledge of God and divine things, and a holy disposition, and all grace are conferred and upheld.

And though means are made use of in conferring grace on men's souls, yet 'tis of God that we have these means of grace, and 'tis God that makes them effectual. 'Tis of God that we have the holy Scriptures; they are the Word of God. 'Tis of God that we have ordinances, and their efficacy depends on the immediate influence of the Spirit of God. The ministers of the gospel are sent of God, and all their sufficiency is of him. II Cor. 4:7, "We have this treasure in earthen vessels, that the excellency of the power may be of God, and not of us." Their success depends entirely and absolutely on the immediate blessing and influence of God.

1. The redeemed have all of the *grace* of God. It was of mere grace that God gave us his only begotten Son. The grace is great in proportion to the dignity and excellency of what is given: the gift was infinitely precious, because it was of a person infinitely worthy, a person of infinite glory; and also because it was of a person infinitely near and dear to God. The grace is great in proportion to the benefit we have given us in him: the benefit is doubly infinite in that in him we have deliverance from an infinite, because an eternal misery, and do also receive eternal joy and glory. The grace in bestowing this gift is great in proportion to our unworthiness to

whom it is given; instead of deserving such a gift, we merited infinitely ill of God's hands. The grace is great according to the manner of giving, or in proportion to the humiliation and expense of the method and means by which way is made for our having of the gift. He gave him to us dwelling amongst us; he gave him to us incarnate, or in our own nature; he gave him to us in our nature, in the like infirmities, in which we have it in our fallen state, and which in us do accompany, and are occasioned by, the sinful corruption of our nature. He gave him to us in a low and afflicted state; and not only so but he gave him to us slain that he might be a feast for our souls.

The grace of God in bestowing this gift is most free. It was what God was under no obligation to bestow: he might have rejected fallen man, as he did the fallen angels. It was what we never did anything to merit: 'twas given while we were yet enemies, and before we had so much as repented. It was from the love of God that saw no excellency in us to attract it; and it was without expectation of ever being requited for it.

And 'tis from mere grace that the benefits of Christ are applied to such and such particular persons. Those that are called and sanctified are to attribute it alone to the good pleasure of God's goodness, by which they are distinguished. He is sovereign and hath mercy on whom he will have mercy, and whom he will he hardens.

Man hath now a greater dependence on the grace of God than he had before the fall. He depends on the free goodness of God for much more than he did then: then he depended on God's goodness for conferring the reward of perfect obedience; for God was not obliged to promise and bestow that reward: but now we are dependent on the grace of God for much more: we stand in need of grace, not only to bestow glory upon us, but to deliver us from hell and eternal wrath. Under the first covenant we depended on God's goodness to give us the reward of righteousness; and so we do now. And not only so, but we stand in need of God's free and sovereign grace to give us that righteousness; and not only so, but we stand in need of his grace to pardon our sin, and release us from the guilt and infinite demerit of it.

And as we are dependent on the goodness of God for more now than under the first covenant, so we are dependent on a much greater, more free and wonderful goodness. We are now more dependent on God's arbitrary and sovereign good pleasure. We were in our first estate dependent on God for holiness: we had our original righteousness from him; but then holiness was not bestowed in such a way of sovereign good pleasure as it is now. Man was created holy, for it became God to create holy all the reasonable creatures he created: it would have been a disparagement to the holiness of God's nature, if he had made an intelligent creature unholy. But now when man is made holy, it is from mere and arbitrary grace; God may forever deny holiness to the fallen creature if he pleases, without any disparagement to any of his perfections.

And we are not only indeed more dependent on the grace of God, but our dependence is much more conspicuous, because our own insufficiency and helplessness in ourselves is much more apparent, in our fallen and undone state, than it was before we were either sinful or miserable. We are more apparently dependent on God for holiness, because we are first sinful, and utterly polluted, and afterward holy: so the production of the effect is sensible, and its derivation from God more obvious. If man was ever holy and always was so, it would not be so apparent, that he had not holiness necessarily, as an inseparable qualification of human nature. So we are more apparently dependent on free grace for the favor of God, for we are first justly the objects of his displeasure, and afterwards are received into favor. We are more apparently dependent on God for happiness, being first miserable, and afterwards happy. 'Tis more apparently free and without merit in us, because we are actually without any kind of excellency to merit, if there could be any such thing as merit in creature-excellency. And we are not only without any true excellency, but are full of, and wholly defiled with, that which is infinitely odious. All our good is more apparently from God, because we are first naked and wholly without any good, and afterward enriched with all good.

2. We receive all of the *power* of God. Man's redemption is often spoken of as a work of wonderful power as well as grace. The great power of God appears in bringing a sinner from his low state, from the depths of sin and misery, to such an exalted state of holiness and happiness. Eph. 1:19, "And what is the exceeding greatness of his power to us-ward who believe, according to the working of his mighty power."

We are dependent on God's power through every step of our redemption. We are dependent on the power of God to convert us, and give faith in Jesus Christ, and the new nature. 'Tis a work of creation: "If any man be in Christ, he is a new creature" (II Cor. 5:17). "We are created in Christ Jesus" (Eph. 2:10). The fallen creature can't attain to true holiness, but by being created again. Eph. 4:24, "And that ye put on the new man, which after God is created in righteousness and true holiness." 'Tis a raising from the dead. Col. 2:12–13, "Wherein also ye are risen with him through the faith of the operation of God, who hath raised him from the dead." Yea, 'tis a more glorious work of power than mere creation, or raising a dead body to life, in that the effect attained is greater and more excellent. That holy and happy being, and spiritual life which is reached in the work of conversion, is a far greater, and more glorious effect, than mere being and life. And the state from whence the change is made, of such a death in sin, and total corruption of nature, and depth of misery, is far more remote from the state attained, than mere death or non-entity.

'Tis by God's power also that we are preserved in a state of grace. I Pet. 1:5, "Who are kept by the power of God through faith unto salvation." As grace is at first from God, so 'tis continually from him, and is maintained by him, as much as light in the atmosphere is all day long from the sun, as well as at first dawning, or at sun-rising.

Men are dependent on the power of God, for every exercise of grace, and for carrying on that work in the heart, for the subduing of sin and corruption, and increasing holy principles, and enabling to bring forth fruit in good works, and at last bringing grace to its perfection, in making the soul completely amiable in Christ's glorious likeness, and filling of it with a satisfying joy and blessedness; and for the raising of the body to life, and to such a perfect state, that it shall be suitable for an habitation and organ for a soul so perfected and blessed. These are the most glorious effects of the power of God, that are seen in the series of God's acts with respect to the creatures.

Man was dependent on the power of God in his first estate, but he is more dependent on his power now; he needs God's power to do more things for him, and depends on a more wonderful exercise of his power. It was an effect of the power of God to make man holy at the first; but more remarkably so now, because there is a great deal of opposition and difficulty in the way. 'Tis a more glorious effect of power to make that holy that was so depraved and under the dominion of sin, than to confer holiness on that which before had nothing of the contrary. 'Tis a more glorious work of power to rescue a soul out of the hands of the devil, and from the powers of darkness, and to bring it into a state of salvation, than to confer holiness where there was no prepossession or opposition. Luke 11:21–22, "When a strong man armed keepeth his palace, his goods are in peace: but when a stronger than he shall come upon him, and overcome him, he taketh from him all his armor wherein he trusted, and divideth his spoils." So 'tis a more glorious work of power to uphold a soul in a state of grace and holiness, and to carry it on till it is brought to glory, when there is so much sin remaining in the heart, resisting, and Satan with all his might opposing, than it would have been to have kept man from falling at first, when Satan had nothing in man.

Thus we have shown how the redeemed are dependent on God for all their good as they have all *of* him.

Second. They are also dependent on God for all, as they have all *through* him. 'Tis God that is the medium of it, as well as the author and fountain of it. All we have, wisdom, and the pardon of sin, deliverance from hell, acceptance into God's favor, grace and holiness, true comfort and happiness, eternal life and glory, we have from God by a mediator; and this mediator is God; which mediator we have an absolute dependence upon, as he *through* whom we receive all. So that here is another way wherein we have our dependence on God for all good. God not only gives us the mediator, and accepts his mediation, and of his power and grace bestows the things purchased by the mediator, but he is the mediator.

Our blessings are what we have by purchase; and the purchase is made of God, the blessings are purchased of him, and God gives the purchaser; and not only so but God is the purchaser. Yea, God is both the purchaser and the price; for Christ, who is God, purchased these blessings for us, by offering up himself as the price of our salvation. He purchased eternal life by the sacrifice of himself. Heb. 7:27, "He offered up himself." And 9:26, "He hath appeared to take away sin by the sacrifice of himself." Indeed it was the human nature that was offered; but it was the same person with the divine, and therefore was an infinite price: it was looked upon as if God had been offered in sacrifice.

As we thus have our good *through* God, we have a dependence on God in a respect that man in his first estate had not. Man was to have eternal life then through his own righteousness; so that he had partly a dependence upon what was in himself; for we have a dependence upon that *through* which we have our good, as well as that *from* which we have it: and though man's righteousness that he then depended on was indeed from God, yet it was his own, it was inherent in himself; so that his dependence was not so immediately on God. But now the righteousness that we are dependent on is not in ourselves, but in God. We are saved through the righteousness of Christ: he "is made unto us righteousness"; and therefore is prophesied of, Jer. 23:6, under that name of "the Lord our righteousness." In that the righteousness we are justified by is the righteousness of Christ, it is the righteousness of God. II Cor. 5:21, "That we might be made the righteousness of God in him."

Thus in redemption, we han't only all things *of* God, but *by* and *through* him. I Cor. 8:6, "But to us there is but one God, the Father, of whom are all things, and we in him; and one Lord Jesus Christ, by whom are all things, and we by him."

Third. The redeemed have all their good *in* God. We not only have it *of* him and *through* him, but it consists *in* him; he *is* all our good.

The good of the redeemed is either objective or inherent. By their objective good I mean, that extrinsic object, in the possession and enjoyment of which they are happy. Their inherent good is that excellency or pleasure which is in the soul itself. With respect to both of which the redeemed have all their good in God, or which is the same thing, God himself is all their good.

1. The redeemed have all their *objective* good in God. God himself is the great good which they are brought to the possession and enjoyment of by redemption. He is the highest good, and the sum of all that good which Christ purchased. God is the inheritance of the saints; he is the portion of their souls. God is their wealth and treasure, their food, their life, their dwelling place, their ornament and diadem, and their everlasting honor and glory. They have none in heaven but God; he is the great good which

the redeemed are received to at death, and which they are to rise to at the end of the world. The Lord God, he is the light of the heavenly Jerusalem; and is the "river of the water of life" that runs, and the tree of life that grows, "in the midst of the paradise of God" [Rev. 2:7]. The glorious excellencies and beauty of God will be what will forever entertain the minds of the saints, and the love of God will be their everlasting feast. The redeemed will indeed enjoy other things; they will enjoy the angels, and will enjoy one another: but that which they shall enjoy in the angels, or each other, or in anything else whatsoever, that will yield them delight and happiness, will be what will be seen of God in them.

2. The redeemed have all their *inherent* good in God. Inherent good is twofold; 'tis either *excellency* or *pleasure*. These the redeemed not only derive from God, as caused by him, but have them in him. They have spiritual excellency and joy by a kind of participation of God. They are made excellent by a communication of God's excellency: God puts his own beauty, i.e. his beautiful likeness upon their souls: they are made "partakers of the divine nature," or moral image of God (II Pet. 1:4). They are holy by being made partakers of God's holiness (Heb. 12:10). The saints are beautiful and blessed by a communication of God's holiness and joy as the moon and planets are bright by the sun's light. The saint hath spiritual joy and pleasure by a kind of effusion of God on the soul. In these things the redeemed have communion with God; that is, they partake with him and of him.

The saints have both their spiritual excellency and blessedness by the gift of the Holy Ghost, or Spirit of God, and his dwelling with them. They are not only caused by the Holy Ghost, but are in the Holy Ghost as their principle. The Holy Spirit becoming an inhabitant, is a vital principle in the soul: he acting in, upon and with the soul, becomes a fountain of true holiness and joy, as a spring is of water, by the exertion and diffusion of itself. John 4:14, "But whosoever drinketh of the water that I shall give him shall never thirst; but the water that I shall give him shall be in him a well of water springing up into everlasting life." Compared with ch. 7:38–39, "He that believeth on me, as the scripture hath said, out of his belly shall flow rivers of living water. (But this spake he of the Spirit, which they that believe on him should receive.)" The sum of what Christ has purchased for us, is that spring of water spoken of in the former of those places, and those rivers of living water spoken of in the latter. And the sum of the blessings, which the redeemed shall receive in heaven, is that "river of water of life," that proceeds from the throne of God and the Lamb (Rev. 22:1). Which doubtless signifies the same with those rivers of living water, explained, John 7:38–39, which is elsewhere called the "river of God's pleasures." Herein consists the fullness of good, which the saints receive of Christ. 'Tis by partaking of the Holy Spirit, that they have communion with Christ in his fullness. God hath given the Spirit, not by measure unto him; and they do receive of his fullness, and grace for grace. This is the sum of the saints' inheritance: and therefore that little of the Holy Ghost which believers have in this world, is said to be the earnest of their inheritance. II Cor. 1:22, "Who hath also sealed us, and given us the Spirit in our hearts." And ch. 5:5, "Now he that hath wrought us for the selfsame thing is God, who also hath given unto us the earnest of the Spirit." And Eph. 1:13–14, "Ye were sealed with that Holy Spirit of promise, which is the earnest of our inheritance, until the redemption of the purchased possession."

The Holy Spirit and good things are spoken of in Scripture as the same; as if the Spirit of God communicated to the soul, comprised all good things. Matt. 7:11, "How much more shall your heavenly Father give good things to them that ask him?" In Luke it is, ch. 11:13, "How much more shall your heavenly Father give the Holy Spirit to them that ask him?" This is the sum of the blessings that Christ died to procure, and that are the subject of gospel promises. Gal. 3:13–14, "He was made a curse for us, that we might receive the promise of the Spirit through faith." The Spirit of God is the great promise of the Father. Luke 24:49, "Behold, I send the promise of my Father upon you." The Spirit of God therefore is called "the Spirit of promise" (Eph. 1:33). This promised thing Christ received, and had given into his hand, as soon as he had finished the work of our redemption, to bestow on all that he had redeemed. Acts 2:13, "Therefore being by the right hand of God exalted, and having received of the Father the promise of the Holy Ghost, he hath shed forth this, which ye both see and hear." So that all the holiness and happiness of the redeemed is *in*

God. 'Tis in the communications, indwelling and acting of the Spirit of God. Holiness and happiness is in the fruit, here and hereafter, because God dwells in them, and they in God.

Thus 'tis God that has given us the Redeemer, and 'tis of him that our good is purchased: so 'tis God is the Redeemer, and the price: and 'tis God also that is the good purchased. So that all that we have is *of* God, and *through* him, and *in* him. Rom. 11:36, "For *of* him, and *through* him, and *to* him" (or "*in* him") "are all things": the same in the Greek that is here rendered "to him," is rendered "in him" (I Cor. 8:6).

II. God is glorified in the work of redemption by this means, viz. by there being so great and universal a dependence of the redeemed on him.

First. Man hath so much the greater occasion and obligation to notice and acknowledge God's perfections and all-sufficiency. The greater the creature's dependence is on God's perfections, and the greater concern he has with them, so much the greater occasion has he to take notice of them. So much the greater concern anyone has with and dependence upon the power and grace of God, so much the greater occasion has he to take notice of that power and grace. So much the greater and more immediate dependence there is on the divine holiness, so much the greater occasion to take notice of and acknowledge that. So much the greater and more absolute dependence we have on the divine perfections, as belonging to the several persons of the Trinity, so much the greater occasion have we to observe and own the divine glory of each of them. That which we are most concerned with, is surely most in the way of our observation and notice; and this kind of concern with anything, viz. dependence, does especially tend to commend and oblige the attention and observation. Those things that we are not much dependent upon, 'tis easy to neglect; but we can scarce do any other than mind that which we have a great dependence on. By reason of our so great dependence on God, and his perfections, and in so many respects; he and his glory are the more directly set in our view, which way soever we turn our eyes.

We have the greater occasion to take notice of God's all-sufficiency, when all our sufficiency is thus every way of him. We have the more occasion to contemplate him as an infinite good, and as the fountain of all good. Such a dependence on God *demonstrates* God's all-sufficiency. So much as the dependence of the creature is on God, so much the greater does the creature's emptiness in himself appear to be: and so much the greater the creature's emptiness, so much the greater must the fullness of the Being be, who supplies him. Our having all *of* God, shows the fullness of his power and grace: our having all *through* him, shows the fullness of his merit and worthiness; and our having all *in* him demonstrates his fullness of beauty, love and happiness.

And the redeemed by reason of the greatness of their dependence on God, han't only so much the greater occasion, but obligation to contemplate and acknowledge the glory and fullness of God. How unreasonable and ungrateful should we be, if we did not acknowledge that sufficiency and glory, that we do absolutely, immediately and universally depend upon?

Second. Hereby is demonstrated how great God's glory is considered comparatively, or as compared with the creature's. By the creature's being thus wholly and universally dependent on God, it appears that the creature is nothing, and that God is all. Hereby it appears that God is infinitely above us; that God's strength, and wisdom, and holiness are infinitely greater than ours. However great and glorious the creature apprehends God to be, yet if he be not sensible of the difference between God and him, so as to see that God's glory is great compared with his own, he will not be disposed to give God the glory due to his name. If the creature in any respects sets himself upon a level with God, or exalts himself to any competition with him, however he may apprehend that great honor and profound respect may belong to God from those that are more inferior, and at a greater distance, will not be so sensible of its being due from him. So much the more men exalt themselves, so much the less will they surely be disposed to exalt God. 'Tis certainly a thing that God aims at in the disposition of things in the affair of redemption (if we allow the Scriptures to be a revelation of God's mind), that God should appear full, and man in himself empty, that God should appear all, and man nothing. 'Tis God's declared design that others should not "glory in his presence," which implies that 'tis his design to advance his own comparative glory. So much the more man "glories in God's presence," so much the less glory is ascribed to God.

Third. By its being thus ordered, that the creature should have so absolute and universal a dependence on God, provision is made that God should have our whole souls, and should be the object of our undivided respect. If we had our dependence partly on God, and partly on something else, man's respect would be divided to those different things on which he had dependence. Thus it would be if we depended on God only for a part of our good, and on ourselves, or some other being, for another part; or if we had our good only *from* God, and *through* another that was not God, and *in* something else distinct from both, our hearts would be divided between the good itself, and him *from* whom, and him *through* whom we received it. But now there is no occasion for this, God being not only he *from* or *of* whom we have all good, but also *through* whom, and one that is that good itself, that we have from him, and through him. So that whatsoever there is to attract our respect, the tendency is still directly towards God, all unites in him as the center.

USE.

I. We may here observe the marvelous wisdom of God, in the work of redemption. God hath made man's emptiness and misery, his low, lost and ruined state into which he is sunk by the fall, an occasion of the greater advancement of his own glory, as in other ways so particularly in this, that there is now a much more universal and apparent dependence of man on God. Though God be pleased to lift man out of that dismal abyss of sin and woe into which he has fallen, and exceedingly to exalt him in excellency and honor, and to an high pitch of glory and blessedness, yet the creature hath nothing in any respect to glory of; all the glory evidently belongs to God, all is in a mere, and most absolute and divine dependence on the Father, Son, and Holy Ghost.

And each person of the Trinity is equally glorified in this work: there is an absolute dependence of the creature on every one for all: all is *of* the Father, all *through* the Son, and all *in* the Holy Ghost. Thus God appears in the work of redemption as "all in all." 'Tis fit that he that "is, and there is none else," should be the Alpha and Omega, the first and the last, the all and the only, in this work.

II. Hence those doctrines and schemes of divinity that are in any respect opposite to such an absolute, and universal dependence on God, do derogate from God's glory, and thwart the design of the contrivance for our redemption. Those schemes that put the creature in God's stead, in any of the mentioned respects, that exalt man into the place of either Father, Son, or Holy Ghost, in anything pertaining to our redemption; that however they may allow of a dependence of the redeemed on God, yet deny a dependence that is so absolute and universal; that own an entire dependence on God for some things, but not for others; that own that we depend on God for the gift and acceptance of a Redeemer, but deny so absolute a dependence on him for the obtaining of an interest in the Redeemer; that own an absolute dependence on the Father for giving his Son, and on the Son for working out redemption, but not so entire a dependence on the Holy Ghost for conversion, and a being in Christ, and so coming to a title to his benefits; that own a dependence on God for means of grace, but not absolutely for the benefit and success of those means; that own a partial dependence on the power of God, for the obtaining and exercising holiness, but not a mere dependence on the arbitrary and sovereign grace of God; that own a dependence on the free grace of God for a reception into his favor, so far that it is without any proper merit, but not as it is without being attracted, or moved with any excellency; that own a partial dependence on Christ, as he through whom we have life, as having purchased new terms of life, but still hold that the righteousness through which we have life is inherent in ourselves, as it was under the first covenant: and whatever other way any scheme is inconsistent with our entire dependence on God for all, and is each of those ways, of having all *of* him, *through* him, and *in* him, it is repugnant to the design and tenor of the gospel, and robs it of that which God accounts its luster and glory.

III. Hence we may learn a reason why faith is that by which we come to have an interest in his redemption; for there is included in the nature of faith, a sensibleness, and acknowledgment of this absolute dependence on

God in this affair. 'Tis very fit that it should be required of all, in order to their having the benefit of this redemption, that they should be sensible of, and acknowledge the dependence on God for it. 'Tis by this means that God hath contrived to glorify himself in redemption, and 'tis fit that God should at least have this glory of those that are the subjects of this redemption; and have the benefit of it.

Faith is a sensibleness of what is real in the work of redemption; and as we do really wholly depend on God, so the soul that believes doth entirely depend on God for all salvation, in its own sense, and act. Faith abases men, and exalts God; it gives all the glory of redemption to God alone. It is necessary in order to saving faith, that man should be emptied of himself, that he should be sensible that he is "wretched, and miserable, and poor, and blind, and naked." Humility is a great ingredient of true faith: he that truly receives redemption receives it "as a little child." Mark 10:15, "Whosoever shall not receive the kingdom of heaven as a little child, he shall not enter therein." 'Tis the delight of a believing soul to abase itself and exalt God alone: that is the language of it. Ps. 115:1, "Not unto us, O Lord, not unto us, but to thy name give glory."

IV. Let us be exhorted to exalt God alone, and ascribe to him all the glory of redemption. Let us endeavor to obtain, and increase in, a sensibleness of our great dependence on God, to have our eye to him alone, to mortify a self-dependent, and self-righteous disposition. Man is naturally exceeding prone to exalt himself, and depending on his own power or goodness; as though he were he from whom he must expect happiness, and to have respect to enjoyments alien from God and his Spirit, as those in which happiness is to be found.

And this doctrine should teach us to exalt God alone as by trust and reliance, so by praise. "Let him that glories, glory in the Lord." Hath any man hope that he is converted, and sanctified, and that his mind is endowed with true excellency and spiritual beauty, and his sins forgiven, and he received into God's favor, and exalted to the honor and blessedness of being his child, and an heir of eternal life; let him give God all the glory; who alone makes him to differ from the worst of men in this world, or the miserablest of the damned in hell. Hath any man much comfort and strong hope of eternal life, let not his hope lift him up, but dispose him the more to abase himself, and reflect on his own exceeding unworthiness of such a favor, and to exalt God alone. Is any man eminent in holiness, and abundant in good works, let him take nothing of the glory of it to himself, but ascribe it to him whose "workmanship we are, created in Christ Jesus unto good works."

The Reality of Conversion (1740)

John 3:10–11.
Jesus answered and said unto him, Art thou a master in Israel, and knowest not these things? Verily, verily, I say unto thee, We speak that we do know, and testify that we have seen; and ye receive not our witness.

In these words Christ reproves Nicodemus' ignorance and doubtfulness of the doctrine of the new birth, which he had taught him in the preceding part of the chapter. The arguments of reproof that Christ makes use of are two:

1. Nicodemus' special advantages and obligation to know such things. He was a master in Israel, one that had made it much more his business to acquaint him with the doctrines of religion than the common people ordinarily did, and one whose business it was to instruct others.

2. The certainty of the doctrine of the new birth itself, which is set forth in the eleventh verse, where Christ declares in very strong terms and with an asseveration that, on what he had said about being born again, he spake what he certainly knew to be true. "Verily, verily, I say unto thee, We speak that we do know, and testify that we have seen."

DOCTRINE.

There is such a thing as conversion.

The doctrine of conversion, or of the new birth, is one of the great and fundamental doctrines of the Christian religion, as appears by Christ's manner of teaching it and insisting on it in his discourse with Nicodemus, in the text and context. It is a doctrine that 'tis of infinite importance that men should know and believe, because men's conversion, or being born again, is by Christ's express declaration absolutely necessary to their salvation. But it is a doctrine that is much caviled at and objected against, and a doctrine that unregenerate men are very apt to doubt of, for they have never had experience of any such thing.

It is with this doctrine as 'tis with the doctrines that treat of things that are in another world, that are invisible things and therefore are things that are hard to be believed. What is wrought in the soul in saving conversion is as much unseen to a natural man as heaven is and, therefore, as it is with the doctrine of another world, men are very ready to suspect all that is said about it and to look upon it as a kind of dream and to be raising many objections against it. So unexperienced men are ready to suspect what is said about conversion is either from lying and dissimulation or from their fancy and vain imagination. And there are many difficulties and objections that they raise against [it] and say on frequent occasions, as Nicodemus did: "How can these things be?"

I shall therefore now endeavor to offer some plain reasons to natural men, tending to their conviction of the reality of such a thing as conversion. Here I would show in particular how several things are manifest which, being put together, make it manifest that there is such a thing as conversion, or such a change as we have commonly been taught to understand by the word "conversion."

I. Man's happiness consists in his union with his Creator. Reason teaches this. For 'tis manifest that man was not made for no higher happiness than the brute creatures (consisting only in the enjoyments of external things or sensitive objects), because he is made with faculties so exceeding diverse. If man had no higher faculties than his external—as 'tis with the brutes—then we might with some reason suppose that he was made for no higher happiness than what consists in the objects of those senses. But seeing it is not [so], but he has those faculties that are so much superior, by which [he] is capable of the knowledge of his Creator, which the beasts give not the least signs of any apprehension of, we must suppose that it must be something of an higher kind that man's happiness consists in; and this can be in no other than union with his Creator. For how unreasonable would it be to suppose that a creature that is capable of knowing his Creator should be happy in a state of alienation from his Creator, or while he and that Being that gave him being (and upholds him every moment and that he depends upon every way) are at odds and in a state of distance, opposition and war one with another?

II. Reason teaches that man never can be happy in union with and the enjoyment of his Creator with an unholy nature, for holiness of nature is conformity of nature to God. But certainly reason teaches that no men have union with God without conformity to God. Amos 3:3, "Can two walk together, except they be agreed?" 'Tis unreasonable to suppose that God would ever admit any person into union with him, to dwell with him and enjoy him, whose nature is contrary to his. For that would be to admit that to union with him that must necessarily be abominable to him, for God's nature must abominate that which is of a contrary nature. And none can think that God would receive to union with him and the enjoyment of him that [which] his nature abhors. Ps. 5:4, "For thou art not a God that hast pleasure in wickedness: neither shall evil dwell with thee."

And besides, if it could be so that God would be willing that men that are of natures contrary to his should dwell with him and enjoy [him], yet it could not be, because it would be impossible in its own nature. For in such a case God would not only abhor men, but men would abhor God. For men's nature necessarily abhors that that is contrary to their nature. And if they abhor God, it is impossible that they should be happy in him. No man can take pleasure and receive happiness in the enjoyment of that which he hates. That which a man's nature abhors, 'tis no pleasure to him to be near it and to be united to it but, on the contrary, he loves to have it at a distance.

III. Experience shows that mankind are, as they are born into the world, universally of an unholy nature and, therefore, they can't be made holy but by a change of nature.

IV. Reason teaches that men's nature, that they are born with, can't be changed but by a supernatural work of the Creator upon them.

V. If we consider how great things this change is wrought for, reason teaches that it must be a great change.

VI. The testimony of Scripture is express that there must be such a change.

VII. [By] what has been visible and apparent in many thousands of persons, it is manifest that there is such a thing as men's natures being changed so as to make 'em holy, that there has appeared in great multitudes such evidences of an exceeding great change of heart that are great evidences to all that will use their reason that there is such a thing as such a change wrought by a supernatural power upon them. However there may be many that have professed such a change in whom the effects of it have not been so visible to others, yet there have been instances of others in whom there have been effects that have fully answered such a profession, and that not only two or three but many hundreds and thousands, yea, many ten thousands. What has been visible in two sorts of persons is especially evidential:

First. What has been visible in many notoriously vicious.
Second. Martyrs.

First. There have been many instances at one time and another of a most remarkable alteration made in those that heretofore were notoriously vicious, profligate livers, many that have had all religion in contempt and have lived in all manner of profaneness and debauchery, that have appeared more like beasts and devils than like men, that have afterwards [been] wonderfully seized and convinced and wrought so upon that their lives have been so changed that, instead of living such a vain, wicked life as they did before, there have appeared in them all the marks of an eminently humble, devout, spiritual and heavenly life.

Such instances especially abounded in the first times of the gospel, by the preaching of the apostles, and in the time of the Reformation from popery. There were great numbers in the times of the apostles that were fornicators and idolaters and adulterers, and effeminate and abusers of themselves with mankind, and thieves and covetous, drunkards and revilers and extortioners, that afterwards were washed and sanctified and justified in the name of the Lord Jesus and by the Spirit of God, as appears by I Cor. 6:9–11. And there have been many instances of cruel persecutors that have been wonderfully stopped in their cruelty, seized by the Spirit of God, and have been changed into humble and meek and zealous Christians. The apostle Paul was an eminent instance of this. And such a change of life as has been made in many han't only been visible for a while, but it has been durable. They have persisted in a course of holy living to the end of life, through all the changes and trials of it.

Now such a remarkable change in great numbers of persons is much more evidential of the reality of conversion in general than it is of conversions in individuals. When we see a great multitude that are thus remarkably changed in life and hold it to the end of life, 'tis a greater evidence that there is such a thing as change of heart than that either this or that man in particular is the subject of that change. For if it might so happen (through the extraordinary concurrence of some peculiar circumstances) that some one man might so dissemble as remarkably to change his outward life and behavior, and appear (in all that could possibly be seen) to behave himself like an eminent saint, and persevere in it without change of heart, yet it is much less supposable that it should thus happen in a great multitude.

Second. What has been visible in the martyrs. What has been seen in many thousands of them carries in it great evidence of such a thing as a change of nature by a supernatural power. In their enduring such sufferings for a good conscience and the glory of Christ, a very great alteration in life, and manifestations of holiness of heart in doings is a great argument of a change of heart. But manifestations of holiness in suffering is a yet greater change because suffering is a greater trial of what is in the heart than doings without suffering.

If unbelievers, and those that doubt whether there be any such thing as conversion, were to have their choice of the circumstances in which they would choose to observe those that pretend to such a change, in order to have the best evidences from their behavior of the reality of that change, they could not choose any circumstances that would better serve such a purpose than suffering circumstances, or circumstances wherein the sincerity of their pretenses must be tried by great sufferings for Christ's sake. But many thousands—yea, and millions—of professing Christians that have had this trial have acquitted themselves so under it as to give the most remarkable evidences of a supernatural love to God and weanedness from the world, for they have been tried with the most extreme sufferings and cruel tortures that man could invent. And the sufferings of many of them have been lengthened out to a very great length. Their persecutors have kept 'em under trying torments that, if possible, they might conquer them by wearing out of their spirits. But yet they have rather chosen to undergo all and have held out in suffering unto the death rather than deny Christ.

Such has been their faith and their love and their courage that their enemies could not by any means overcome it, though they had 'em in their hands to execute their will upon them. And very often have they suffered all with the greatest composedness of spirit, yea, and with cheerfulness. And many of them have appeared exceeding joyful under their torments and have glorified in tribulation.

And thus it has been not only with some few persons—or with here and there an exempt instance—that have braved it out through an extraordinary stoutness and ruggedness of spirit; but so it has been with multitudes of all sort: many that have been under the decays of old age, long after the strength of nature has begun to fail and they were in that state wherein are wont very much to lose their natural courage; and also in women and even children and persons of a delicate and weak constitution. Such as these have, by their faith and love to Christ and courage in his cause, conquered the greatest and cruelest monarchs of the earth. In all the most dreadful things that their power could inflict upon them, they have rather chosen to suffer such affliction than in the least to depart from their dear Lord and Savior.

Whoever reads the histories that give an account of these things must needs acknowledge, if they don't put [out] the light of reason, that those persons had something in them far above nature, that they were influenced by some supernatural and powerful principle that men naturally don't experience. And many of those that have thus patiently and joyfully suffered such things, before their change were very loose, vain persons, contemners of all religion. Yea, many that once were cruel persecutors themselves have been seized with conviction and have then at last borne witness to Christ and his gospel by a patient suffering his will, a remarkable instance of which we have in the blessed apostle Paul.

And the faith, steadfastness and cheerfulness of the martyrs in the Christian church in all ages of it carries in it the evidence of a continuation of miracles to manifest the reality of such a thing as conversion. If we consider it in all its circumstances, it is wonderful and does as truly show the finger of God as the miracles that were wrought in the days of Christ and the apostles. There are the professors of no other religion besides the

Christian that show anything like it to vouch for the truth of their religion; but it has [been] Christians, the followers of Jesus, that have been thus persecuted and have been thus patient under their sufferings.

What else can [be] thought of that can be supposed to be a cause sufficient to answer such an effect but only some mighty work of God on their hearts, changing their natures and infusing principles that strengthened them and carried 'em far beyond the strength of nature? What else should have such an effect, not only on two [or] three persons of very peculiar natural tempers and constitutions, but on thousands of all sorts, all ages, all conditions of life, and both sexes, strong and weak, men, women and children, bond and free?

It requires something above nature to make a man love an unseen object so as cheerfully to lose all things and suffer all things for his sake. Nature don't work in that manner. It may work so as to cause men to have a strong love to an object they have seen with their bodily eyes and have conversed with. But 'tis beyond the power of nature to beget such a love to an object that they are told of, of which they are informed that he lived on earth many hundred years ago and lives now in [an] invisible world. Nature may operate so as to cause transient affections about that which they are so informed of, but not to knit the heart so strongly to an unseen object as to have such great effects as these.

There is no kind of love in the world that has had such great, visible effects in men as love to Christ has had, though he be an unseen object, which [is] an evidence of a divine work in the hearts of men, infusing that love into them. Thus the voice of reason, Scripture and experience, and the testimony of the best of men do all concur in it, that there must be such a thing as conversion. Reason teaches it so much that, unless we deny the being of God, we can't avoid acknowledging such a thing as conversion. For if there be a God, he is doubtless the governor and judge of the world, and will receive his reasonable creatures there to himself to be happy in him or exclude 'em from his presence according as they are conformed to him by the holiness of their nature or not. And therefore seeing man naturally is unholy, there must be a change of nature in order to their being happy in God.

The Scripture does so teach this doctrine of conversion that, if we deny it, we do in effect renounce the Scriptures. We had as good deny the whole as deny what the Scripture teaches us about the necessity of conversion or the turning of the heart from sin to God. If we deny what the Scripture says of this, the rest can be of no significancy to us.

Experience does so much teach that there is such a thing as conversion that multitudes of Christians don't only manifest their having actually been the subjects of such a change in their talk, but in their behavior; not only in their behavior in prosperity, but under the greatest imaginable sufferings, and that in a constant manner, without wavering—which is the greatest evidence, in any case, that one man can give another of his sincerity.

If this doctrine of conversion had not been confirmed by the voice of reason, if it were a doctrine the truth of which was very difficult to reason, yet God's own voice in his Word determining the matter might be enough with us. If there be a God, doubtless he has revealed his mind to fallen man concerning the way of his recovery and how he may come to [be] happy in him. But where have we any such revelation but in the Scriptures? But if the Scriptures teach such a doctrine, surely God knows better than men. But not only God's word, but man's reason and the experience of many ages does manifest that there must be such a change of the heart and nature of man as this.

VIII. It would be unreasonable to reject the testimonies of all that declare their experience of such a change in themselves. If they were only fools and are persons remarkably weak in understanding, {then perhaps we could reject their testimonies}. If they were commonly found not to be men of probity, and whose word was not to be depended on in other things, [then perhaps we could reject their testimonies]. The things they testify they must be supposed capable of knowing whether they have felt or not.

Such things as [these] natural men know themselves to be entire strangers to and can't work up in their own hearts. And there are great multitudes agreeing, very distant one from another, in [the] experience professed here; [and] are, as to what is essential, the same. That professed {is also the same}. The same is professed in different ages. And if we may believe their testimony, the experience holds. These new feelings of a sense of divine things (love, humility, submission) never wholly leave them. Things that once they could not experience anything of, now from time to time they do experience.

[*Obj.*] The great objection that many make, is that many that have thought themselves (and have been thought by others) to be converted have carried themselves so ill.

[*Answ.*] The ill carriages, if rightly considered, confirm what the Scripture has told us concerning conversion.

1. The Scripture has told us there should be offenses, should be wolves in sheep's clothing.

2. That Scripture teaches us that men are often deceived concerning themselves and others. "[Thine enemies. . . . have taken crafty counsel against thy people, and consulted against thy] hidden ones" [Ps. 83:2–3]. "[But he is a Jew, which is one inwardly; and circumcision is that of the heart, in the spirit, and not in the letter; whose] praise is not of men, but of God," Rom. 2:29. There are sepulchers men walk over and discern not, Luke 11:44. "That which is highly esteemed amongst men is abomination [in the sight of God]," Luke 16:15. Foolish virgins take lamps as well as wise [Matt. 25:1–13].

3. Though the godly have a body of sin and death and are liable sometimes to carry themselves very ill, that we ben't capable of judging we are warned against it.

4. Many counterfeits don't make [a thing] not true. How can this objection be of force? How can there being many counterfeits prove that it's nothing true? [This is like saying that there are] many specious lies and therefore all [statements are] false; [or that there is] much unfaithfulness [and therefore] no honesty; [or that] because many things that shine like gold are not gold, therefore there is no true gold; [or that] many things that glister like diamonds are not true diamonds, [and therefore there are no true diamonds].

5. How does that prove that those that do carry themselves well, and give the greatest and strongest evidences in their behavior and sufferings, that they are not converted?

APPLICATION.

The only *Use* that I would make of this doctrine is of *Exhortation,* to exhort those that remain in a natural condition earnestly to seek conversion. If there be such a thing as conversion, 'tis the most important thing in the world; and they are happy that have been the subjects of it and they most miserable that have not (because they hang over the pit of hell and are in danger every day of being eternally lost). So certainly as there is such a thing as conversion, so certainly all you that [are] in an unconverted state have the wrath of God abiding on you, and are every day in danger of that misery in hell that is unalterable, and without the least hope of deliverance. If there really be such a thing as conversion, then you that are unconverted can't reasonably have any rest in the condition that you are in.

Therefore let me now earnestly exhort you to seek deliverance from your present state by being the subjects of a true and saving conversion to God. And under this use I would take a method somewhat diverse from that which is more usual. I would first give some directions to you what to do that you may be converted, and then would conclude with some considerations tending to move you to comply with those directions.

[*First.* Directions.]

1. Take heed of long halting between two opinions. Take heed you don't live without coming to any determination what you will do. If you are unresolved whether there be such a thing as conversion, don't be contented to continue undetermined in so great a question. How unreasonable is it. Does it not infinitely concern you to come to some resolution? Have you such abundance of time to spare? Don't remain unresolved what you had best to do, whether best to reform your life or no. [It is] best to be [either] in earnest or not. Come to some determination in your mind. I Kgs. 18:21, "How long halt ye between two opinions? if the Lord be God, follow him: but if Baal, then follow him." So I say, if it be best for you to follow your lusts, [then follow them; but if it be best for you to follow the Lord, then follow him].

2. Don't put off in hopes of future advantages. Don't do as Felix did who, when Paul reasoned with him of the great things of religion, sent away the Apostle for the present and talked of sending for him at a more

convenient season (Acts 24:25). Don't put off because you are now young and you hope that you shall have a more convenient season when you are settled in the world. Many that have done so never have lived to be settled in this world, but their state has been settled and fixed for eternity and hell has been made their settled habitation before the time came that they laid out in their minds. Don't put off in hope that hereafter you shall have more leisure and less temptation. Difficulties in this affair are wont to increase and not diminish the older persons grow. Don't put off hoping to see another time of the pouring of the Spirit of God on this town. It is a thing that you are altogether uncertain of, whether there ever will be another pouring out of the Spirit in your lifetime. And if there should, 'tis uncertain whether you will have any benefit of it. Don't put off waiting for the Spirit of God to awaken you and stir you up to seek salvation. This will be dreadful presumption in you. The way for you to have the needed influences of the Spirit of God is for you to be [in] the use of all appointed means, and to watch at wisdom's gates, and wait at the posts of her doors [Prov. 8:34].

3. You must submit to those things that seem to you to be hard things. You must never expect to be in an hopeful way to obtain conversion till you are brought to comply with those things that seem very hard to corrupt nature. Many men study a great deal to find out a way how to obtain the kingdom of heaven easily, or how to make their salvation and their ease agree together. But let us rack our inventions never so much, we never shall make it out. The gate by which persons enter into life will be a strait gate still. The time that is spent in endeavors to find a wide gate is spent very unprofitably. And many persons, while they are busily employing themselves this way, suddenly drop down and sink into hell, and so all their projects and hopes are brought to an end.

Things needful to be done in order to salvation may seem hard things on several accounts. Some duties are hard as they are very contrary to those desires and inclinations that are natural to them. Men must deny themselves of those things that seem sweet to them and that they have very pleasing, taking ideas of and strong desires after, and that their natures do importunately solicit them for, so that they don't know how to say nay to their importunities.

Some things that need to be done by men in order to their salvation seem very hard to them on account of the labor of them. They love ease. It is very cross to them to comply with hard and constant labor in the business of religion. That is a new work, a work that hitherto they han't been used to and a business with respect to which they have always hitherto indulged themselves in their ease. It looks a great thing to them to take upon [them] so much new trouble in addition to all they had been used to before.

Many things that belong to religion seem hard to men because they are very contrary to their natural temper. It is cross to their humor and seems very much out of their way to go and do this or that. So it may be contrary to some persons' natural disposition to enter upon religious conversation. Some are of a very reserved temper and it is very contrary to them to open their hearts to others to tell of their inward difficulties and temptations when, indeed, it is exceeding needful for them.

Some things seem hard to men by reason of their circumstances. Duties that may be easy to persons in some circumstances may seem very difficult in others. Many things that are requisite in order to conversion seem very hard to them by reason of their being so contrary to their pride. So it seems hard to men oftentimes to hear the religious conversation from their pious friends and acquaintances, and especially to take a reproof from 'em. So it seems hard to men oftentimes, when they have erred and in any respect wronged their neighbor, to come back and confess their fault to him. And it seems hard to many through their pride to ask advice under their spiritual difficulties. And it seems hard to some to come to the Lord's Supper because, if they do, they must pass under an examination with respect to their knowledge, and their pride makes 'em averse to that, lest they should be thought ignorant.

Many of the commands of God in his holy Word seem hard sayings to men that seek conversion. They spend a great deal of time in thinking of them and endeavoring to find out some excuse for their neglect of them. But they are long before they comply with them, and may never yield to them. But if you would obtain saving conversion, you must yield to those things that seem very hard to you. Why will you stand so long considering and hesitating when life and death are set before [you]? There is indeed no room for hesitation. There is a must in the case: you must take up the cross, as heavy as it is and as averse as you are to bear the burden of it.

4. Beware of being blinded concerning your practices by the deceitfulness of sin. This is one great hindrance of conversion and what, without doubt, prevents the conversion of multitudes. You had need keep the most strict and watchful and jealous eye upon your own heart with respect to this. Beware, lest through perverse reasonings you put evil for good and {good for evil}.

Beware that you ben't deceived concerning your past sins. Doubtless many of you have heretofore done those things that have been very ill in the sight of God, and abominable to his pure eyes, under a notion that it was lawful. Men, when they have done thus, especially when they have continued any time in any way of sin under this notion, are under strong prejudice in favor of their former deceits. They have allowed such and such things heretofore as lawful and it is therefore difficult for 'em now to see the evil of them and to condemn them. And so they are kept from that conviction of their own guilt that is needful for them. There is great guilt lies upon them by reason of the wicked practices they have indulged themselves in, and the first thing needful in order to the removal of guilt is their being convinced of their guilt. But this they are hindered from by their vain deceit. And therefore beware of such a deceit.

And beware that you ben't deceived concerning your future practices. Beware that you don't still do those things that are provoking to God and pernicious to your soul under a notion of there being no hurt in them. Take heed of bending your principles to your practices and, as it were, straining and forcing your opinions to agree with your dispositions. When men make their practices a rule to their principles, they proceed the backward way, a way that is the reverse of that which should be. And in such a way you are likely to fall behind and to be broken and snared and taken.

The wit of man has scarce ever been employed in anything more than in wresting the rules of God's Word and in finding out ways how to make their principle and corrupt practices agree. But this has a great tendency to prevent any saving good to the soul. Men's deceiving themselves thus about their practices don't hinder those practices being ruinous and destructive to them, as appears by Prov. 14:12, "There is a way that seems right unto a man, but the end thereof are the ways of death." Its seeming right to him don't hinder its leading of him to eternal death and damnation. The prophet Isaiah denounces woe to such. Is. 5:20, "Woe to them that call evil good, and good evil; that put darkness for light, and light for darkness; that put bitter for sweet, and sweet for bitter!"

And that men are so desperately inclined to deal deceitfully with God and their own consciences in those things is doubtless one main hindrance of the true and thorough conversion of sinners to God, and one great reason of warnings and counsels being so ineffectual. It prevents thorough reformation, which is very needful in order to conversion and is a great step towards it. Heb. 3: 12–13, "Take heed, brethren, lest there be in any of you an evil heart of unbelief, in departing from the living God. But exhort one another daily, while it is called Today; lest any of you be hardened through the deceitfulness of sin." II Cor. 11:3, "I fear, lest by any means, as the serpent beguiled Eve through his subtlety, so your minds should be corrupted from the simplicity that is in Christ."

5. Beware that you don't flatter yourself that you don't allow any known sin when, indeed, it is otherwise. Don't flatter yourself concerning these and those practices that you allow yourself in, that if they be sin they ben't known sins, when indeed you sin against light. Men very often will foolishly plead that, if they do sin in such and such things, 'tis a sin of ignorance. They plead that they are satisfied that 'tis lawful when, at the same time, they would not dare to do those things if they expected very speedily to be called to appear before God to give an account. And they will also plead concerning things that they do that they don't deny to be evil that, though they do 'em, yet they don't allow themselves in them, when indeed they do allow themselves in them. They go on in the practice of them and have no serious and fixed intention of any other. Such kind of things as these are great hindrances to any saving effect of the means of grace on the souls of men.

6. Be directed to avoid doubtful things, i.e. things that you are at a loss about whether they are lawful or not. If you are tempted to anything that is pleasing to your bodily appetites or would gratify your love of profit or honor but are doubtful in your own mind whether it be lawful or not; if

you can't satisfy yourself so but that, when you have done, there will remain a secret doubt whether you han't now been guilty of that which is wickedness in the sight of God: in such a case you had far better (for the safety of your own soul) to let alone. What says the Apostle? Rom. 14:23, "He that doubtest is damned if he eat." 'Tis best not to taste of fruit, though never so sweet, that you do but suspect is forbidden. Don't do such doubtful things and so disquiet your conscience and expose your own soul merely for the sake of a moment's pleasure, or in compliance with your company, or for a little worldly profit or honor.

7. As you would avoid whatsoever would be any impediment to your conversion, avoid not only those things that are in themselves sinful, but also things that lead to sin. Christ directs you to watch and pray against temptation (Matt. 21:41). And therefore take heed that you don't run yourself into temptation. One great hindrance of men's conversion, which prevents the means of grace from ever being effectual to that end, are the snares of the world. Therefore, as you would not have your conversion hindered, you should, as much as in you lies, avoid those snares.

If there be any practice that is customary that you can see no evil in considered in itself, yet if you have found by experience that it has proved of ill consequence to you—either by very much taking off your mind from the concerns of your soul, or indisposing you to secret prayer or any other duties of religion, or by leading you into those acts or speeches that are sinful—or if you have reason to think that the tendency of it is to lead to sin—from what is to be observed of the consequences of it in others or by reasons that you have heard offered in the preaching of the Word—then strictly avoid those things, as you would lay aside every weight and would have every clog and hindrance in the way of your conversion removed out of the way.

8. Don't seek conversion only in a way of doing duties to God, but also duties to men. The way to obtain saving conversion is thoroughly to reform your life and to seek God's grace in a way of all duty, of both tables of the law. You are not to think that all that you have to do in seeking conversion is reading and praying and hearing and meditating and attending ordinances; but if you would be in a likely way to be converted you must seek it also in duties of justice and charity to men, in a dutiful

behavior to your parents, duties of love to your brethren and sisters, duties to your husbands or wives or children, duties of meekness, justice and charity to your neighbors. You should strictly avoid all malice, strife, envy and backbiting and should abound in acts of love and seek to do what good you can.

Indeed, you should not do those things to make a righteousness of them. Neither should you avoid 'em and so live in sin for fear you should make a righteousness of them, any more than you should avoid reading, hearing and praying for fear you should make a righteousness of them. Reading and praying and attending ordinances are not a means of conversion by any virtue or power in those duties, but because they are the appointed way in which God will be sought and waited upon and will bestow his grace and blessing. And so are moral duties towards men a way that God has appointed for men to seek his grace, inasmuch as attending duties and ordinances of the Word of God.

We find in Scripture that a way of attending duties to men has been owned and succeeded with spiritual discoveries. So it was with the centurion. We have an account of his being one remarkable for acts of love and kindness to the people amongst whom he lived. Luke 7:5, "he loveth our nation, and hath built us a synagogue." And in this way he found favor with Christ. He came to him with a miraculous and wonderful manifestation of his grace to him when he healed his servant. So Cornelius, in the way of doing much alms to the people as well as praying to God, always obtained favor of God and, [by] a very wonderful discovery of God's grace to him and all his family, had those things discovered to him by which he and all his family were saved, and became the first fruits of the Gentiles, the first that were called in that calling of the Gentiles (Acts 10:4 and 11:14).

If we compare external duties towards God and moral duties towards men, the preference is to be given to the latter, as is declared in the Scriptures. For God "will have mercy, and not sacrifice" (Matt. 9:13).

9. If you would be in a likely way to obtain salvation, don't look to men as though they were to be your rule, but look to the rules of God's Word. If there be any that make a great profession and are reputed saints, or if they are accounted persons of great experience, don't think that you may do all

that you see such do. Consider that God has never set forth them to be your rule. He has given you something else for your rule and that is his own, holy Word that is pure and wholly right.

We ought to have respect to the good examples of others. But there is no example, excepting only the example of our Lord Jesus Christ, that ought to have the force of a rule with us. We should not be over-busy in observing how reputed saints carry themselves, to watch for their halting and mark all their faults and blemishes, to lay them as stumbling blocks for ourselves to fall over. If we can see anything in them that is agreeable to the rules of God's Word, we should be stirred up by it also to follow the same rule. But as to their errors, whether small or great, 'tis safest for us to let 'em alone. There may be difficulties in them that we can't solve. Nor is it necessary that we should. We are not appointed to be their judges; to their own Master they stand or fall. We have a sufficient and sure rule for our direction without determining anything about their ill carriages one way or the other. God has appointed us to be doers of the law, and not judges, as Jas. 4:11.

10. Be directed to make the best of bad times. There is a great deal of difference in times with respect to the advantage persons are under to obtain conversion. A time of a general striving of the Spirit of God is a blessed season for this purpose, a glorious opportunity to obtain conversion. But when it is a very dead time it is far otherwise. The stream then is strong the other way. Everything seems to pull men back and hinder men in this business. 'Tis now such a time amongst us. But you must consider that a great many persons die in bad times. Death is as common in bad times as good ones. It don't wait for men to have a time of the outpouring of the Spirit of God to die in. Conversion is therefore as necessary in bad times as good ones.

Therefore, as the work is more difficult, there is need of the more care and watchfulness and the greater labor and diligence. You must be the more watchful against the temptations and ill examples of such an evil time. You must row up this stream and, the stronger the stream is against you, you must put to the more strength. The apostles exhorted the Jews to save themselves from that untoward generation (Acts 2:40).

11. Beware that you don't hearken to the devil while you are seeking your

salvation. When any person sets about this business, the devil is wont to be exceeding busy with him. He lays himself out to his utmost by his wiles and temptations to hinder their success—for he is afraid that he shall lose one of the subjects of his kingdom—and suggests many things to them to embarrass and ensnare their minds. He endeavors sometimes to flatter them and at other times to discourage them. {They try} in vain to use means {to overcome his temptations and attain their salvation; this} only makes them worse. {They find that it is} best to leave off secret prayer {rather than to rely on such means for salvation}. 'Tis not worth their while to attend such and such ordinances and duties. [The devil suggests to them that they] have committed unpardonable sin {and that the} day of grace is past. {Indeed, he} often suggests very blasphemous thoughts. If you would be in an hopeful way to obtain conversion, don't hearken to any such like temptations of Satan. Such suggestions are commonly from the devil. He is your enemy. Jas. 4:7, "Resist the devil." Be exhorted by no means to yield to him; but turn away from him after the example of Christ. Resist all his temptations.

Hear what God says, the counsels that are given you from his holy Word that will be a sure guide to you, that will lead you in a safe way. But if you hearken to the devil, he will soon lead you over precipices and into pits, into the mire, and by which means your soul shall perish. And if Satan suggests blasphemous thoughts to you, the best way is not to stand to dispute with him or so much as to give him the hearing. Don't enter in any contest with him; but turn away your ear from him and let your mind be intent on something else more profitable to you than anything concerning those things that he makes an handle of to perplex you with dreadful, blasphemous thoughts.

12. Take heed that nothing beside the great concern of your soul should insensibly steal away and swallow up the care and concern of your mind. There are many objects that you are encompassed with that are very apt to draw away the heart and get possession of the mind and, oftentimes, all a person's convictions and all that they have done in seeking conversion is overthrown and lost by this means. Something or other happens that drives the affection and fills up their thoughts and time, and so the word of God is choked as with thorns that spring up among the seed that has been

sown. Sometimes 'tis some pleasure that steals in and overcharges the heart; sometimes some worldly business, new affair; sometimes something new in a person's circumstances; sometimes something of a public nature that becomes a matter of common talk. Therefore take heed that your heart ben't unawares overcharged with such things, which will set you further off from the kingdom of God than ever. Luke 21:34, "take heed to yourselves, lest at any time [your hearts be overcharged with surfeiting, and drunkenness, and cares of this life, and so that day come upon you unawares]."

13. Take heed that you don't flatter yourself with anything that you imagine looks peculiarly promising in your particular [case]. 'Tis probable that everyone is ready to do so. All men in a natural condition are ready to think they see something that makes it especially hopeful concerning them that they shall be converted before they die and so shall not go to hell at last. Some, it may be, flatter themselves in their own wisdom, whereby they are able to contrive likely ways for themselves; some in the steadfastness of their resolutions; some in their godly relations and the many prayers they have put up for them; some in one thing and some in another. This is what proves pernicious and ruinous to multitudes. Ps. 36:2, "he flattereth himself in his own eyes, till his iniquity be found to be hateful." Flattering themselves in such things keeps 'em from having those awakenings and that sense of their danger that is needful in order to their conversion, and so keeps 'em from being so thorough to escape that which they are in danger of. Therefore be exceeding watchful against such self-flattery.

14. Labor to be so thorough in the use of means for your conversion that your conscience mayn't hereafter accuse [you] of any willful negligence. Let the event be what it will, if it should be so at last that you should not have success, if it should be so that you should, when you come to lie upon a deathbed, have no hopeful evidences of your being in a safe estate, yet take heed that at that time your conscience mayn't accuse you as being your own destroyer by a foolish neglect of anything that you ought to have done and might have done. Do what you can. "Whatever your hand finds to do, do it with your might" (Cant. 9:10). Let no ordinance nor any duty whatsoever be neglected by you. Make the best improvement of every

ordinance and every providence and every advantage and talent that God has put into your hands.

15. If you would be in a likely way to be converted, look not at secret things but to things that are revealed. Deut. 29:29, "The secret things belong unto the Lord our God: but those things which are revealed belong unto us and to our children forever, that we may do all the words of this law."

Don't perplex your mind with the secret decrees of God, and particularly about the eternal decrees of God with respect to yourself, prying into those secrets which are hidden from men and angels, laboring to unseal that book which is sealed with seven seals and which no man in heaven or earth is worthy or able to open or to look thereon. When men get into a way of perplexing their minds with such things, they are in a very unhappy way. The devil has 'em in a dismal snare. Therefore diligently avoid such a snare and let the revealed will of God be enough for you. Mind what God commands you, what counsels and direction he gives. Let your whole heart be intent upon those things. This is the way for you to prosper. But if you entangle and tease your mind with thoughts about the secret, eternal counsels of God, you will be out of the way of your duty and in the way to your own mischief and will expose yourself to ruin.

16. Don't look so much at what you have done as what you have to do. Don't make much of your past doings or spend time in thinking what pains you have taken—how much more you have done than others, how much you have done without success, how many prayers you have made and God has not heard you, how long you have sought and yet han't found, and the like—but forget the things that are behind, as the apostle Paul did (Phil. 3:13). You have enough to think of that more concerns you, and that is what you have yet to do: what God still requires of you while your day of grace and opportunity lasts; what advantages you have still in your hands and how you shall make the best improvement of them. This is the way for you to make progress and be successful at last.

17. Take heed that you don't trust either in anything that you have done or can do for, when you have done all, you have done nothing, nothing that can make any atonement for the least of your sins or that [is] worthy

to be offered as a price for the least of God's favors. None of it is worthy of God's acceptance, as that he should bestow one favorable look upon it. Nothing is done from love to him and, if it were all done from love to him, yea, and ten thousand times as much, still all would deserve no regard from God from such a rebel as you have been. You would not in the least deserve any pity by it, as that God should save you from eternal misery or bestow the least dram of grace upon you or that he should have any manner of regard to any of your prayers or cries. For sin is a thing of infinite demerit and, therefore, if you can fill of millions of ages in prayers and sufferings and watchfulness and labor, it would be nothing, for nothing short of an infinite merit can be an atonement for your sin.

Thus I have given you the best directions that I am able in order to your obtaining a saving conversion to God. Let me now entreat you to endeavor to follow them. Don't carelessly forget directions that you hear from time to time in order to your conversion. I could wish that all that are desirous of obtaining conversion would keep these directions (or some others that are of like nature) always by them, and frequently think of them, and make it their constant care to conform themselves to 'em.

[*Second.*] I conclude with two or three considerations that I would set before you very briefly to move you to follow these directions:

1. Consider what these directions are for. They are for your life. Here are applicable those words of the wise man in Prov. 4:13, "Take fast hold of instruction; let her not go: keep her; for she is thy life." It is for your life that I have been giving you directions, for life in the highest sense of the word, for ten thousand times more than temporal life. 'Tis for your salvation from eternal death and for your obtaining everlasting life, a life of glory, no mean or ordinary life, but a life of the greatest honor and blessedness, in the possession of a crown and kingdom, to live and reign forever and ever.

2. There is no one person that hears me now but that is under a possibility of conversion: old, young, bond and free, poor, wicked. You are all under a possibility of salvation; otherwise God would not have set open the doors of his house to you this day. You all appear here to have salvation offered to you in the name of Christ, all [are] naturally capable of this

change, and all are in the enjoyment of these means. Christ opens his arms to receive you all. Prov. 8:4, "Unto you, O men, [I call; and my voice is to the sons of man]."

3. If you follow these directions, in all probability you will be converted. This appears by Prov. 2, at [the] beginning [vv. 1–5]: "My son, if thou wilt receive my words, and hide my commandments with thee. . . . Then shalt thou understand the fear of the Lord, and find the knowledge of God." These directions are agreeable to God's word and, therefore, are his directions: so that, if you will follow them, you will be in God's own way: so that, you that are desirous of being converted and are much concerned for fear you should be damned, you have now heard of a way how you may in all likelihood be converted, and may be delivered from hell, and may be better prepared for death, and may be happy and blessed forever.

To the Mohawks at the Treaty, August 16, 1751

These honorable gentlemen treat in the name {of King George}, but I in the name of Jesus Christ. . . .

II Peter 1:19.
We have also a more sure word of prophecy, whereunto ye do well that ye take heed, as unto a light that shineth in a dark place, until the day dawn, and the day star arise in your hearts.

When God first made man, he had a principle of holiness in his heart.

That holiness that was in him was like a light that shone in his heart, so that his mind was full of light.

But when man sinned against God, he lost his holiness, and then the light that was in his mind was put out.

Sin and the devil came in and took possession of his heart, and his mind was full of darkness.

But the consequence was that the world of mankind sank down more and more into darkness, and most of the nations of the world by degrees quite lost the knowledge of the true God.

Some worshipped [the] sun and moon and stars, some worshipped images of gold and silver, brass and iron, wood and stone.

Some worshipped serpents and other beasts.

And some worshipped the devil, that used to come to 'em, and appear to 'em, and make 'em believe that he was the true God.

And other nations that had some remembrance of the God that made the world yet were very much in the dark. They did not know what he was.

Knew very little about another world and what was like to become of men after they are dead.

The "honorable gentlemen" were British representatives negotiating at Albany, New York, with the Mohawks to establish a political alliance. Edwards preached this sermon as missionary to the Indians at Stockbridge, Massachusetts, where some of the Mohawks were to settle.

Nor did they know anything, how men that had sinned and had offended God should be reconciled to him and obtain his favor.

And many nations were very ignorant and blind and did not know much more than the beasts.

In this state the world was very miserable, not knowing anything, what they should do to be saved.

And so the greater part of the world from generation to generation was blinded by the devil and led down to destruction.

But the great God took pity on mankind and gave 'em the holy Scriptures to teach men and to be in this world as a light shining in a dark place.

God first made known himself to Moses and other prophets, and directed them to write a part of the Bible.

And after many ages, he sent his own Son into the world to die for sinners and more fully to instruct the world.

This was about 1,750 years ago.

And then Christ directed his apostles to write the Word in a more clear manner, and so the Bible was finished.

And Christ commanded that his word contained in the Bible should be oped to all nations, and that all should be instructed out of it.

And this is the great light that God has given to teach mankind concerning the God that made 'em and concerning another world.

Now those nations that have the Scripture, they enjoy light. The Lord Jesus shines upon them like a bright and glorious sun.

But the nations that have not the Bible live in great darkness, and the devil, the prince of darkness, reigns over 'em.

But here you must note this: of them that have the Bible, there are two sorts.

There are some that are truly good men, and they not only have the light shining round about 'em, but the light shines into their hearts.

And there are others that are wicked men that will not regard the Scripture, and they, although the light shines round about 'em, yet it don't shine into 'em but are perfectly dark within.

Those last receive no benefit by the Scripture. The Scripture does 'em no good.

But 'tis their own fault. They have great opportunity to be made happy if they would but improve it.

Therefore there are these two things one ought to do:

1. We should seek to know the Word of God, that we might be instructed by it.

2. We should receive it into our hearts and practice according to it.

Now, therefore, mind the Apostle's counsel in the text. Give heed to this sure word of God till "the day dawn, and the day star arise in your hearts."

Your forefathers have for a great many ages lived in great darkness.

And since the white people came over the seas and have settled in these parts of the world, they have not done their duty to you. They have greatly neglected you.

So that although 'tis about 140 years since the white people came over here, there are but few of the poor Indians have been thoroughly instructed to this very day.

But few of your children have been taught to read.

And therefore you know but little of the Word of God, for you ben't able to read it.

This has been a shameful neglect of the white people, by which the great God has undoubtedly been made very angry.

For God is a merciful God, and would have all men be saved and come to the knowledge of the truth.

Jesus Christ gave command that the gospel should be preached to all nations.

The Christian religion teaches kindness and love to all mankind.

And therefore the white people have not behaved like Christians, that they have shown no more love to your souls.

The French, they pretend to teach the Indians religion, but they won't teach 'em to read. They won't let 'em read the Word of God. They are afraid that if they should read the Scripture, they would know that their ways are not agreeable to the Scripture.

And therefore they refuse to open the Bible to the Indians, but keep it just shut up.

When the Bible is hid from 'em, they can cheat 'em and make 'em believe what they have a mind to.

And many of the English and Dutch are against your being instructed. They choose to keep you in the dark for the sake of making a gain of you.

For as long as they keep you in ignorance, 'tis more easy to cheat you in trading with you.

And some have taken wrong ways in instructing the Indians.

And they have baptized 'em and given the sacrament to 'em before they have been well instructed, and while they have lived in their drunkenness.

Whereas baptism and the sacrament are privileges which God has appointed only for his people, such as are virtuous men.

And no wonder many white people flatter the Indians in their wickedness: for they live in wickedness and flatter one another in it.

But you have been neglected long enough. 'Tis now high time that some more effectual care should be taken that you may be really brought into the clear light, and know as much as the English do.

And the great God seems mercifully to have moved the hearts of many of the English of late, especially in England, to give much money for this end.

And we do no more than our duty in it, for it was once with our forefathers as 'tis with you. They formerly were in great darkness and knew no more than the Indians when the white people first came over here.

But God put it into the hearts of others to come and instruct the English in the Word of God, and so to bring 'em into the light.

This good we had by the kindness of God to us, and therefore we ought to be ready to show this kindness to you.

We are no better than you in no respect, only as God has made us to differ and has been pleased to give us more light. And now we are willing to give it to you.

Now, therefore, don't content yourselves to live in darkness any longer.

Consider wisely what is best for yourselves, and take that course that will tend most for your good and the good of your children.

Religion is the greatest concern of mankind. The temporal concerns that they treat with you about at Albany from year to year are mere childish trifles in comparison of this.

For by and by you must all die and go into another world, and then none of the things of this world will do you any good. But the things of religion, in their effects and consequences, last forever.

When you are dead, your eyes will be open. Then this world will look little to you, and you shall know that religion is infinitely the greatest concern.

'Tis because men are blind that they are not more concerned for the good of their souls and the souls of their poor children.

'Tis because they are blind that they go in drunkenness and spend away their lives in wickedness.

The devil blinds men's eyes and tries to his utmost to keep 'em in the dark, that he may destroy 'em.

I have read of some nations, that when they take children captives in war, they keep 'em well for a while and feed 'em with the best till they are fat, and then kill 'em and eat 'em.

So the devil does by wicked men.

Now, therefore, look well about you and consider what is best for yourselves and your children.

There never was such an opportunity for you to be brought into the light as there is now.

We invite you to come and enjoy the light of the Word of God, which is ten thousand times better than [the] light of the sun.

There is such a thing as this light's shining into the heart, as it does into the hearts of all good men.

And when it does so, it changes their hearts and makes 'em like to Jesus Christ.

'Tis as when you hold a glass out in the light of the sun, the glass will shine with a resemblance of the sun's brightness.

Like a sweet and beautiful flower in the spring.

Before the heart of a man is sanctified, the heart won't receive the light of the Word of God.

A wicked man that hears the Word of God and won't receive it is like a piece of dung in the light of the sun. It sends forth a stink, but reflects no light.

When the light of God's Word shines into the heart, it gives new life to the soul.

You see how it is [in] the spring. When the sun shines on the earth and trees, it gives 'em new life, makes the earth looks green. It causes flowers to appear and give a good smell.

So it is in the heart of a man when the light of God's Word shines into it.

Wisdom and knowledge in religion is better than silver or gold and all the riches of the world.

The light, when it shines into the heart, is sweeter than the honey, and the gospel will be a pleasant sound to you when you come to understand it.

Therefore if you would be a wise and an happy people, put yourselves in the way of receiving this light.

You love your children: therefore take care for their instruction, that they may be the children of the light, the children of God, and not the children of the devil.

If you never have this light shine into the heart, you must dwell forever in darkness, in another world, with the devil, the prince of darkness, in hell.

And there is a burning heat but no light.

But if you receive this light into your hearts, you will be prepared to die and fitted to dwell in heaven, which is a world of light. And there you yourselves will shine forth forever as the sun in the kingdom of Jesus Christ.

He That Believeth Shall Be Saved (1751)

Mark 16:15–16.
Go ye into all the world and preach the gospel to every creature.
He that believeth and is baptized shall be saved;
but he that believeth not shall be damned.

Before Christ came, there was but one nation that worshipped the true God, which was the nation of the Jews. All other nations in the world worshipped idols, the sun, moon, and stars, and worshipped images, and worshipped the devil.

The nations of the world first of all worshipped the true God that made heaven and earth, and continued to do so for some time after the flood.

But in two or three hundred years after the flood, they began by degrees to grow more wicked and to forget the true God. The devil drew 'em away to worship other things that were no gods.

And then [God] called Abraham and separated him from the rest of the world, that he might keep up the knowledge of him, and of the true religion, in his posterity.

And after this, all the world, besides the Jews, who were Abraham's posterity, fell away to the worship of idols and had wholly lost the true religion.

And so all continued worshipping idols for about 1,500 years, till Christ came.

When [Christ] first came, which was about 1,750 years ago, he preached the gospel to the Jews only, and so continued until the Jews put him to death.

But after he rose from the dead, then he bid his disciples go into all the world, and not only preach the gospel to the Jews, but to teach all nations and preach the gospel to every creature, as we are told in the text.

The Jews, because they had been the people of God for so long a time, were proud of their privileges, and thought that no other people could be saved but they.

But Christ tells his disciples that all that believed and was baptized, of whatever nation, should be saved, and that he that believed not should be damned.

And so we have an account afterwards of how the disciples afterwards went all about the world preaching the gospel to all nations.

And by degrees a great many nations threw away their idols and turned to the Christian religion.

So that in about three hundred years after Christ, a great part of the world, all the greatest and strongest nations of the world, became Christians. And there was the greatest change and alteration in the world that ever was.

Christ was the light of the world. The preaching of the gospel was like the rising of the sun in the morning that drove away all darkness and filled the world with light.

Before this, the English were ignorant and dark, just like the Indians were before the English came here.

Christ in the text tells his disciples what they must preach to all nations and how men of all nations might come to be saved.

He tells them that they that believe in him shall be saved, and they that don't believe shall be damned.

This forenoon I shall speak from those words, "He that believeth shall be saved."

And here I shall do two things: I shall first show what is meant by believing in Christ, and then will show how that believing in Christ is the way to be saved.

I. What is meant by believing in Christ.

For a man to believe in Christ is to come to him with all the heart, to take him for his Savior and give himself to him, to be one of his people and to have all his dependence on Christ to make him happy.

There are a great many that are called Christians that are baptized, and keep sabbath days, and go to meeting, who don't truly believe in Christ.

There are a great many that own the Christian religion, and say they believe there is but one God, and that Christ is the Son of God and Savior of sinners, that don't truly believe in Christ.

They that are wicked men, that walk in wicked ways, let 'em say what they will, don't truly believe in the Lord Jesus Christ.

Such as these don't believe in Christ with all their hearts. They in their hearts never came to Christ, to be his people and take him for their Savior.

They that truly believe in Christ, they know Christ. God opens their eyes to see how great and how glorious he is, and how good and how lovely he is.

If a man be blind and don't see how excellent Christ is, he will never come to him and accept of him as a Savior with all his heart.

They that truly believe in Christ, they see the excellency of the great things that the Word of God teaches about Christ and the way of being saved by him. And they are fully convinced 'tis the word of God.

They that truly believe in Christ, they see what wicked miserable creatures they be, and so they see their need of a Savior to deliver [them] from this misery.

They who don't know their misery and don't see their need of Christ won't come to him with all their hearts.

If a sick man that is like to die don't know that he is dangerously sick, and thinks he is pretty well, he won't go with all his heart to the physician to cure him.

They that believe in Christ, they see that they can't help themselves, that if Christ don't save 'em they must perish.

And they see how exceeding sinful they be, all over sinful, and that they deserve to be damned.

They that don't see how wicked they be, and how they deserve to perish, can't come with all their hearts to Christ to save 'em.

They that truly believe in Christ, they see that he is able to save him, that there is enough in him for 'em.

When they see how great and glorious he is, that will convince them that for so glorious a person to die was a thing great enough to answer for all their sins.

And they see that his love and mercy and pity is enough for such poor, wicked, miserable creatures as they are.

They that truly believe in Christ, they see how lovely he is, and they love him with all their hearts.

They that don't love Christ never will come to him with all their hearts to save 'em.

They that do truly believe in Christ, they give themselves to him to be his people. They give their hearts to him. They are made willing to give up themselves to him wholly in soul and body forever.

They that do truly believe in Christ, they in their hearts forsake all for Christ, forsake all their sins, forsake the world, and are willing to leave all for Christ.

They that truly believe in Christ, they are willing to forsake father and mother, wife and children, brothers and sisters, houses and lands, yea, and their own lives, rather than to forsake Christ [Matt. 19:29].

Thus I have told you what it is to believe in Christ.

I come now, in the

II. Second place, to show how that thus believing in Christ is the only way to be saved by Christ.

All that are saved, are saved for Christ's sake alone. God saves 'em wholly on Christ's account. But God won't save any for Christ's sake whose hearts don't come to him for salvation.

We can never pay God for the sins we have committed against him by anything we can do. Christ has done it for us. And therefore our hearts must go to Christ for salvation, and we must not go nowhere else.

Christ has suffered for us, and has satisfied for our sin, and has paid down a sufficient price for our salvation. He has done all. There is nothing for us to do now but only believe in Christ, and with all our hearts to come to him for salvation.

If Adam had never fallen, then he would have had eternal life on his own account, and for his own goodness. But now, since we have fallen and lost our goodness, we are saved only for Christ's sake.

We now are not saved for our goodness. You must never expect to be saved for your good deeds. For your goodness can never pay for your badness.

It makes God very angry when such wicked creatures as we are expect to be saved for our goodness.

If men do never so much in religion—if they read the Bible, pray never so much, keep the sabbath never so well, come to meeting, if [they are] honest, if they give to the poor—they must not think that these things pay for their sins, and that God will save 'em for this.

We must see our own vileness and wickedness, and lie down in the dust before God, and own we deserve nothing but to be cast into hell.

And we must come to Christ and trust in him only, and not in our own righteousness, for salvation.

We can't be saved without being good, but 'tis not because our goodness is sufficient, or can do anything of itself. But 'tis because all whose hearts come to Christ will be good, and if men ben't good, their hearts never will come to Christ.

Though Christ has paid for all our sins and has done enough for our salvation without anything of ours, yet God won't save any for Christ's sake but such as belong to Christ.

God don't look on any as belonging to Christ whose hearts don't come to him.

They whose hearts come to Christ, they are joined to Christ, and so they belong to him and therefore are saved for his sake.

They who believe in Christ, their hearts are joined to Christ, and so in the Scripture they are called members of his body [I Cor. 6:15, 12:12]. Christ is the head and they are the members.

And sometimes in the Bible Christ is compared to a tree, and they who believe on him to the branches [Hos. 14, John 15:5].

And sometimes Christ is called the husband, and the soul of a believer [is compared] to his wife [Cant. 4:8–12, 5:1], because as the heart of a wife is joined to her husband, so is the believer's heart joined to Christ's.

And the great reason why God is willing to save good men is not because of their goodness, or for anything they do—for they are sinful unworthy creatures—but because they are joined to Christ.

All that are joined to Christ and belong to Christ, God will save 'em for Christ's sake. For God infinitely loves Christ, and Christ has done enough and suffered enough for their salvation.

This is the great difference between the way of getting eternal life which God proposed to Adam before the fall, and that which is now.

If Adam had never sinned, he will have been made happy for his own goodness. But now we can be saved only by believing in Christ.

I showed in the forenoon how all that believe in Christ shall be saved. I would now show how they that don't believe shall be damned.

I told you in the forenoon what it was for a man to believe in Christ: how it is to come to him with all the heart, to take him for a Savior, and to give himself to be his, to be one of his people, and to look to him for all his happiness.

They that don't thus come to Christ can never be saved. Not one man can ever be saved in any other way. All the rest shall be damned.

Two things:

I. Show what it is to be damned.

II. Give the reasons why every man that don't believe in Christ [shall be damned].

[I.] To be damned is to be perfectly deprived of all good and to suffer perfect misery to all eternity as the fruit of the wrath of God for sin.

They that are damned are lost. God throws them away and never will take any care of them, or show 'em any mercy.

They shall be separated from God. They that are saved shall come near to God to dwell with him, but they that are damned shall be driven away from him.

God will love those that are saved, but they that are damned, God will be angry with them, and hate 'em and be their enemy forever.

They shall have no part with the saints in heaven. They shall see them at a great distance, but shall never come nigh them.

They shall be deprived of all the good things of this world, and they shall have no good things in another world, so that they shall have nothing. They shall be wholly deprived of all good.

They shall wish and long for many things, but they shall have nothing. They shall have perfect darkness, and not the least beam of light.

And they shall suffer all misery. They shall be filled full of misery. They shall be like a cup thrown all over into the water, that is filled as full as it can hold.

When they die and the soul goes out of the body, God will send no angels to take care of it, and he will let the devils take it.

The devils will fly upon it like hungry bears and wolves, and shall carry the soul down into hell.

There the soul shall be cast into a great fire and shall be tormented continually without any rest, day or night.

That fire is not like our fires in this world. Those fires are fires kindled by men, but that fire will be the fire of the wrath of the great God.

And at the end of the world, the dead body shall be raised and the soul shall be joined to it again.

And then the body and soul both shall be cast into a great fire along with the devils.

There shall be no end of this misery. After thousands and thousands of thousands of years, it will be but just beginning, no nearer to an end.

God will have no pity upon 'em. If they pray to him, he won't hear their prayers. He won't hear their cries and shrieks.

Now in this world God stands ready to pity sinners if they will hearken to him and come to Christ. But if they won't hearken, he will not pity 'em in another world.

They shall have no way to escape, find no way out, nor will they find any to help 'em.

They shall have no friends. God won't be their friend. Christ will not be their friend. The angels [will not be their friends]. Good men [will not be their friends]. Those that were their friends in this world [will not be their friends]. The devils {will not be their friends}, but will be like wolves and serpents to torment 'em. Others that be in hell along with them {will not be their friends], will hate 'em, [will] torment one another. They that used to be their friends in this world [will not be their friends in hell]. Fathers [will not be their friends].

So that they will have no hope when they think of eternity before 'em. They shall have no hope, and O! how will that sink their hearts.

II. Reasons why every man that don't believe in Christ shall be damned.

All men have sinned and deserve to be damned. All men are naturally full of sin.

And there [is] no other Savior of sinners, no way of salvation, but by Christ.

And therefore all they that don't belong to Christ must be damned.

But none belong to Christ but they that there are joined to him.

But none are joined to Christ but only they whose hearts come to Christ, and so believe in him.

They that don't believe in Christ can't be saved by Christ, because they won't have him for their Savior.

If they are baptized, and go to meeting, and seem to show respect to Christ, yet God looks at the heart. He sees that, and he sees that their hearts despise Christ.

And therefore God don't look upon 'em as belonging to Christ. God don't count 'em the people of Christ, nor have they any part in him.

And if they have no part in Christ, nothing that they can do, none of their goodness, can save 'em.

For 'tis Christ's death and his goodness that satisfies for sin and buys heaven, and not their goodness.

APPLICATION.

[I.] Now therefore, let everyone look into himself, and search his own heart, and see whether he does truly believe in the Lord Jesus Christ.

Don't think it enough that you come to meeting, [were] baptized; that you are honest, keep sabbath days, don't get drunk.

You must do these things, must keep the sabbath, {must not get drunk, etc.}. But those things alone won't do. You must give your whole hearts to Christ. Have your eyes ever been opened to see the glorious excellency of Jesus Christ?

Has the light of the Word of God ever shined into your heart so that to see the excellence of that Word that teaches Christ and the work of salvation by him?

Has that Word of Christ been made sweeter to you than the honey and honeycomb?

Is the Word of Christ sweet food to your soul, that puts new life into you and is better than silver and gold?

Do you see your need you have of Christ? Do you [see] what poor, wicked, miserable creatures you are?

Do you see that all your goodness, all your prayers, and all that you do, is not worthy to be accepted of God, and can never pay for your sins?

Is your heart broken for your sin? And do you see what a filthy, vile, abominable creature you be?

Do you see that you don't deserve any mercy, that you deserve to be cast into hell forever and ever for your wickedness?

Do you see that you are like a poor little infant that can't help yourself, and that therefore you need the help of Christ?

And does your whole heart go to Christ, and him alone, as your Savior?

Do you give your heart to Christ, and are you willing with all your heart to give yourself to Christ, to be his people forever and ever?

Are you willing to forsake all for Christ?

The Scripture says that he that believes in Christ is like a man that [buys] one pearl of great price [Matt. 13:46].

Are you willing to forsake all your sins, forsake all the world for Christ?

Now, in the

II. Second place, I advise all poor sinners to come to Christ for salvation and give them with all their hearts to him.

You are poor miserable creatures. You are in danger of going to hell, and stand in great need of Christ.

There is no other way for you to be saved. God never appointed any other Savior but he.

You must come to Christ. You can't do without him. If you don't come to him, you must be damned forever and ever.

You have a better opportunity than many others. You have the gospel preached to you. You are instructed in the way of salvation by him. And many others have no such privilege.

Christ in his Word calls you to come to him. He invites, he bids you come, and welcome.

If you are a great sinner, a wicked person, if you have done wickedness a thousand times, yet Christ is ready to receive you if you will come to him.

Christ calls all, men and women, young and old, and little children. All are invited to look to him that they may be saved.

Christ gave directions {to his disciples} to preach the gospel to every creature under heaven.

Christ has provided a great feast. {He has} set his door wide open. Whosoever will, may come.

You may come and eat without money. Come for nothing. Christ has paid the price, and you may come for nothing.

Nothing is required of you for your escaping eternal burnings and having all the glory of heaven, but only to come to Christ for it with all your heart.

You may have Christ for your Savior and may have all heaven, only if you will give Christ your hearts.

Christ stands at the door and knocks. If you will open the door, he will come in and he will give himself to you, and all that he has.

Now is your opportunity, while life lasts. Christ never will invite you and offer himself to you anymore after you are dead.

The Scriptures say if you won't hear now while Christ calls to you, he won't hear you when you call to him in your misery, but will laugh at your calamity and mock you when you cry in great distress [Prov. 1:26].

Christ this day calls and invites you. I am his servant, and I invite you to come to him.

Therefore make haste. Delay not. Give your heart to Christ and he will save you from hell, and all heaven shall be yours.

A Divine and Supernatural Light, Immediately Imparted to the Soul By the Spirit of God, Shown to Be Both a Scriptural, and Rational Doctrine (1734)

Matthew 16:17.
And Jesus answered and said unto him, Blessed art thou, Simon Barjona: for flesh and blood hath not revealed it unto thee, but my Father which is in heaven.

Christ says these words to Peter, upon occasion of his professing his faith in him as the Son of God. Our Lord was inquiring of his disciples, who men said that he was; not that he needed to be informed, but only to introduce and give occasion to what follows. They answer, that some said he was John the Baptist, and some Elias, and others Jeremias or one of the prophets. When they had thus given an account, who others said he was, Christ asks them, who they said he was. Simon Peter, whom we find always zealous and forward, was the first to answer; he readily replied to the question, "Thou art Christ, the Son of the living God" [v. 16].

Upon this occasion Christ says as he does *to* him and *of* him in the text: in which we may observe,

1. That Peter is pronounced blessed on this account. "Blessed art thou"—"Thou art an happy man, that thou art not ignorant of this, that I am Christ, the Son of the living God. Thou art distinguishingly happy. Others are blinded, and have dark and deluded apprehensions, as you have now given an account, some thinking that I am Elias, and some that I am Jeremias, and some one thing, and some another; but none of them thinking right, all of them misled. Happy art thou, that art so distinguished as to know the truth in this matter."

2. The evidence of this his happiness declared; viz. that God, and he only, had revealed it to him. This is an evidence of his being blessed,

(1) First, as it shows how peculiarly favored he was of God, above others, q.d. "How highly favored art thou, that others that are wise and great men, the Scribes, Pharisees, and rulers, and the nation in general, are left in darkness, to follow their own misguided apprehensions, and that thou shouldst be singled out, as it were by name, that my heavenly Father should thus set his love on thee, Simon Barjona. This argues thee blessed, that thou shouldst thus be the object of God's distinguishing love."

(2) Secondly, it evidences his blessedness also, as it intimates that this knowledge is above any that flesh and blood can reveal. "This is such knowledge as my Father which [is] in heaven only can give: it is too high and excellent to be communicated by such means as other knowledge is. Thou art blessed, that thou knowest that which God alone can teach thee."

The original of this knowledge is here declared; both negatively and positively. Positively, as God is here declared the author of it. Negatively, as 'tis declared that flesh and blood had not revealed it. God is the author of all knowledge and understanding whatsoever: he is the author of the knowledge, that is obtained by human learning: he is the author of all moral prudence, and of the knowledge and skill that men have in their secular business. Thus it is said of all in Israel that were wise-hearted, and skilled in embroidering, that God had filled them with the spirit of wisdom (Ex. 28:3).

God is the author of such knowledge; but yet not so but that flesh and blood reveals it. Mortal men are capable of imparting the knowledge of human arts and sciences, and skill in temporal affairs. God is the author of such knowledge by those means: flesh and blood is made use of by God as the mediate or second cause of it; he conveys it by the power and influence of natural means. But this spiritual knowledge, spoken of in the text, is what God is the author of, and none else: he reveals it, and flesh and blood reveals it not. He imparts this knowledge immediately, not making use of any intermediate natural causes, as he does in other knowledge.

What had passed in the preceding discourse, naturally occasioned Christ to observe this; because the disciples had been telling, how others did not know him, but were generally mistaken about him, and divided and confounded in their opinions of him: but Peter had declared his assured faith that he was the Son of God. Now it was natural to observe, how it was not flesh and blood, that had revealed it to him, but God; for if this knowledge were dependent on natural causes or means, how came it to pass that they, a company of poor fishermen, illiterate men, and persons of low education, attained to the knowledge of the truth; while the Scribes and Pharisees, men of vastly higher advantages, and greater knowledge and sagacity in other matters, remained in ignorance? This could be owing only to the gracious distinguishing influence and revelation of the Spirit of God. Hence, what I would make the subject of my present discourse from these words, is this:

DOCTRINE.

There is such a thing, as a spiritual and divine light, immediately imparted to the soul by God, of a different nature from any that is obtained by natural means.

In what I say on this subject at this time, I would:

I. Show what this divine light is.

II. How it is given immediately by God, and not obtained by natural means.

III. Show the truth of the doctrine.

And then conclude with a brief improvement.

I. I would show what this spiritual and divine light is. And in order to it would show,

First, in a few things what it is not. And here,

1. Those convictions that natural men may have of their sin and misery is not this spiritual and divine light. Men in a natural condition may have convictions of the guilt that lies upon them, and of the anger of God, and their danger of divine vengeance. Such convictions are from light or sensibleness of truth: that some sinners have a greater conviction of their guilt and misery than others, is because some have more light, or more of an apprehension of truth, than others. And this light and conviction may be from the Sprit of God; the Spirit convinces men of sin: but yet nature is

much more concerned in it than in the communication of that spiritual and divine light, that is spoken of in the doctrine; 'tis from the Spirit of God only as assisting natural principles, and not as infusing any new principles. Common grace differs from special, in that it influences only by assisting of nature; and not by imparting grace, or bestowing anything above nature. The light that is obtained, is wholly natural, or of no superior kind to what mere nature attains to; though more of that kind be obtained, than would be obtained if men were left wholly to themselves. Or in other words, common grace only assists the faculties of the soul to do that more fully, which they do by nature; as natural conscience, or reason, will by mere nature make a man sensible of guilt, and will accuse and condemn him when he has done amiss. Conscience is a principle natural to men; and the work that it doth naturally, or of itself, is to give an apprehension of right and wrong; and to suggest to the mind the relation that there is between right and wrong, and a retribution. The Spirit of God, in those convictions which unregenerate men sometimes have, assists conscience to do this work in a further degree, than it would do if they were left to themselves: he helps it against those things that tend to stupefy it, and obstruct its exercise. But in the renewing and sanctifying work of the Holy Ghost, those things are wrought in the soul that are above nature, and of which there is nothing of the like kind in the soul by nature; and they are caused to exist in the soul habitually, and according to such a stated constitution or law, that lays such a foundation for exercises in a continued course, as is called a principle of nature. Not only are remaining principles assisted to do their work more freely and fully, but those principles are restored that were utterly destroyed by the fall; and the mind thenceforward habitually exerts those acts that the dominion of sin had made it as wholly destitute of, as a dead body is of vital acts.

The Spirit of God acts in a very different manner in the one case, from what he doth in the other. He may indeed act upon the mind of a natural man; but he acts in the mind of a saint as an indwelling vital principle. He acts upon the mind of an unregenerate person as an extrinsic occasional agent; for in acting upon them he doth not unite himself to them; for notwithstanding all his influences that they may be the subjects of, they are still "sensual, having not the Spirit" (Jude 19). But he unites himself with the mind of a saint, takes him for his temple, actuates and influences him as a new, supernatural principle of life and action. There is this difference; that the Spirit of God, in acting in the soul of a godly man, exerts and communicates himself there in his own proper nature. Holiness is the proper nature of the Spirit of God. The Holy Spirit operates in the minds of the godly, by uniting himself to them, and living in them, and exerting his own nature in the exercise of their faculties. The Spirit of God may act upon a creature, and yet not in acting communicate himself. The Spirit of God may act upon inanimate creatures; as, "The Spirit moved upon the face of the waters" [Gen. 1:2] in the beginning of the creation: so the Spirit of God may act upon the minds of men, many ways, and communicate himself no more than when he acts upon an inanimate creature. For instance, he may excite thoughts in them, may assist their natural reason and understanding, or may assist other natural principles, and this without any union with the soul, but may act, as it were, as upon an external object. But as he acts in his holy influences, and spiritual operations, he acts in a way of peculiar communication of himself; so that the subject is thence denominated *spiritual.*

2. This spiritual and divine light don't consist in any impression made upon the imagination. 'Tis no impression upon the mind, as though one saw anything with the bodily eyes: 'tis no imagination or idea of an outward light or glory, or any beauty of form or countenance, or a visible luster or brightness of any object. The imagination may be strongly impressed with such things; but this is not spiritual light. Indeed when the mind has a lively discovery of spiritual things, and is greatly affected with the power of divine light, it may, and probably very commonly doth, much affect the imagination: so that impressions of an outward beauty or brightness, may accompany those spiritual discoveries. But spiritual light is not that impression upon the imagination, but an exceeding different thing from it. Natural men may have lively impressions on their imaginations; and we can't determine but that the devil, who transforms himself into an angel of light, may cause imaginations of an outward beauty, or visible glory, and of sounds and speeches, and other such things; but these are things of a vastly inferior nature to spiritual light.

3. This spiritual light is not the suggesting of any new truths, or propo-

sitions not contained in the Word of God. This suggesting of new truths or doctrines to the mind, independent of any antecedent revelation of those propositions, either in word or writing, is inspiration; such as the prophets and apostles had, and such as some enthusiasts pretend to. But this spiritual light that I am speaking of, is quite a different thing from inspiration: it reveals no new doctrine, it suggests no new proposition to the mind, it teaches no new thing of God, or Christ, or another world, not taught in the Bible; but only gives a due apprehension of those things that are taught in the Word of God.

4. 'Tis not every affecting view that men have of the things of religion that is this spiritual and divine light. Men by mere principles of nature are capable of being affected with things that have a special relation to religion, as well as other things. A person by mere nature, for instance, may be liable to be affected with the story of Jesus Christ, and the sufferings he underwent, as well as by any other tragical story: he may be the more affected with it from the interest he conceives mankind to have in it: yea, he may be affected with it without believing it; as well as a man may be affected with what he reads in a romance, or sees acted in a stage play. He may be affected with a lively and eloquent description of many pleasant things that attend the state of the blessed in heaven; as well as his imagination be entertained by a romantic description of the pleasantness of fairy land, or the like. And that common belief of the truth of the things of religion, that persons may have from education, or otherwise, may help forward their affection. We read in Scripture of many that were greatly affected with things of a religious nature, who yet are there represented as wholly graceless, and many of them very ill men. A person therefore may have affecting views of the things of religion, and yet be very destitute of spiritual light. Flesh and blood may be the author of this: one man may give another an affecting view of divine things with but common assistance; but God alone can give a spiritual discovery of them.

But I proceed to show,

Secondly, positively, what this spiritual and divine light is.

And it may be thus described: a true sense of the divine excellency of the things revealed in the Word of God, and a conviction of the truth and reality of them, thence arising.

This spiritual light primarily consists in the former of these, viz. a real sense and apprehension of the divine excellency of things revealed in the Word of God. A spiritual and saving conviction of the truth and reality of these things, arises from such a sight of their divine excellency and glory; so that this conviction of their truth is an effect and natural consequence of this sight of their divine glory. There is therefore in this spiritual light,

1. A true sense of the divine and superlative excellency of the things of religion; a real sense of the excellency of God, and Jesus Christ, and of the work of redemption, and the ways and works of God revealed in the gospel. There is a divine and superlative glory in these things; an excellency that is of a vastly higher kind, and more sublime nature, than in other things; a glory greatly distinguishing them from all that is earthly and temporal. He that is spiritually enlightened truly apprehends and sees it, or has a sense of it. He don't merely rationally believe that God is glorious, but he has a sense of the gloriousness of God in his heart. There is not only a rational belief that God is holy, and that holiness is a good thing; but there is a sense of the loveliness of God's holiness. There is not only a speculatively judging that God is gracious, but a sense how amiable God is upon that account; or a sense of the beauty of this divine attribute.

There is a twofold understanding or knowledge of good, that God has made the mind of man capable of. The first, that which is merely speculative or notional: as when a person only speculatively judges, that anything is, which by the agreement of mankind, is called good or excellent, viz. that which is most to general advantage, and between which and a reward there is a suitableness; and the like. And the other is that which consists in the sense of the heart: as when there is a sense of the beauty, amiableness, or sweetness of a thing; so that the heart is sensible of pleasure and delight in the presence of the idea of it. In the former is exercised merely the speculative faculty, or the understanding strictly so-called, or as spoken of in distinction from the will or disposition of the soul. In the latter the will, or inclination, or heart, are mainly concerned.

Thus there is a difference between having an opinion that God is holy and gracious, and having a sense of the loveliness and beauty of that holiness and grace. There is a difference between having a rational judgment that honey is sweet, and having a sense of its sweetness. A man may have the former, that knows not how honey tastes; but a man can't have the latter, unless he has an idea of the taste of honey in his mind. So there is a difference between believing that a person is beautiful, and having a sense of his beauty. The former may be obtained by hearsay, but the latter only by seeing the countenance. There is a wide difference between mere speculative, rational judging anything to be excellent, and having a sense of its sweetness, and beauty. The former rests only in the head, speculation only is concerned in it; but the heart is concerned in the latter. When the heart is sensible of the beauty and amiableness of a thing, it necessarily feels pleasure in the apprehension. It is implied in a person's being heartily sensible of the loveliness of a thing, that the idea of it is sweet and pleasant to his soul; which is a far different thing from having a rational opinion that it is excellent.

2. There arises from this sense of divine excellency of things contained in the Word of God, a conviction of the truth and reality of them: and that either indirectly, or directly.

(1) First, indirectly, and that two ways:

1. As the prejudices that are in the heart, against the truth of divine things, are hereby removed; so that the mind becomes susceptive of the due force of rational arguments for their truth. The mind of man is naturally full of prejudices against the truth of divine things: it is full of enmity against the doctrines of the gospel; which is a disadvantage to those arguments that prove their truth, and causes them to lose their force upon the mind. But when a person has discovered to him the divine excellency of Christian doctrines, this destroys the enmity, removes those prejudices, and sanctifies the reason, and causes it to lie open to the force of arguments for their truth.

Hence was the different effect that Christ's miracles had to convince the disciples, from what they had to convince the Scribes and Pharisees. Not that they had a stronger reason, or had their reason more improved; but their reason was sanctified, and those blinding prejudices, that the Scribes and Pharisees were under, were removed by the sense they had of the excellency of Christ, and his doctrine.

2. It not only removes the hindrances of reason, but positively helps reason. It makes even the speculative notions the more lively. It engages the attention of the mind, with the more fixedness and intenseness to that kind of objects; which causes it to have a clearer view of them, and enables it more clearly to see their mutual relations, and occasions it to take more notice of them. The ideas themselves that otherwise are dim, and obscure, are by this means impressed with the greater strength, and have a light cast upon them; so that the mind can better judge of them. As he that beholds the objects on the face of the earth, when the light of the sun is cast upon them, is under greater advantage to discern them in their true forms, and mutual relations, than he that sees them in a dim starlight or twilight.

The mind having a sensibleness of the excellency of divine objects, dwells upon them with delight; and the powers of the soul are more awakened, and enlivened to employ themselves in the contemplation of them, and exert themselves more fully and much more to purpose. The beauty and sweetness of the objects draws on the faculties, and draws forth their exercises: so that reason itself is under far greater advantages for its proper and free exercises, and to attain its proper end, free of darkness and delusion. But,

(2) Secondly, a true sense of the divine excellency of the things of God's Word doth more directly and immediately convince of the truth of them; and that because the excellency of these things is so superlative. There is a beauty in them that is so divine and godlike, that is greatly and evidently distinguishing of them from things merely human, or that men are the inventors and authors of; a glory that is so high and great, that when clearly seen, commands assent to their divinity, and reality. When there is an actual and lively discovery of this beauty and excellency, it won't allow of any such thought as that it is an human work, or the fruit of men's invention. This evidence, that they, that are spiritually enlightened, have of the truth of the things of religion, is a kind of intuitive and immediate evidence. They believe the doctrines of God's word to be divine, because they see divinity in them, i.e. they see a divine, and transcendent, and most evidently distinguishing glory in them; such a glory as, if clearly seen, don't leave room to doubt of their being of God, and not of men.

Such a conviction of the truth of religion as this, arising, these ways, from a sense of the divine excellency of them, is that true spiritual conviction that there is in saving faith. And this original of it, is that by which it is most essentially distinguished from that common assent, which unregenerate men are capable of.

II. I proceed now to the second thing proposed, viz. to show how this light is immediately given by God, and not obtained by natural means. And here,

First. 'Tis not intended that the natural faculties are not made use of in it. The natural faculties are the subject of this light: and they are the subject in such a manner, that they are not merely passive, but active in it; the acts and exercises of man's understanding are concerned and made use of in it. God, in letting in this light into the soul, deals with man according to his nature, or as a rational creature; and makes use of his human faculties. But yet this light is not the less immediately from God for that; though the faculties are made use of, 'tis as the subject and not as the cause; and that acting of the faculties in it, is not the cause, but is either implied in the thing itself (in the light that is imparted), or is the consequence of it. As the use that we make of our eyes in beholding various objects, when the sun arises, is not the cause of the light that discovers those objects to us.

Second. 'Tis not intended that outward means have no concern in this affair. As I have observed already, 'tis not in this affair, as it is in inspiration, where new truths are suggested: for here is by this light only given a due apprehension of the same truths that are revealed in the Word of God; and therefore it is not given without the Word. The gospel is made use of in this affair: this light is the "light of the glorious gospel of Christ" (II Cor. 4:4). The gospel is as a glass, by which this light is conveyed to us. I Cor. 13:12, "Now we see through a glass." But,

Third. When it is said that this light is given immediately by God, and not obtained by natural means, hereby is intended, that 'tis given by God without making use of any means that operate by their own power, or a natural force. God makes use of means; but 'tis not as mediate causes to produce this effect. There are not truly any second causes of it; but it is produced by God immediately. The Word of God is no proper cause of this effect: it don't operate by any natural force in it. The Word of God is only made use of to convey to the mind the subject matter of this saving instruction: and this indeed it doth convey to us by natural force or influence. It conveys to our minds these and those doctrines; it is the cause of the notion of them in our heads, but not of the sense of the divine excellency of them in our hearts. Indeed a person can't have spiritual light without the Word. But that don't argue, that the Word properly causes that light. The mind can't see the excellency of any doctrine, unless that doctrine be first in the mind; but the seeing the excellency of the doctrine may be immediately from the Spirit of God; though the conveying of the doctrine or proposition itself may be by the Word. So that the notions that are the subject matter of this light, are conveyed to the mind by the Word of God; but that due sense of the heart, wherein this light formally consists, is immediately by the Spirit of God. As for instance, that notion that there is a Christ, and that Christ is holy and gracious, is conveyed to the mind by the Word of God: but the sense of the excellency of Christ by reason of that holiness and grace, is nevertheless immediately the work of the Holy Spirit. I come now,

III. [In the third place,] to show the truth of the doctrine; that is, to show that there is such a thing as that spiritual light that has been described, thus immediately let into the mind by God. And here I would show briefly, that this doctrine is both scriptural, and rational.

First, 'tis scriptural. My text is not only full to the purpose, but 'tis a doctrine that the Scripture abounds in. We are there abundantly taught, that the saints differ from the ungodly in this, that they have the knowledge of God, and a sight of God, and of Jesus Christ. I shall mention but few texts of many: I John 3:6, "Whosoever sinneth, hath not seen him, nor known him." III John 1:11, "He that doth good, is of God: but he that doth evil, hath not seen God." John 14:19, "The world seeth me no more; but ye see me." John 17:3, "And this is eternal life, that they might know thee, the only true God, and Jesus Christ whom thou hast sent." This knowledge, or sight of God and Christ, can't be a mere speculative knowledge; because it is spoken of as a seeing and knowing, wherein they differ from the ungodly. And by these scriptures it must not only be a different knowledge in degree and circumstances, and different in its effects; but it must be entirely different in nature and kind.

And this light and knowledge is always spoken of as immediately given of God. Matt. 11:25–27, "At that time Jesus answered and said, I thank thee, O Father, Lord of heaven and earth, because thou hast hid these things from the wise and prudent, and hast revealed them unto babes: even so, Father; for so it seemed good in thy sight. All things are delivered unto me of my Father, and no man knoweth the Son but the Father; neither knoweth any man the Father, save the Son, and he to whomsoever the Son will reveal him." Here this effect is ascribed alone to the arbitrary operation, and gift of God, bestowing this knowledge on whom he will, and distinguishing those with it, that have the least natural advantage or means for knowledge, even babes, when it is denied to the wise and prudent. And the imparting the knowledge of God is here appropriated to the Son of God, as his sole prerogative. And again, II Cor. 4:6, "For God, who commanded the light to shine out of darkness, hath shined in our hearts, to give the light of the knowledge of the glory of God in the face of Jesus Christ." This plainly shows, that there is such a thing as a discovery of the divine superlative glory and excellency of God and Christ; and that peculiar to the saints: and also that 'tis as immediately from God, as light from the sun: and that 'tis the immediate effect of his power and will; for 'tis compared to God's creating the light by his powerful word in the beginning of the creation; and is said to be by the Spirit of the Lord, in the eighteenth verse of the preceding chapter. God is spoken of as giving the knowledge of Christ in conversion, as of what before was hidden and unseen, in that [place], Gal. 1:15–16, "But when it pleased God, who separated me from my mother's womb, and called me by his grace, to reveal his Son in me." The Scripture also speaks plainly of such a knowledge of the Word of God, as has been described, as the immediate gift of God. Ps. 119:18, "Open thou mine eyes, that I may behold wondrous things out of thy law." What could the Psalmist mean, when he begged of God to open his eyes? was he ever blind? might he not have resort to the law and see every word and sentence in it when he pleased? And what could he mean by those "wondrous things"? was it the wonderful stories of the creation, and deluge, and Israel's passing through the Red Sea, and the like? were not his eyes open to read these strange things when he would? Doubtless by "wondrous things" in God's law, he had respect to those distinguishing and wonderful excellencies, and marvelous manifestations of the divine perfections, and glory, that there was in the commands and doctrines of the Word, and those works and counsels of God that were there revealed. So the Scripture speaks of a knowledge of God's dispensation, and covenant of mercy, and way of grace towards his people, as peculiar to the saints, and given only by God, Ps. 25:14, "The secret of the Lord is with them that fear him; and he will show them his covenant."

And that a true and saving belief of the truth of religion is that which arises from such a discovery, is also what the Scripture teaches. As John 6:40, "And this is the will of him that sent me, that every one that seeth the Son, and believeth on him, may have everlasting life." Where it is plain that a true faith is what arises from a spiritual sight of Christ. And John 17:6–8, "I have manifested thy name unto the men which thou gavest me out of the world . . . Now they have known that all things whatsoever thou hast given me are of thee; for I have given unto them the words which thou gavest me, and they have received them, and have known surely that I came out from thee, and they have believed that thou didst send me." Where Christ's manifesting God's name to the disciples, or giving them the knowledge of God, was that whereby they knew that Christ's doctrine was of God, and that Christ himself was of him, proceeded from him, and was sent by him. Again, John 12:44–46, "Jesus cried, and said, He that believeth on me, believeth not on me, but on him that sent me; and he that seeth me seeth him that sent me. I am come a light into the world, that whosoever believeth on me should not abide in darkness." Their believing in Christ and spiritually seeing him, are spoken of as running parallel.

Christ condemns the Jews, that they did not know that he was the Messiah, and that his doctrine was true, from an inward distinguishing taste and relish of what was divine, in Luke 12:56–57. He having there blamed the Jews, that though they could "discern the face of the sky and of the earth," and signs of the weather, that yet they could not discern those times; or as 'tis expressed in Matthew [16:3], "the signs of those times"; he adds, "Yea, and why even of your own selves judge ye not what is right?" i.e. without extrinsic signs. "Why have ye not that sense of true excellency, whereby ye may distinguish that which is holy and divine? Why have ye not that savor of the things of God, by which you may see the distinguishing glory, and evident divinity of me and my doctrine?"

The apostle Peter mentions it as what gave them (the apostles) good and well-grounded assurance of the truth of the gospel, that they had seen the divine glory of Christ. II Pet. 1:16, "For we have not followed cunningly devised fables, when we made known unto you the power and coming of our Lord Jesus Christ, but were eyewitnesses of his majesty." The Apostle has respect to that visible glory of Christ which they saw in his transfiguration: that glory was so divine, having such an ineffable appearance and semblance of divine holiness, majesty, and grace, that it evidently denoted him to be a divine person. But if a sight of Christ's outward glory might give a rational assurance of his divinity, why may not an apprehension of his spiritual glory do so too? Doubtless Christ's spiritual glory is in itself as distinguishing, and as plainly showing his divinity, as his outward glory; and a great deal more: for his spiritual glory is that wherein his divinity consists; and the outward glory of his transfiguration showed him to be divine, only as it was a remarkable image or representation of that spiritual glory. Doubtless therefore he that has had a clear sight of the spiritual glory of Christ, may say, I have not followed cunningly devised fables, but have been an eyewitness of his majesty, upon as good grounds as the Apostle, when he had respect to the outward glory of Christ, that he had seen. But this brings me to what was proposed next, viz. to show that,

Secondly, this doctrine is rational.

1. 'Tis rational to suppose that there is really such an excellency in divine things, that is so transcendent and exceedingly different from what is in other things, that if it were seen would most evidently distinguish them. We can't rationally doubt but that things that are divine, that appertain to the Supreme Being, are vastly different from things that are human; that there is that God-like, high, and glorious excellency in them, that does most remarkably difference them from the things that are of men; insomuch that if the difference were but seen, it would have a convincing, satisfying influence upon any one, that they are what they are, viz. divine. What reason can be offered against it? Unless we would argue that God is not remarkably distinguished in glory from men.

If Christ should now appear to anyone as he did on the Mount at his transfiguration; or if he should appear to the world in the glory that he now appears in in heaven, as he will do at the day of judgment; without doubt, the glory and majesty that he would appear in, would be such as would satisfy everyone, that he was a divine person, and that religion was true: and it would be a most reasonable, and well-grounded conviction too. And why may there not be that stamp of divinity, or divine glory on the Word of God, on the scheme and doctrine of the gospel, that may be in like manner distinguishing and as rationally convincing, provided it be but seen? 'Tis rational to suppose, that when God speaks to the world, there should be something in his word or speech vastly different from men's word. Supposing that God never had spoken to the world, but we had notice that he was about to do it; that he was about to reveal himself from heaven, and speak to us immediately himself, in divine speeches or discourses, as it were from his own mouth; or that he should give us a book of his own inditing; after what manner should we expect that he would speak? Would it not be rational to suppose, that his speech would be exceeding different from men's speech, that he should speak like a God; that is, that there should be such an excellency and sublimity in his speech or word, such a stamp of wisdom, holiness, majesty, and other divine perfections, that the word of men, yea of the wisest of men, should appear mean and base in comparison of it? Doubtless it would be thought rational to expect this, and unreasonable to think otherwise. When a wise man speaks in the exercise of his wisdom, there is something in everything he says, that is very distinguishable from the talk of a little child. So, without doubt, and much more, is the speech of God (if there be any such thing as the speech of God), to be distinguished from that of the wisest of men; agreeable to Jer. 23:28–29. God having there been reproving the false prophets that prophesied in his name, and pretended that what they spake was his word, when indeed it was their own word, says, "The prophet that hath a dream, let him tell a dream; and he that hath my word, let him speak my word faithfully. What is the chaff to the wheat? saith the Lord. Is not my word like as a fire? saith the Lord; and like a hammer that breaketh the rock in pieces?"

2. If there be such a distinguishing excellency in divine things, 'tis rational to suppose that there may be such a thing as seeing it. What should hinder but that it may be seen? 'Tis no argument that there is no such thing as a distinguishing excellency, or that, if there be, that it can't be

seen, that some don't see it; though they may be discerning men in temporal matters. It is not rational to suppose, if there be any such excellency in divine things, that wicked men should see it. 'Tis not rational to suppose, that those whose minds are full of spiritual pollution, and under the power of filthy lusts, should have any relish or sense of divine beauty, or excellency; or that their minds should be susceptive of that light that is in its own nature so pure and heavenly. It need not seem at all strange, that sin should so blind the mind, seeing that men's particular natural tempers and dispositions will so much blind them in secular matters; as when men's natural temper is melancholy, jealous, fearful, proud, or the like.

3. 'Tis rational to suppose that this knowledge should be given immediately by God, and not be obtained by natural means. Upon what account should it seem unreasonable, that there should be any immediate communication between God and the creature? 'Tis strange that men should make any matter of difficulty of it. Why should not he that made all things, still have something immediately to do with the things that he has made? Where lies the great difficulty, if we own the being of a God, and that he created all things out of nothing, of allowing some immediate influence of God on the creation still? And if it be reasonable to suppose it with respect to any part of the creation, 'tis especially so with respect to reasonable, intelligent creatures; who are next to God in the gradation of the different orders of beings, and whose business is most immediately with God; who were made on purpose for those exercises that do respect God, and wherein they have nextly to do with God: for reason teaches that man was made to serve and glorify his Creator. And if it be rational to suppose that God immediately communicates himself to man in any affair, it is in this. 'Tis rational to suppose that God would reserve that knowledge and wisdom, that is of such a divine and excellent nature, to be bestowed immediately by himself, and that it should not be left in the power of second causes. Spiritual wisdom and grace is the highest and most excellent gift that ever God bestows on any creature: in this the highest excellency and perfection of a rational creature consists. 'Tis also immensely the most important of all divine gifts: 'tis that wherein man's happiness consists, and on which his everlasting welfare depends. How

rational is it to suppose that God, however he has left meaner goods and lower gifts to second causes, and in some sort in their power, yet should reserve this most excellent, divine, and important of all divine communications, in his own hands, to be bestowed immediately by himself, as a thing too great for second causes to be concerned in? 'Tis rational to suppose that this blessing should be immediately from God; for there is no gift or benefit that is in itself so nearly related to the divine nature, there is nothing the creature receives that is so much of God, of his nature, so much a participation of the Deity: 'tis a kind of emanation of God's beauty, and is related to God as the light is to the sun. 'Tis therefore congruous and fit, that when it is given of God, it should be nextly from himself, and by himself, according to his own sovereign will.

'Tis rational to suppose, that it should be beyond a man's power to obtain this knowledge, and light, by the mere strength of natural reason; for 'tis not a thing that belongs to reason, to see the beauty and loveliness of spiritual things; it is not a speculative thing, but depends on the sense of the heart. Reason indeed is necessary in order to it, as 'tis by reason only that we are become the subjects of the means of it; which means I have already shown to be necessary in order to it, though they have no proper causal influence in the affair. 'Tis by reason, that we become possessed of a notion of those doctrines that are the subject matter of this divine light; and reason may many ways be indirectly, and remotely an advantage to it. And reason has also to do in the acts that are immediately consequent on this discovery: a seeing the truth of religion from hence, is by reason; though it be but by one step, and the inference be immediate. So reason has to do in that accepting of, and trusting in Christ, that is consequent on it. But if we take reason strictly, not for the faculty of mental perception in general, but for ratiocination, or a power of inferring by arguments; I say if we take reason thus, the perceiving of spiritual beauty and excellency no more belongs to reason, than it belongs to the sense of feeling to perceive colors, or to the power of seeing to perceive the sweetness of food. It is out of reason's province to perceive the beauty or loveliness of anything: such a perception don't belong to that faculty. Reason's work is to perceive truth, and not excellency. 'Tis not ratiocination that gives men the perception of the beauty and amiableness of a countenance; though it may be many ways indirectly an advantage to it; yet 'tis no more reason that immediately perceives it, than it is reason that perceives the sweetness of honey: it depends on the sense of the heart. Reason may determine that a countenance is beautiful to others, it may determine that honey is sweet to others; but it will never give me a perception of its sweetness.

[IMPROVEMENT.]

I will conclude with a very brief improvement of what has been said.

I. This doctrine may lead us to reflect on the goodness of God, that has so ordered it, that a saving evidence of the truth of the gospel is such, as is attainable by persons of mean capacities, and advantages, as well as those that are of the greatest parts and learning. If the evidence of the gospel depended only on history, and such reasonings as learned men only are capable of, it would be above the reach of far the greatest part of mankind. But persons, with but an ordinary degree of knowledge, are capable, without a long and subtile train of reasoning, to see the divine excellency of the things of religion: they are capable of being taught by the Spirit of God, as well as learned men. The evidence that is this way obtained, is vastly better and more satisfying, than all that can be obtained by the arguings of those that are most learned, and greatest masters of reason. And babes are as capable of knowing these things, as the wise and prudent; and they are often hid from these, when they are revealed to those. I Cor. 1:26–27, "For ye see your calling, brethren, how that not many wise men after the flesh, not many mighty, not many noble, are called: But God hath chosen the foolish things of the world."

II. This doctrine may well put us upon examining ourselves, whether we have ever had this divine light, that has been described, let into our souls. If there be such a thing indeed, and it ben't only a notion, or whimsy of persons of weak and distempered brains, then doubtless 'tis a thing of great importance, whether we have thus been taught by the Spirit of God; whether the light of the glorious gospel of Christ, who is the image of God, hath shined into us, giving us the light of the knowledge of the glory of God in the face of Jesus Christ; whether we have seen the Son, and believed on him, or have that faith of gospel doctrines which arises from a spiritual sight of Christ.

III. All may hence be exhorted, earnestly to seek this spiritual light. To influence and move to it, the following things may be considered.

First. This is the most excellent and divine wisdom, that any creature is capable of. 'Tis more excellent than any human learning; 'tis far more excellent, than all the knowledge of the greatest philosophers, or statesmen. Yea, the least glimpse of the glory of God in the face of Christ doth more exalt and ennoble the soul, than all the knowledge of those that have the greatest speculative understanding in divinity, without grace. This knowledge has the most noble object that is, or can be, viz. the divine glory, and excellency of God, and Christ. The knowledge of these objects is that wherein consists the most excellent knowledge of the angels, yea, of God himself.

Second. This knowledge is that which is above all others sweet and joyful. Men have a great deal of pleasure in human knowledge, in studies of natural things; but this is nothing to that joy which arises from this divine light shining into the soul. This light gives a view of those things that are immensely the most exquisitely beautiful, and capable of delighting the eye of the understanding. This spiritual light is the dawning of the light of glory in the heart. There is nothing so powerful as this to support persons in affliction, and to give the mind peace and brightness, in this stormy and dark world.

Third. This light is such as effectually influences the inclination, and changes the nature of the soul. It assimilates the nature to the divine nature, and changes the soul into an image of the same glory that is beheld. II Cor. 3:18, "But we all with open face, beholding as in a glass the glory of the Lord, are changed into the same image, from glory to glory, even as by the Spirit of the Lord." This knowledge will wean from the world, and raise the inclination to heavenly things. It will turn the heart to God as the fountain of good, and to choose him for the only portion. This light, and this only, will bring the soul to a saving close with Christ. It conforms the heart to the gospel, mortifies its enmity and opposition against the scheme of salvation therein revealed: it causes the heart to embrace the joyful tidings, and entirely to adhere to, and acquiesce in the revelation of Christ as our Savior: it causes the whole soul to accord and symphonize with it, admitting it with entire credit and respect, cleaving to it with full inclination and affection. And it effectually disposes the soul to give up itself entirely to Christ.

Fourth. This light, and this only, has its fruit in an universal holiness of life. No merely notional or speculative understanding of the doctrines of religion, will ever bring to this. But this light, as it reaches the bottom of the heart, and changes the nature, so it will effectually dispose to an universal obedience. It shows God's worthiness to be obeyed and served. It draws forth the heart in a sincere love to God, which is the only principle of a true, gracious and universal obedience. And it convinces of the reality of those glorious rewards that God has promised to them that obey him.

I Know My Redeemer Lives (1740)

Job 19:25.
For I know that my redeemer liveth.

In saying this, Job seems to have an eye to the reproaches that his three friends cast upon him and so much insist upon, viz. that he was an hypocrite and wicked man. He says in the two foregoing verses, "Oh that my words were now written! oh that they were printed in a book! That they were graven with an iron pen and lead in the rock for ever!" I. e. "Those words that I am now going to say," which are said in the verse of the text and two next verses: "I know that my Redeemer liveth, and that he shall stand at the latter day upon the earth." He wishes that those words were written and so graven that they might never wear out, to that end, that it might be remembered that he said 'em, even till the event proves 'em to be true; that men in the latter day, when Christ should come to stand upon the earth, might remember how positive he was of his interest in him, and that he would then appear as his Redeemer, notwithstanding all the uncharitable and reproachful suggestions of his three friends to the contrary; and that then it might be seen who was in the right, they or he: they that said he was an hypocrite, or he who was so positive to the contrary.

Job's wish is accordingly fulfilled. God so ordered it that his words should afterwards be written in a book by the direction of his own Holy Spirit, viz. in this book where we find them, where they have remained for more than three thousand years, and are more durable than if they were engraven with an iron pen and lead in a rock, and will remain till his words are fulfilled; even till Job's Redeemer stands at the latter day on the earth, and he whose body has long ago been destroyed with worms shall see God in his flesh, and shall see him for himself.

There are two things that I would now take notice of concerning these words of Job:

1. What is the privilege that he professes himself [to] be the subject of, viz. that he knows that his Redeemer lives; and,

2. How much he values this privilege professed. How precious the matter of his profession is to him, that he should so desire to have his words by which he makes the profession so written or engraven that they may remain forever in indelible characters. He speaks of his privilege with an air of triumph, as that which he comforts himself in and glories in in the midst of his great affliction, under which his skin was already destroyed with sore boils all over him, from the crown of {his head to the sole of his foot} [Job 2:7], and wherein he was so deserted by his former friends and so despised and reproached by them as a wicked man and a notorious hypocrite.

DOCTRINE.

It is a matter of great comfort and rejoicing to any person, whatever circumstances he is in, when he can say that he knows that his Redeemer lives.

First, I would take notice of the several things contained in this profession; and second, show how it is matter of great comfort and rejoicing to anyone when they can say thus.

I. I would show what is implied when anyone can say that he knows that his Redeemer lives.

First. It implies that he knows that Christ is the appointed Redeemer and Savior of man. It implies a knowledge of Christ's divine mission; that he was no impostor, but indeed a person sent from God to reveal his mind and will. It implies a knowing that he is the Messiah, as he professed himself to be, and that he is the person that God has pitched upon and sent into the world, and that he might be the Savior of men from their sins and from eternal destruction. It implies what Peter professed in the sixth [chapter] of John, v. 69: "And we believe and are sure that thou art the Christ, the Son of the living God."

It implies that he knows the truth of the gospel, and that that can be said of him that Christ said of his disciples to his Father, in John 17:7–8, "Now they have known that all things whatsoever thou hast given me are of thee. For I have given unto them the words which thou gavest me; and they have received them, and have known surely that I came out from thee, and they have believed that thou didst send me."

And [it] implies a knowing that the Scriptures are the Word of God, and that that Word is true, and that the way of salvation revealed in the Scriptures is the very way of life, and "that there is no other name given under heaven among men, whereby we must be saved" [Acts 4:12], but the name of Christ.

Second. Another thing contained in that knowledge that is professed in the text, is knowing that Christ lives. This signifies four things:

1. A knowing that he is in possession of life in himself. It implied in Job's time that he was the living God; that he was not as those idols were that the heathen worshipped, that were things without life. And now, in the days of the gospel, it implies that we know that Christ is risen from the dead, and so is alive as God-man. And so that that is true that Christ says of himself, in Rev. 1:18, "I am he that liveth, and was dead." If Christ were not risen, he could not be our Savior. The Apostle says in I Cor. 15:17–18, if Christ ben't risen, then our faith is vain, and we are yet in our sins; and they that "are fallen asleep in Christ are perished."

2. Knowing his sufficiency as the author and fountain of life. The insufficiency of false gods is often represented in Scripture by that, that they were things without life: dumb idols, lifeless sticks and stones, and so not able to help those that trusted in them. But the sufficiency of the true God and his ability to save those that trust in him is often represented by that, that he is the living God.

And the sufficiency of Christ to save us and give us life is represented by the same thing. He is a sufficient Savior because he is a living Savior. Heb. 7:25, "Wherefore he is able also to save them to the uttermost that come unto God by him, seeing he ever liveth to make intercession for them."

Christ tells his disciples in John 14:19 that because he lives, they shall live also. He is sufficient for them as a fountain of life to them. And in this Job comforts himself, that though he should die and worms should destroy his body, that yet his Redeemer lives, and so is sufficient to restore him to life, that he might still see his Savior in his flesh at the latter day.

3. It implies a knowing his faithfulness and unchangeableness as a

Savior. There are many that have formerly appeared to be friends to others that live still, but yet their friendship don't live. As men they live, but as friends they are dead. Job professes his faith in that Christ [that] not only lives himself, but lives as his friend and Redeemer. His promise lives. His word is established as a sure record in heaven, and his faithfulness to his promise lives. His mercy lives. He is a Redeemer of the same grace and mercy that ever he was, and his love to him that believes on him lives. For whom he loves, he loves to the end. He hath loved them with an everlasting love.

He lives as the fountain of their good and happiness, a living spring whose stream never dries up. This Job comforts himself in. He in himself was a mutable being, subject to great changes. He had passed under great changes already. He was suddenly brought down from a state of health and wealth and great earthly glory to a state of the greatest meanness, and poverty, and disease and wounds. His skin was destroyed already with sore boils. And he should still be the subject of a greater change; for that body that was now diseased should die. Those worms that were in his noisome sores had already devoured his skin, as in the seventh [chapter] of Job, v. 5: "My flesh is clothed with worms and clods of dust; my skin is broken, and become loathsome." And his body should yet become the subject of a greater change, in that the time would soon come that the worm that had destroyed his skin should destroy his body. But though he was subject to such changes, yet that was his comfort, that his Redeemer was unchangeable.

4. It implies a knowing that he is an everlasting Savior, that he will live forever, and that his power and his mercy and his truth will be forever more. This Job comforts himself in. He wishes that his words were so written or engraven that they might remain forever, as his Redeemer shall live forever. Though he should die and be devoured with worms, yet this is his rejoicing, that his Redeemer should never die, but should live forever more; agreeable to Rev. 1:18, "I am he that liveth, and was dead; and, behold, I am alive for evermore."

Third. The third thing contained in the privilege spoken of in the doctrine, is knowing that Christ is our Redeemer. Thus Job professed not only that he knew that Christ was a Redeemer, and that he lived, but also that he was his Redeemer; that when he should see him standing on the latter day on the earth, {though after his skin worms destroy his body, yet in his flesh shall he see God} [Job 19:26].

It implies not only that we know that Christ is a divine and glorious person, but that he, with all his glories, is ours. Not only a knowing that he lives, but that he lives for us; that he is risen from the dead and ascended into heaven in our name, and as our forerunner; that he has loved us and died for us; agreeable to the profession which the Apostle made, Gal. 2:20, "Who loved me, and gave himself for me."

'Tis a knowing not only that he has promised such and such unspeakable blessings to them that believe, but knowing that we do believe, and so that the promises are made to us, and that the glory shall be bestowed upon us.

I come, in the

II. Second place, to show how it is matter of comfort and rejoicing in all circumstances when any person can say this.

First. 'Tis reasonable ground of comfort and rejoicing in all circumstances. Whether persons are rich or poor, if they can say as holy Job said in the text, they have reason to rejoice; if they are destitute of those conveniences and comforts of life that others have, and meet with great difficulties, and are driven to great straits; are often hungry and han't food to satisfy their hunger, and know not which way to turn to provide themselves clothing for themselves and their families: yet if they can say that they know their Redeemer lives, they have enough. They are richer than earthly kings commonly are. They have food to eat that others know not of, that is of a most refreshing and satisfying nature. They feed daintily and live highly, for they live upon the bread which came down from heaven. They live upon angels' food.

If they are looked upon [as] mean and are despised in the world, are less regarded than their neighbor, their words are not so much heard, they han't so much respect shown 'em: yet if they can say, "I know that my Redeemer liveth," they have reason to set their hearts at rest about the esteem of men. God has given better honor than that which is of men. They are highly advanced in honor. They are God's children, and heirs to a glorious crown.

If they labor under infirmity of body and a broken constitution, and are some of those that never eat with pleasure, and don't know what it is to enjoy health and the common comforts of life that others do, yet if they can say, "I know that my Redeemer liveth," they have enough to strengthen 'em with strength in their souls. They have that in their spirit that may well sustain their infirmity and make 'em strong in weakness.

If they have painful and distressing disease, and have wearisome days and nights appointed to 'em, yet if they can say, "I know that my Redeemer liveth," they have that which may well quiet 'em and comfort, and make 'em exceeding joyful in all their tribulation. Though they have outward pain, yet they may have inward pleasure and peace that passes all understanding.

If they are exercised with some bereavements, and God has taken away very dear friends, pleasant companions, or children, or God has taken from them loving and prudent parents that were great comforts and blessings to them, yet if they can say, "I know that my Redeemer liveth," they may have comfort in their mourning. They have no reason to mourn as others. Their hearts have no cause to sink under their bereavements. The consideration that their Redeemer lives may be sufficient to give them the oil of joy for mourning, and the garments of praise instead of the spirit of heaviness.

If they think of their sins, if the dreadful corruption of their hearts is discovered to them, and the sins of their practice in all their multitude and in their blackest aggravation stand before them, staring them in the face, yet if they can say, "I know that my Redeemer liveth," they need not be distressed with their sins, let 'em be never so many and great. The view of them may well humble them, but not discourage them in the least; and instead of sinking with the thoughts of their sin, they may well thereby have their hearts so much the more enlarged in praise, and glorying in God's mercy and the love of Christ, and say triumphantly, "I have an advocate with the Father, even Jesus Christ the righteous," and in the Lord Jehovah have I righteousness (I John 2:1).

If the town or land where they live is threatened with public calamities and judgments, either mortal sickness or the grievousness of war, they may glory in this, and say, "The Lord is our refuge and strength, and present help" [Ps. 46:1]. "We have a strong city; salvation will God appoint for walls and bulwarks" [Is. 26:1].

If they are exercised with the temptation and assaults of the devil, yet their consideration may well fill them with courage and carry 'em above the fears of that powerful cruel adversary, and laugh at all his rage, and give them strength to tread on the lion and adder, and to trample under foot the young lion and dragon.

If they are the subjects of cruel profanations, and are delivered up in the hands of persecutors, yet if they can say, "I know that my Redeemer liveth," they may, notwithstanding, rejoice and be exceeding glad and have cause to sing in the dungeon and triumph in flames.

If they are on a deathbed and there is no prospect of any other but their soon leaving all things here below, parting with all their dear friends, and leaving their bodies to be eaten with worms, yet they may with joy use Job's language in the text and context: "I know that my Redeemer liveth, and that he shall stand at the latter day upon the earth: and though after my skin worms destroy my body, yet in my flesh shall I see God" [Job 19:25–26].

If they should see their world coming to an end, yet if they would say, "I know that my Redeemer liveth," they might even then say, "I will not fear though the earth be moved and the mountains {shake}" [Ps. 18:7].

Second. If anyone can say, "I know that my Redeemer liveth," it won't only be just ground of comfort, but it will actually and infallibly give comfort and rejoicing in all circumstances. All they that can say, "I know that my Redeemer liveth," at some particular season, can't say so at all times. Faith is not always in that degree of exercise in them, but when it is it infallibly has that effect to give comfort and rejoicing to the soul. And nothing in their circumstances can keep 'em from their joy "no man taketh from them" [John 16:22]. Faith is in its nature a supporting and joyful grace. We read, Rom. 15:13, "All joy and peace in believing." And when faith is in exercise to a full degree, the soul is steadfast and immovable. The building stands strong and unshaken in all storms and tempests. The soul with whom it is thus dwells on high, and his place of defense is the munitions of rocks [Is. 33:16], and his bread and his waters are sure and fail not. He is like a tree that spreadeth out her roots by a river that always supplies it with sap, and therefore is green and flourishing in the greatest drought. Jer. 17:7–8, "Blessed is the man that trusteth in the Lord, and whose hope the Lord is. For he shall be as a tree planted by the waters, and that spreadeth out her roots by the river, and shall not see when heat comes, but her leaf shall be green; neither shall cease from yielding fruit." We read of "joy unspeakable and full of glory" from that sight that faith gives. I Pet. 1:8, "Whom having not seen, ye love, in whom, though now ye see him not, yet believing, ye rejoice with joy unspeakable and full of glory."

So we read of rejoicing "in hope of the glory of God" through the influence of faith and glorying in tribulation, in the fifth chapter of Romans [vv. 1–3].

Where there is that riches of the full assurance of understanding, it will infallibly be accompanied with the spirit of adoption: that spirit of love which delivers from and casts our servile fear, and is the seal and earnest of the Spirit in our hearts, and his witness that we are the children of God.

But the following reasons may be given of the doctrine:

Reason 1. He that can say, "I know that my Redeemer liveth," he knows him to be better than all. For as has been observed already, 'tis implied that he knows that he is the Christ, the Son of the living God. He sees in him that glory and excellency that is delightful and ravishing. That beauty is so great, so divine, that the sight of it, when it is so clearly seen, is above [all] things sweet. It fills the soul with a light so divine and powerful that it is impossible but the soul should be withal filled with peace and pleasantness. A sinking dullness and sorrow is not consistent with such bright light. What can be better to the soul than to see the face of the only begotten Son of God, that is full of grace and truth? And while the soul has that light, it will have comfort. In vain is the rage of Satan, or any of his instruments, to the contrary.

And besides, there being this further implied, that the soul, at the same time that it sees the divine glory of this Savior and knows him to be better than all, also knows that he is his Redeemer and can say, "My beloved is mine, and I am his." It must needs give it comfort, whatever else it is deprived of. If the believer is destitute of riches, yea, and of food and raiment, or if he be deprived of earthly friends, yet if he sees it and knows that he has Christ, and that he is his and will always be his, and never can be deprived of him, this must cause him to possess himself in quietness and comfort.

[*Reason*] 2. He that can say, "I know that my Redeemer liveth," he knows that his Redeemer is above all and able to do all things for him. If he be persecuted, he knows that his Redeemer is above his persecutors. If he be tempted by the devil, and he sees that the powers of hell rage against him, he knows that his Redeemer is above all the devils in hell, and that he is able to deliver him from their hands. He knows that his foundation is sure and his refuge strong, and that his Redeemer is round about him as the mountains were round about Jerusalem, and that his name is a strong tower, and his salvation that is appointed for his walls and bulwarks is as mountains of brass.

If he has affliction in the world, and is in the midst of storms, he knows that his Redeemer is above the storms of the world, and can restrain them and quell them when he pleases. 'Tis but for him to say "Peace, be still," and all 'tis calm. If he be tossed like a vessel on the tempestuous sea, he knows that his Redeemer is in the ship, and therefore knows he can't sink.

If death approaches with its most grim and ghastly countenance, yet he knows that his Redeemer is above death, and therefore is not terrified with it, but can look upon it with a calm, pleasant countenance and say, "O death, where is thy sting? O grave, where is thy victory?" [I Cor. 15:55–56].

[*Reason*] 3. He that can say, "I know that my Redeemer liveth," he knows that he loves him and pities him under all suffering. He knows that he has loved him from eternity, and he knows that he still loves him, and will love him, to eternity. He knows that he is the object of the free and unchangeable love of his Redeemer. And he knows that as a father pities his children, so his Redeemer pities him under affliction, and that he knows his soul in adversity, and that a woman may sooner forget her sucking child than Christ; that he has graven him as it were upon the palms of his hands, and that in all his affliction he is afflicted. And this must needs be a most supporting and comforting consideration under all afflictions.

[*Reason*] 4. He that can say, "I know that my Redeemer liveth," he knows that his Redeemer will fulfill his promises to him. He finds in his

Word many great and precious promises, and they are precious to him; he is persuaded of them and embraces them.

He knows that he will never leave him nor forsake him. He knows that Christ will not forsake his people, and never will cast off his inheritance. He knows that he will defend him and will not suffer him to be utterly cast down. He knows that he will order that which he sees to be best for him, and that he will never take away his loving-kindness from him, nor suffer his faithfulness to fail. He knows that none can ever pluck him out of Christ's hands. He knows that Christ will at last make [him] a conqueror over all his enemies and will subdue them under his feet, and that the time will soon come that he will wipe all tears from his eyes, and there shall be no more death, neither sorrow nor crying, and is "persuaded that neither life, nor death, nor angels, nor principalities, nor powers, nor things past, nor things to come, nor height, nor depth, nor any other creature, shall be able to separate him from the love of God, which is in Christ Jesus his Lord" [Rom. 8:38–39].

APPLICATION.

I. This may well lead those that are Christless persons to reflect on their miserable state, which is so exceeding distant from that privilege spoken of in the doctrine. So blind are you, and dark is your mind, with respect to spiritual things that you don't yet know whether Christ be a Redeemer or no of God's appointing, or whether there be any Redeemer at all. You have all your days been told of a Redeemer, and been instructed in the doctrine of his salvation, but yet never knew and don't know to this day whether there be a word of truth in all that you have heard about him. 'Tis a question that you never yet have fully resolved, whether Christ be the Son of God. You have always halted between two opinions with respect to it, and so you do to this very day.

You have all your days been in the school of Christ, but you are one of them that have been ever learning, and never are yet "come to the knowledge of the truth" [II Tim. 3:7]. And though Christ be the most glorious object that ever was exhibited or manifested in this [world], and be the light and glory of heaven and the brightness of God's glory, yet [you] have always been blind, and never would see any form or comeliness in him, or beauty wherefore you should desire him.

You are ignorant of him as the Lord and fountain of life. You don't know that he lives. You han't determined in your mind whether ever he rose from the dead or not.

And you not only don't know that he is your Redeemer, but you either do or may know that he is not. You have no interest in him. You are without Christ, and without any Redeemer. You are a poor, undone, perishing sinner, and have none that you have any interest in to appear before God for you.

You stand in as much need of a Redeemer as others. You are a poor captive in the hands of the devil. You are a poor prisoner in the hands of justice, and have no interest in any Savior. Those that can say, "I know that my Redeemer lives," have that which may abundantly comfort them, whatever circumstances they are in. But what comfort can a poor creature in your condition take under any circumstances? What comfort can you have in the thoughts of dying without a Redeemer? The thoughts of it may well be amazing to you. What can you have to give you any reasonable comfort when you consider how many sins you have been guilty of, and have no mediator to make satisfaction for you? Your sins may well appear more frightful than so many devils to you. What reasonable comfort can you take under any affliction when you have to consider that those afflictions are from the hand of an angry God, and that you have no Redeemer to stand between God and you? And if you have any comfort in your present state in outward prosperity, your rejoicing is madness. You can have no reasonable comfort in anything in the state that you are now in.

II. This doctrine may lead such persons to consider their folly who trust in such redeemers as shall perish. They that trust in Christ, and know that they do so, may say that they know that their Redeemer lives. Whatever changes they pass under, and though they should die and worms devour their bodies, yea, though heaven and earth should come to an end, yet still their Redeemer lives. But what will they do that trust in men, whose breath is in his nostrils, that make flesh their arm? What will they do that trust in their own righteousness? What will become of this, and the hope that is built upon it, when death comes? The hail shall sweep away such lying refuges, and the waters shall overflow such hiding places. Death, that will cut them off, will at one blow cut off all their confidence and dash their false hopes in pieces. "For what is the hope of the hypocrite, when God taketh away his soul" (Job 27:8).

III. I would hence exhort those that hope that they have an interest in Christ to seek that assurance of faith and hope that Job expresses in the text, that they may be able to say with him, "I know that my Redeemer lives."And here I shall particularly insist on the last thing that it was observed was implied in such a profession, viz. knowing that he is your Redeemer, or being assured of an interest in him. Here consider:

First. If you have an interest in Christ and yet don't know it, in many respects you will fail of the benefit of it while in this world. He that has an interest in Christ and don't know it, he can't have the comfort of it. He is under great restraint in his rejoicing in Christ. He durst not rejoice in him as his Savior. When he does rejoice in him and gives himself a liberty for a while to salve himself in Christ's love, yet such a thought as this is ready to come across him: "It may be I am only an hypocrite; I have been taking comfort in the love and promises of a Savior, but it may be I am deceived and have comforted myself in that which don't belong to me, and instead of rejoicing have cause of sorrow and trembling from the consideration of my miserable condition."

As long as the saints are at a loss whether Christ is their Redeemer or no, it tends to make 'em afraid to take comfort. When they meet with texts of Scripture that hold forth the wonderful mercy and love of Christ to believers, they will be afraid to take the comfort of them, lest they should take that to themselves that don't belong to 'em. And if they do sometimes allow themselves to take comfort in them, then it [is] with restraint and fear, lest they do what they have no warrant for. They dare not so much as give God thanks for giving them an interest in Christ, though that be so much the greatest mercy that ever they received, for fear they should give God thanks for a mercy they never received.

Christ came into the world to die, that he might deliver those who through fear of death are all their lifetime subject to bondage. But the saints that don't know that they have an interest in Christ will be subject to bondage through fear of death still. They will shrink at the thoughts of dying, for they know that death will finish and determine all things that relate to their salvation; that then they must appear before an all-seeing, heart-searching Judge that will pass a sentence upon them that can't be altered; and that if they should be found mistaken, then it will be too late to rectify the mistake. And if they are mistaken, they shall be undone forever; and therefore not being certain whether they are in a good estate or no, the thoughts of dying must needs be terrible. 'Tis a great thing to leap off from this stage into eternity, to launch forth into that boundless ocean; and he that is going to fetch that leap will be afraid unless he [is] fully assured that he has good security as to the event. It is enough to terrify the soul to leap forth into an uncertain eternity.

And thus, doubtless, many truly godly persons have lived under a great deal of fear and sorrow, and also have had much sorrow and exercising fear on a death bed, and so failed of much of the sensible benefit of their interest in Christ while they lived, and never could fully take the comfort of it till after they were dead, because they did not know that Christ was their Redeemer. They hoped he was, but were not assured of it.

This may well stir us up earnestly to seek, that we may obtain a certainty of an interest in Christ.

Second. Let it be considered how much more such an assurance would be for your comfort than any of those temporal good things that men are wont to spend their time and strength in the pursuit of. You don't begrutch to labor hard all the year round for the obtaining temporal good things. For those things you exercise your skill and contrivance, and [for] those things you willingly labor under the burning heat of the sun in the summer, and for those things you will expose yourselves to the piercing cold of the winter, and will go forth in rain and snow. For those things many of you often make long journeys, and are long absent from home, and suffer a great many difficulties abroad, and are not sparing of your strength. Nor are you ever weary, but continue still to pursue the same things. But if you could obtain that which Job makes profession of—to know that your Redeemer lives—how much more comfort might you have in it than in all those temporal things. It would be better to you than the most flourishing estate. It would be a greater comfort to you than to have the most plentiful crops and gainful bargains, and the greatest stores of good things in your houses.

It would afford you a great deal more comfort than to think that you had plentifully laid in for the winter, and the greatest abundance stored up in your barns and cellars, and had also wherewith well to set off your children, or to set 'em up comfortably in the world, and to leave 'em large portions when you died.

If you could say, "I know that my Redeemer liveth," then you would have this to think of: that you knew you was well provided for against the day of death and the day of judgment. You would know that you had enough for time and eternity, and could say with the Psalmist, "The Lord is my shepherd, I shall not want"; I have a table prepared for me, and "my cup runneth over"; and "though I walk through the valley of the shadow of death, I will fear none evil" [Ps. 23:1, 4–5]. Such thoughts as these would cast a light upon all your enjoyments and all your circumstances, and you could not help rejoicing evermore. For what can be more joyful to a man than to know that he is safe from the dreadful eternal destruction that the greater part of the world are exposed to, to know that he is out of the reach of the sting of death and the power of hell, to know that there is a glorious almighty God, and this God is his God; to know that Christ is the judge of heaven and earth, and yet to know that He is his Redeemer; to know that there is a day of judgment, and also to know that then they shall stand at the right hand of Christ; to know that there is a heaven of eternal glory, and to know that this is a kingdom prepared for them; to know that God has loved 'em before the foundation of the world, that their names were written on Christ's heart then, and that he died out of love to them and will love them to eternity?

Such considerations will surely give strong consolation, and will tend to make everything pleasant to him. Such an assurance will be a great help to you to come with boldness at all times to the throne of grace, for then you will know that when you go to him, you go to a Father, and you won't be afraid to call him Father. And when you speak to Christ, you won't be afraid to use such a style as this: "My Lord, my Redeemer, my dear Savior." And this will make prayer and other duties of religion pleasant to you.

This will especially tend to make the Lord's Supper a delightful ordinance to you, for you will know that person whose body and blood is there represented is your Savior, and that that death and those sufferings that are there commemorated were for your sake. And then, when you take Christ's body and blood, and eat and drink, you take what is your own. You eat that bread that came down from heaven for you, you drink that blood that was shed for you. This assurance will greatly open the way for a more free, full, and sweet converse between Christ and your soul. It will make the promises of the gospel abundantly the more sweet to you when you know that those promises are made to you. And the Bible, that is all over full of those precious promises, will be a sweet book to you. And thus your life will be filled up with the sweetest, and best, and most durable and reasonable comforts, and your life will close with peace and comfort, and nothing shall make you afraid.

Seeing, therefore, you don't begrutch to take so much pains, with so much assiduity and constancy, for the enjoyments of this world, why will you not take as much pains for that, which if you obtained it, would yield you so much more comfort than any or all of them?

Third. Let it be considered that such an assurance would not only be most comfortable, but also very profitable to your soul. It would be a great strengthening to you against temptations. It would give you courage to go through with difficult duties, and to bear sufferings for Christ's sake. For what can tend to give the child courage more than for the father to stand by, speaking comfortably to him, manifesting his love and acceptance?

If you know that Christ is your king, and know that he has loved you from eternity, and that he has laid down his life for you, it will greatly draw forth your heart in love to him. It will tend to quicken and warm your heart, and greatly to enliven your graces, and to engage your heart in Christ's service. The Apostle, speaking of his labors and sufferings for Christ's sake, says, II Cor. 5:14, "The love of Christ constraineth us." The consideration of Christ's having loved him and died for him had a powerful confirming influence upon him to engage him in the service of Christ. It will cause you to do your duty with the greater cheerfulness and will draw you on in the way of [holiness], so as that you may not only walk but run in the way of God's commandments.

It will be a great help to an heavenly life, if you know that Christ, who is in heaven at the right hand of God, is your Redeemer and your treasure. It will have a tendency to keep your heart there, and to take it off from things that are here below.

Fourth. This is a privilege that many of God's saints have attained to. Job professes it, and David often professes it in the Psalms. He often speaks positively that the Lord is his shepherd (Ps. 23:1), and Ps. 16:5, "The Lord is the portion of mine inheritance and of my cup."

The apostle Paul often speaks in the most positive terms, as in II Tim. 1:12, "I know whom I have believed." And he says positively, Gal. 2:20, that Christ died for him; and that for him to live was Christ, and to die would be gain, in Phil. 1:21. And near the close of his life, he speaks confidently, II Tim. 2:4, 7–8, "I have fought a good fight."

Not only the eminent saints that we read of in the Scriptures, but there have been many in all ages of the church that have obtained to this privilege.

Fifth. 'Tis not a privilege attainable only by a few, but that which in the use of proper means might ordinarily be obtained by the saints. And that is evident, because 'tis a privilege that is set forth in the Scripture for all to seek. All are commanded to seek it. II Pet. 1:10, "Give diligence to make your calling and election sure." And not only so, but they that have it not are much blamed that they han't it. II Cor. 13:5, "Know ye not your own selves, how that Christ is in you, except you be reprobates."

This would not be, unless the saints might, in the use of due and proper means, with proper care and diligence, ordinarily obtain. It is manifest by those scriptures that assurance is a prize that God has set up for all Christians to run for, and that striving after it is part of the work that all Christians have to do that han't obtained it, and if they don't attain it, they are much to blame.

Now how much may those considerations well quicken to think how excellent the privilege, and to think that is attainable, and that you may reasonably hope to obtain it in the due use of proper means in order [to] it, and so may come to say as well as holy Job, "I know that my Redeemer liveth."

But I proceed now briefly to consider what are the proper means to be used in order to an attaining to this privilege. And before I come to particulars, I would observe in the general:

To use self-examination alone, without any other means, is not the way for persons to attain to this privilege. Though there be sure rules of trial given in the Word of God, and the revelation which God has made of the qualifications of those that have an interest in Christ be very full and clear, and self-examination ought by no means to be left undone; yet for Christians to use no other means to obtain assurance, but only to examine themselves, is not the way to be successful—and that however good rules may be given for 'em to examine themselves by, and however strict and frequent they may be in examination of themselves.

But in order to persons' enjoying this glorious privilege, four things are ordinarily requisite:

1. That troublers be cast out and kept out. As long as persons secretly allow themselves in some practice or way that is disagreeable to a Christian spirit and Christian rules, and offensive to the pure eye of God, some lust that has some secret vent covered over with false pleas and carnal reasonings, it will be in the heart as Achan was in the camp of Israel [Josh. 7]. It must be a continual troubler that will cause God to hide his face and will darken evidences of grace, and the light of God's countenance and assurance of his favor is not to be expressed. All the self-examinations in the world won't satisfy the soul of its good estate till the Achan is destroyed, and when that is slain, another must not be admitted. There must be the most careful and strict watch kept up against all ways of sin, either in our behavior towards God or man, either at home or abroad, alone and with company, in God's house or elsewhere. And there must be a close walk with God in a way of universal obedience. They that walk closely with God will be in the way to have much communion with him, and to know their interest in him. The Psalmist says, Ps. 119:6, "Then shall I not be ashamed, when I have respect to all thy commandments," which implies that then he should be bold, being assured of his own sincerity.

2. Another thing requisite is that grace be not in low degrees. If persons have only very small degrees and exercises of grace, the consequence will be that it will be difficultly seen. And this is the very reason that many saints live so much in doubt. Their souls are sickly, and grace is in a very

feeble, low state in them. They have very weak exercises of it, and hence they can't be satisfied fully whether they have any or no.

But if persons are strong in grace and have commonly the lively actings of grace, it is easily seen and known. Grace is a very distinguishable thing from everything else in itself, and the reason why sometimes it is so difficult to distinguish it, is that there is so little of it to be seen. But when its exercises are vigorous and lively, they plainly show themselves.

And besides, the stronger grace is, the more clear the eye is to discern and distinguish between that which is true and that which is counterfeit. And moreover, the more gracious the soul is, the more does Christ delight to commune with it and manifest himself to it, and the more will he bestow his special rounds and favors on it. So that strength of grace, and the lively exercises of it, every way tend to promote assurance. And therefore those that would obtain assurance should not rest in past attainments, but should press forward with all their might, striving earnestly after higher degrees and actings of grace. They should make this their great and main business; their lives, their strength and their all should be devoted to it.

Thus they should seek greater acquaintance with Christ, that they may see more of his divine glory. We must first see how glorious a Redeemer he is, and how happy we should therefore be if he were our Redeemer, before we see and know that he is our Redeemer.

We should strive after a strong faith and the lively actings of it. A true hope is the daughter of faith. Faith is the root of which hope is the branch, and according to the strength of the root, so is the branch more or less flourishing. There never is a true assurance of hope without an assurance of faith. If we would know that Christ is our Redeemer, we must first know that he is the Redeemer that God has appointed, and that he lives and is a sufficient faithful Redeemer, able and willing to save to the uttermost.

And we must strive that we may grow in love to Christ. The spirit of love is the spirit of a child that cries, "Abba, Father." 'Tis the spirit of adoption, and when it is in strong exercise it casteth out fear and gives assurance. I John 4:18, "There is no fear in love."

There is nothing that does more naturally tend to encourage and assure the heart than to feel the strong and lively actings of a holy childlike love to God. It naturally, irresistibly causes us to look on God as our Father when we feel such lively actings of the spirit of a child towards him. Such a lively exercise of the spirit of adoption, or spirit of love, is the very thing that in Scripture is called the seal of the Spirit, and "the earnest of the Spirit" (II Cor. 1:22), and the witness of the Spirit of God "with our spirit, that we are the children of God" (Rom. 8:16).

This spirit, that casts out fear, is that which enables the saints to glory and triumph in tribulation (Rom. 5).

'Tis a strong faith and strong love that causes the saints to "rejoice with joy unspeakable and full [of glory]." I Pet. 1:8, "Whom having not seen, ye love; in whom, though now ye see him not, yet believing, ye rejoice with joy unspeakable and full of glory."

And it is not to be expected that persons should obtain assurance in any other way than by obtaining the strong, lively actings of love to Christ in the soul, so as to swallow up all carnal affections and desires.

Again, another grace that you must earnestly seek the increase of is humility and poverty of spirit. There is no grace whatsoever that has so many promises of comfort and of the tokens of God's presence and favor made to it in the Scriptures as such a spirit as this. If you indulge a spirit of pride, a spirit of high conceit of your own godliness or of any other qualification, or an ambitious revengeful spirit, a spirit of high resentment in your behavior among men, you will not be likely ever to obtain a steady assurance.

But if you would obtain this, you must earnestly seek that you may be meek and lowly of heart, and be more and more as a lamb, or dove, or a little child.

You must seek the increase and exercise of those graces in a diligent, constant and laborious attendance on all the appointed means of grace and performance of all duties of piety and charity. You will never be likely to come to any great strength of grace, unless you make progress in it in something of a constant steady manner; and in order to this, your watchfulness and diligence, and labor and prayer, must be constant.

3. Another thing ordinarily requisite in and to assurance is an abounding in holy fruits. The goodness of the fruit confirms the goodness of the

tree, both to ourselves and others. This comforted Hezekiah on his deathbed (Is. 38:3, II Tim. 4:7). The testimony of our own consciences, with respect to our doing good works and living an holy life, is spoken of by the Apostle as that which tends to give us assurance. I John 3:18–19, "My little children, let us not love in word, and in tongue; but in deed and in truth. And hereby we know that we are of the truth, and shall assure our hearts before him." And the apostle Paul mentions diligence in a holy life as what tends to give full assurance of hope. Heb. 6:9–10, "But, beloved, we are persuaded better things of you, and things that accompany salvation, though we thus speak. For God is not unrighteous to forget your work and labor of love, which ye have showed toward his name, in that ye have ministered to the saints, and do minister."

Holy works, and especially works of charity and self-denial, are those that [God] is wont to reward with special tokens of his presence and manifestations of his love and favor.

4. Another thing that is requisite to assurance is frequent and strict self-examination. Some persons never know what a condition they are in, and one reason is they never thoroughly inquire. They don't take thorough pains to acquaint themselves with the rule God has given for us to try ourselves by. They have a hope that it is well with them, and they are too easy and contented with an uncertain hope. They han't obtained any certainty, and they are too willing to go without it, and ben't thoroughly engaged to inquire what their state is. Rules of trial were given that we might use 'em and try ourselves by 'em.

Christians should often be examining themselves. They ought to deal faithfully in it, with a jealous eye over their own hearts, looking to God to help, imploring the influence of his Spirit, that he would help 'em against the boldness and deceitfulness of their hearts, and that he search 'em, and try 'em, and lead 'em in the way everlasting.

The Excellency of Christ (1738)

Revelation 5:5–6.
And one of the elders saith unto me, Weep not: behold the Lion of the tribe of Judah, the root of David, hath prevailed to open the book, and to loose the seven seals thereof. And I beheld, and lo in the midst of the throne, and of the four beasts, and in the midst of the elders, stood a Lamb, as it had been slain.

The visions and revelations that the apostle John had of the future events of God's providence, are here introduced with a vision of the book of God's decrees, by which those events were fore-ordained; which is represented in the first verse of this chapter, as a book in the right hand of him that sat on the throne, "written within, and on the back side, and sealed with seven seals." Books in the form in which they were wont of old to be made, were broad leaves of parchment, or paper, or something of that nature, joined together at one edge, and so rolled up together, and then sealed, or some way fastened together, to prevent their unfolding and opening. Hence we read of the roll of a book, Jer. 36:2. It seems to have been such a book that John had a vision of here; and therefore 'tis said to be "written within, and on the back side," i.e. on the inside pages, and also on one of the outside pages, viz. that that was rolled in, in rolling the book up together. And it is said to be "sealed with seven seals," to signify that what was written in it was perfectly hidden and secret; or that God's decrees of future events are sealed, and shut up from all possibility of being discovered by creatures, till God is pleased to make them known. We find that seven is often used in Scripture as the number of perfection, to signify the superlative, or most perfect degree of any thing; which probably came from that, that on the seventh day God beheld the works of creation finished, and rested and rejoiced in them, as being complete and perfect.

When John saw this book, he tells us he "saw a strong angel proclaiming with a loud voice, who is worthy to open the book, and to loose the seals thereof? And no man in heaven, nor in earth, neither under the earth, was able to open the book, neither to look thereon." And that he wept much, because "no man was found worthy to open and read the book, neither to look thereon." And then tells us how his tears were dried up, viz. "that one of the elders said unto him, weep not: behold the Lion of the tribe of Judah hath prevailed," etc., as in the text. Though no man nor angel, nor any mere creature, was found either able to loose the seals, or worthy to be admitted to the privilege of reading the book, yet this was declared, for the comfort of this beloved disciple, that Christ was found both able and worthy. And we have an account in the succeeding chapters how he actually did it, opening the seals in order, first one, and then another, revealing what God had decreed should come to pass hereafter. And we have an account in this chapter, of his coming and taking the book out of the right hand of him that sat on the throne, and of the joyful praises that were sung to him, in heaven and earth, on that occasion.

Many things might be observed in the words of the text; but 'tis to my present purpose only to take notice of the two distinct appellations here given to Christ.

1. He is called a lion. "Behold the Lion of the tribe of Judah." He seems to be called the Lion of the tribe of Judah, in allusion to what Jacob said, in his blessing of the tribes on his deathbed, who when he came to bless Judah, compares him to a lion. Gen. 49:9, "Judah is a lion's whelp: from the prey my son art thou gone up: he stooped down, he couched as a lion, and as an old lion; who shall raise him up?" And also to the standard of the camp of Judah in the wilderness, on which was displayed a lion, according to the ancient tradition of the Jews. 'Tis much on account of the valiant acts of David, that the tribe of Judah, of which David was, is in Jacob's prophetical blessing compared to a lion; but more especially with an eye to Jesus Christ, who also was of that tribe, and was descended of David, and is in our text called "the root of David"; and therefore Christ is here called "the Lion of the tribe of Judah."

2. He is called a lamb. John was told of a lion that had prevailed to open the book, and probably expected to see a lion in his vision; but while he is expecting, behold a Lamb appears to open the book, an exceeding diverse kind of creature from a lion! A lion is a devourer, one that is wont to make terrible slaughter of others; and no creature more easily falls a prey to him

than a lamb. And Christ is here represented not only as a lamb, a creature very liable to be slain, but a "Lamb as it had been slain," that is, with the marks of its deadly wounds appearing on it.

That which I would observe from the words, for the subject of my present discourse is this, viz.:

[DOCTRINE.]

There is an admirable conjunction of diverse excellencies in Jesus Christ.

The lion and the lamb, though very diverse kinds of creatures, yet have each their peculiar excellencies. The lion excels in strength, and in the majesty of his appearance and voice. The lamb excels in meekness and patience, besides the excellent nature of the creature as good for food, and yielding that which is fit for our clothing, and being suitable to be offered in sacrifice to God. But we see that Christ is in the text compared to both; because the diverse excellencies of both wonderfully meet in him.

In handling this subject, I would

I. Show wherein there is an admirable conjunction of diverse excellencies in Christ.

II. How this admirable conjunction of excellencies appears in Christ's acts.

And then make application.

I. I would show wherein there is an admirable conjunction of diverse excellencies in Jesus Christ. Which appears in three things,

First. There is a conjunction of such excellencies in Christ, as, in our manner of conceiving, are very diverse one from another.

Second. There is in him a conjunction of such really diverse excellencies, as otherwise would have seemed to us utterly incompatible in the same subject.

Third. Such diverse excellencies are exercised in him towards men, that otherwise would have seemed impossible to be exercised towards the same object.

First. There is a conjunction of such excellencies in Christ, as, in our manner of conceiving, are very diverse from one another. Such are the various divine perfections and excellencies that Christ is possessed of. Christ is a divine person, or one that is God; and therefore has all the attributes of God. The difference there is between these is chiefly relative, and in our manner of conceiving them. And those that in this sense are most diverse, do meet in the person of Christ. I shall mention two instances.

1. There do meet in Jesus Christ, infinite highness, and infinite condescension. Christ, as he is God, is infinitely great and high above all. He is higher than the kings of the earth; for he is King of kings, and Lord of lords. He is higher than the heavens, and higher than the highest angels of heaven. So great is he, that all men, all kings and princes, are as worms of the dust before him, all nations are as the drop of the bucket, and the light dust of the balance; yea, and angels themselves are as nothing before him. He is so high, that he is infinitely above any need of us; above our reach, that we cannot be profitable to him, and above our conceptions, that we cannot comprehend him. Prov. 30:4, "What is his name, and what is his Son's name, if thou canst tell?" Our understandings, if we stretch them never so far, can't reach up to his divine glory. Job 11:8, "It is high as heaven, what canst thou do?" Christ is the Creator, and great possessor of heaven and earth: he is sovereign Lord of all: he rules over the whole universe, and doth whatsoever pleaseth him: his knowledge is without bound: his wisdom is perfect, and what none can circumvent: his power is infinite, and none can resist him: his riches are immense and inexhaustible: his majesty is infinitely awful.

And yet he is one of infinite condescension. None are so low, or inferior, but Christ's condescension is sufficient to take a gracious notice of them. He condescends not only to the angels, humbling himself to behold the things that are done in heaven, but he also condescends to such poor creatures as men; and that not only so as to take notice of princes and great men, but of those that are of meanest rank and degree, "the poor of the world" (Jas. 2:5). Such as are commonly despised by their fellow creatures, Christ does not despise. I Cor. 1:28, "Base things of the world, and things that are despised, hath God chosen." Christ condescends to take notice of beggars (Luke 16:22), and of servants, and people of the most despised nations: in Christ Jesus is neither "barbarian, Scythian, bond, nor free"

(Col. 3:11). He that is thus high, condescends to take a gracious notice of little children. Matt. 19:14, "Suffer little children to come unto me." Yea, which is much more, his condescension is sufficient to take a gracious notice of the most unworthy, sinful creatures, those that have no good deservings, and those that have infinite ill deservings.

Yea, so great is his condescension, that it is not only sufficient to take some gracious notice of such as these, but sufficient for every thing that is an act of condescension. His condescension is great enough to become their friend: 'tis great enough to become their companion, to unite their souls to him in spiritual marriage: 'tis great enough to take their nature upon him, to become one of them, that he may be one with them: yea, it is great enough to abase himself yet lower for them, even to expose himself to shame and spitting; yea, to yield up himself to an ignominious death for them. And what act of condescension can be conceived of greater? Yet such an act as this, has his condescension yielded to, for those that are so low and mean, despicable and unworthy!

Such a conjunction of such infinite highness, and low condescension, in the same person, is admirable. We see by manifold instances, what a tendency an high station has in men, to make them to be of a quite contrary disposition. If one worm be a little exalted above another, by having more dust, or a bigger dunghill, how much does he make of himself! What a distance does he keep from those that are below him! And a little condescension, is what he expects should be made much of, and greatly acknowledged. Christ condescends to wash our feet; but how would great men (or rather the bigger worms), account themselves debased by acts of far less condescension!

2. There meet in Jesus Christ, infinite justice, and infinite grace. As Christ is a divine person he is infinitely holy and just, infinitely hating sin, and disposed to execute condign punishment for sin. He is the judge of the world, and is the infinitely just judge of it, and will not at all acquit the wicked, or by any means clear the guilty.

And yet he is one that is infinitely gracious and merciful. Though his justice be so strict with respect to all sin, and every breach of the law, yet he has grace sufficient for every sinner, and even the chief of sinners. And it is not only sufficient for the most unworthy to show them mercy, and bestow some good upon them, but to bestow the greatest good; yea, 'tis sufficient to bestow all good upon them, and to do all things for them. There is no benefit or blessing that they can receive so great, but the grace of Christ is sufficient to bestow it on the greatest sinner that ever lived. And not only so, but so great is his grace, that nothing is too much as the means of this good: 'tis sufficient not only to do great things, but also to suffer in order to it; and not only to suffer, but to suffer most extremely, even unto death, the most terrible of natural evils; and not only death, but the most ignominious and tormenting, and every way the most terrible death that men could inflict; yea, and greater sufferings than men could inflict, who could only torment the body, but also those sufferings in his soul, that were the more immediate fruits of the wrath of God against the sins of those he undertakes for.

Second. There do meet in the person of Christ, such really diverse excellencies, which otherwise would have been thought utterly incompatible in the same subject; such as are conjoined in no other person whatever, either divine, human, or angelical; and such as neither men nor angels would ever have imagined could have met together in the same person, had it not been seen in the person of Christ. I would give some instances.

1. In the person of Christ do meet together, infinite *glory*, and lowest *humility*. Infinite glory, and the virtue of humility, meet in no other person but Christ. They meet in no created person; for no created person has infinite glory: and they meet in no other divine person but Christ. For though the divine nature be infinitely abhorrent to pride, yet humility is not properly predicable of God the Father, and the Holy Ghost, that exist only in the divine nature; because it is a proper excellency only of a created nature; for it conists radically in a sense of a comparative lowness and littleness before God, or the great distance between God and the subject of this virtue; but it would be a contradiction to suppose any such thing in God.

But in Jesus Christ, who is both God and man, these two diverse excellencies, are sweetly united. He is a person infinitely exalted in glory and dignity. Philip. 2:6, "Being in the form of God, he thought it not robbery to be equal with God." There is equal honor due to him with the Father. John 5:23, "That all men should honor the Son, even as they honor the Father." God himself says to him, "Thy throne, O God, is for ever and ever" (Heb. 1:8). And there is the same supreme respect, and divine worship, paid to him by the angels of heaven, as to God the Father; as there, v. 6, "Let all the angels of God worship him."

But however he is thus above all, yet he is lowest of all in humility. There never was so great an instance of this virtue, among either men or angels, as Jesus. None ever was so sensible of the distance between God and him, or had a heart so lowly before God, as the man Christ Jesus (Matt. 11:29). What a wonderful spirit of humility appeared in him, when he was here upon earth, in all his behavior! In his contentment in his mean outward condition, contentedly living in the family of Joseph the carpenter, and Mary his mother, for thirty years together, and afterwards choosing outward meanness, poverty and contempt, rather than earthly greatness; in his washing his disciples' feet, and in all his speeches and deportment towards them; in his cheerfully sustaining the form of a servant through his whole life, and submitting to such immense humiliation at death!

2. In the person of Christ do meet together, infinite majesty, and transcendent *meekness*. These again are two qualifications that meet together in no other person but Christ. Meekness, properly so called, is a virtue proper only to the creature: we scarcely ever find meekness mentioned as a divine attribute in Scripture; at least not in the New Testament; for thereby seems to be signified, a calmness and quietness of spirit arising from humility, in mutable beings, that are naturally liable to be put in a ruffle, by the assaults of a tempestuous and injurious world. But Christ being both God and man, hath both infinite majesty and superlative meekness.

Christ was a person of infinite majesty. It is he that is spoken of, Ps. 45:3, "Gird thy sword upon thy thigh, O most mighty, in thy glory and thy majesty." 'Tis he that is mighty, that rideth on the heavens, and in his excellency on the sky. 'Tis he that is terrible out of his holy places; who is mightier than the noise of many waters, yea, than the mighty waves of the sea; before whom a fire goeth, and burneth up his enemies round about; at whose presence the earth doth quake, and the hills do melt; who sitteth on the circle of the earth, and all the inhabitants thereof are as grasshoppers;

who rebukes the sea and maketh it dry, and drieth up the rivers; whose eyes are as a flame of fire, from whose presence, and from the glory of whose power, the wicked shall be punished with everlasting destruction; who is the blessed and only potentate, the King of kings, and Lord of lords, that hath heaven for his throne, and the earth for his footstool, and is the high and lofty One who inhabits eternity, whose kingdom is an everlasting kingdom, and of whose dominion there is no end.

And yet he was the most marvelous instance of meekness, and humble quietness of spirit, that ever was, agreeable to the prophecies of him, Matt. 21:4–5, "All this was done, that it might be fulfilled which was spoken by the prophet, saying, Tell ye the daughter of Sion, Behold thy King cometh unto thee, meek, and sitting upon an ass, and a colt the foal of an ass." And, agreeable to what Christ declares of himself, Matt. 21:29, "I am meek and lowly of heart." And agreeable to what was manifest in his behavior here in this world. For there never was such an instance seen on earth of a meek behavior, under injuries and reproaches, and towards enemies; who when he was reviled, reviled not again; who was of a wonderful spirit of forgiveness, was ready to forgive his worst enemies, and prayed for them with fervent and effectual prayers. With what meekness did he appear, when in the ring of soldiers, that were condemning and mocking him, when he was silent, and opened not his mouth, but went as a lamb to the slaughter. Thus is Christ a lion in majesty, and a lamb in meekness.

3. There meet in the person of Christ, the deepest reverence towards God, and equality with God. Christ, when he was here on earth, appeared full of holy reverence towards the Father: he paid the most reverential worship to him, praying to him with postures of reverence. Thus we read of his "kneeling down and praying" (Luke 22:41). This became Christ, as he was one that had taken on him the human nature. But at the same time he existed in the divine nature; whereby his person was in all respects equal to the person of the Father. God the Father hath no attribute or perfection, that the Son hath not, in equal degree, and equal glory. These things meet in no other person but Jesus Christ.

4. There are conjoined in the person of Christ, infinite worthiness of good, and the greatest patience under sufferings of evil. He was perfectly innocent, and deserved no suffering. He deserved nothing from God, by

any guilt of his own; and he deserved no ill from men. Yea, he was not only harmless, and undeserving of suffering, but he was infinitely worthy, worthy of the infinite love of the Father, worthy of infinite and eternal happiness, and infinitely worthy of all possible esteem, love, and service from all men. And yet he was perfectly patient under the greatest sufferings, that ever were endured in this world. Heb. 6:15, "After he had patiently endured, he obtained the promise." He suffered not from his Father, for his faults, but ours; and he suffered from men, not for his faults, but for those things, on account of which, he was infinitely worthy of their love and honor; which made his patience the more wonderful, and the more glorious. I Pet. 2:20–24,

> For what glory is it, if when ye be buffeted for your faults, ye shall take it patiently? but if when ye do well, and suffer it, ye take it patiently, this is acceptable with God: for even hereunto were ye called; because Christ also suffered for us, leaving us an example, that we should follow his steps; who did no sin, neither was guile found in his mouth; who when he was reviled, reviled not again, when he suffered he threatened not, but committed himself to him that judgeth righteously: who his own self, bare our sins in his own body, on the tree, that we being dead to sin, should live unto righteousness; by whose stripes ye were healed.

There is no such conjunction of innocence, worthiness, and patience under sufferings, as in the person of Christ.

5. In the person of Christ are conjoined, an exceeding spirit of obedience, with supreme dominion over heaven and earth. Christ is the Lord of all things, in two respects. He is so as he is God-man, and Mediator; and so his dominion is appointed, and given of the Father, and is by delegation from God, and he is as it were the Father's vicegerent. But he is the Lord of all things in another respect, viz. as he is (by his original nature) God. And so he is by natural right, the Lord of all, and supreme over all, as much as the Father. Thus he has dominion over the world, not by delegation, but in his own right: he is not an under-God, as the Arians suppose, but to all intents and purposes, supreme God.

And yet, in the same person, is found the greatest spirit of obedience to the commands and law of God that ever was in the universe; which was manifest in his obedience here in this world. John 14:31, "As the Father gave me commandment, even so I do." John 15:10, "Even as I have kept my Father's commandments, and abide in his love." The greatness of his spirit of obedience appears in the perfection of his obedience, and in his obeying commands of such exceeding difficulty. Never any one received commands from God, of such difficulty, and that were so great a trial of obedience, as Jesus Christ. One of God's commands to him was, that he should yield himself to those dreadful sufferings that he underwent. See John 10:18, "No man taketh it from me, but I lay it down of myself. This commandment received I of my Father." And Christ was thoroughly obedient to this command of God. Heb. 5:8, "Though he were a Son, yet learned he obedience by the things that he suffered." Phil. 2:8, "He humbled himself, and became obedient unto death, even the death of the cross." Never was there such an instance of obedience in man nor angel, as this; though he that obeyed was at the same time, supreme Lord of both angels and men.

6. In the person of Christ are conjoined absolute sovereignty, and perfect resignation. This is another unparalleled conjunction. Christ as he is God, is the absolute sovereign of the world: he is the sovereign disposer of all events. The decrees of God are all his sovereign decrees; and the work of creation, and all God's works of providence, are his sovereign works. 'Tis he that worketh all things according to the counsel of his own will. Col. 1:16–17, "By him, and through him, and to him, are all things." John 5:17, "The Father worketh hitherto, and I work." Matt. 8:3, "I will, be thou clean."

But yet Christ was the most wonderful instance of resignation, that ever appeared in the world. He was absolutely and perfectly resigned, when he had a near, and immediate prospect of his terrible sufferings, and the dreadful cup that he was to drink, the idea and expectation of which, made his soul exceeding sorrowful, even unto death, and put him into such an agony, that his sweat was as it were great drops, or clots of blood, falling down to the ground. But in such circumstances, he was wholly resigned to the will of God. Matt. 26:39, "O my Father, if it be possible, let this cup pass from me! Nevertheless, not as I will, but as thou wilt." V. 42, "O my

Father, if this cup may not pass from me, except I drink it, thy will be done!"

7. In Christ do meet together, self-sufficiency, and an entire trust and reliance on God; which is another conjunction peculiar to the person of Christ. As he is a divine person he is self-sufficient, standing in need of nothing; all creatures are dependent on him, but he is dependent on none, but is absolutely independent. His proceeding from the Father in his eternal generation, or filiation, argues no proper dependence on the will of the Father; for that proceeding was natural and necessary, and not arbitrary. But yet Christ entirely trusted in God: his enemies say that of him, "He trusted in God that he would deliver him" (Matt. 27:43). And the Apostle testifies, I Pet. 2:23, "That he committed himself to God."

Third. Such diverse excellencies are expressed in him towards men, that otherwise would have seemed impossible to be exercised towards the same object; as particularly these three, justice, mercy and truth. The same that are mentioned, Ps. 85:10, "Mercy and truth are met together, righteousness and peace have kissed each other." The strict justice of God, and even his revenging justice, and that against the sins of men, never was so gloriously manifested as in Christ. He manifested an infinite regard to the attribute of God's justice, in that when he had a mind to save sinners, he was willing to undergo such extreme sufferings, rather than that their salvation should be to the injury of the honor of that attribute. And as he is the judge of the world, he doth himself exercise strict justice; he will not clear the guilty, nor at all acquit the wicked in judgment. And yet, how wonderfully is infinite mercy towards sinners displayed in him! And what glorious and ineffable grace and love have been, and are exercised by him, towards sinful men! Though he be the just judge of a sinful world, yet he is also the Savior of the world: though he be a consuming fire to sin, yet he is the light and life of sinners. Rom. 3:25–26, "Whom God hath set forth to be a propitiation, through faith in his blood, to declare his righteousness, for the remission of sins that are past, through the forbearance of God; to declare, I say, at this time, his righteousness, that he might be just, and the justifier of him which believeth in Jesus."

So the immutable truth of God, in the threatenings of his law against the sins of men, was never so manifested, as it is in Jesus Christ; for there never was any other so great a trial of the unalterableness of the truth of God, in those threatenings, as when sin came to be imputed to his own Son. And then in Christ, has been seen already, an actual complete accomplishment of those threatenings; which never has been, nor will be seen in any other instance; because the eternity that will be taken up in fulfilling those threatenings on others, never will be finished. Christ manifested an infinite regard to this truth of God in his sufferings. And in his judging the world, he makes the covenant of works that contains those dreadful threatenings, his rule of judgment: he will see to it that it is not infringed in the least jot or tittle; he will do nothing contrary to the threatenings of the law, and their complete fulfillment. And yet in him we have many great, and precious promises, promises of perfect deliverance from the penalty of the law. And this is the promise that he hath promised us, even eternal life. And in him are all the promises of God, yea, and Amen.

Having thus shown wherein there is an admirable conjunction of excellencies in Jesus Christ, I now proceed,

[II.] Secondly, to show how this admirable conjunction of excellencies appears in Christ's acts.

First. It appears in what Christ did in taking on him our nature. In this act his infinite condescension wonderfully appeared; that he that was God, should become man; that the Word should be made flesh, and should take on him a nature infinitely below his original nature! And it appears yet more remarkably, in the low circumstances of his incarnation: he was conceived in the womb of a poor young woman; whose poverty appeared in that when she came to offer sacrifices of her purification, she brought what was allowed in the law, only in case of poverty; as Luke 2:24, "According to what is said in the law of the Lord, a pair of turtledoves, or two young pigeons." This was allowed only in case the person was so poor, that she was not able to offer a lamb (Lev. 12:8).

And though his infinite condescension thus appeared in the manner of his incarnation, yet his divine dignity also appeared in it; for though he was conceived in the womb of a poor virgin, yet he was there conceived by the power of the Holy Ghost. And his divine dignity also appeared in the holiness of his conception and birth. Though he was conceived in the womb of one of the corrupt race of mankind, yet he was conceived and born without sin; as the angel said to the blessed Virgin, Luke 1:35, "The Holy Ghost shall come upon thee, and the power of the Highest shall overshadow thee; therefore also, that holy thing which shall be born of thee, shall be called the Son of God." His infinite condescension marvelously appeared in the manner of his birth. He was brought forth in a stable, because there was no room for them in the inn. The inn was taken up by others, that were looked upon as persons of greater account. The blessed Virgin being poor and despised, was turned or shut out; though she was in such necessitous circumstances, yet those that counted themselves her betters would not give place to her; and therefore in the time of her travail she was forced to betake herself to a stable; and when the child was born, it was wrapped in swaddling clothes, and laid in a manger; and there Christ lay a little infant; and there he eminently appeared as a lamb. But yet this feeble infant that was born thus in a stable, and laid in a manger, was born to conquer and triumph over Satan, that roaring lion: he came to subdue the mighty powers of darkness, and make a show of them openly; and so to restore peace on earth, and to manifest God's good will towards men, and to bring glory to God in the highest; according as the end of his birth was declared by the joyful songs of the glorious hosts of angels, appearing to the shepherds, at the same time that the infant lay in the manger; whereby his divine dignity was manifested.

Second. This admirable conjunction of excellencies appears in the acts and various passages of Christ's life. Though Christ dwelt on the earth in mean outward circumstances, whereby his condescension and humility especially appeared, and his majesty was veiled; yet his divine dignity and glory did in many of his acts shine through the veil, and it illustriously appeared that he was, not only the Son of man, but, the great God.

Thus in the circumstances of his infancy, his outward meanness appeared; yet there was something then to show forth his divine dignity, in the wise men's being stirred up to come from the east to give honor to him, their being led by a miraculous star, and coming and falling down and worshipping him, and presenting him with gold, frankincense and myrrh. His humility and meekness wonderfully appeared in his subjection to his mother and reputed father, when he was a child: he herein appeared as a lamb. But his divine glory broke forth and shone, when at twelve years old, he disputed with the doctors in the temple: in that he appeared, is some measure, as "the Lion of the tribe of Judah."

And so after he entered on his public ministry, his marvelous humility and meekness was manifested in his choosing to appear in such mean outward circumstances, and in being so contented in them, when he was so poor that he had not where to lay his head, and depended on the charity of some of his followers for his subsistence; as appears by Luke 8, at the beginning. As also in his meek, condescending, and familiar treatment of his disciples; in his discourses with them, treating them as a father his children, yea, as friends and companions: and in his patient bearing such affliction and reproach, and so many injuries from the scribes and Pharisees, and others: in these things he appeared as a Lamb. And yet he at the same time did many ways show forth his divine majesty and glory; particularly in the miracles that he wrought, which were evidently divine works, and manifested omnipotent power, and so declared him to be "the Lion of the tribe of Judah." His wonderful and miraculous works plainly showed him to be the God of nature; in that it appeared by them that he had all nature in his hands, and could lay an arrest upon it, and stop and change its course, as he pleased. In healing the sick, and opening the eyes of the blind, and unstopping the ears of the deaf, and healing the lame, he showed that he was the God that framed the eye, and created the ear, and was the author of the frame of man's body. By the dead's rising at his command, it appeared that he was the author and fountain of life, and that "God the Lord, to whom belong the issues from death." By his walking on the sea in a storm, when the waves were raised, he showed himself to be that God, spoken of [in] Job 9:8, "That treadeth on the waves of the sea." By his stilling the storm, and calming the rage of the sea, by his powerful command, saying, "Peace, be still," he showed himself to be he that has the command of the universe, and to be that God that brings things to pass by the word of his power, that speaks and 'tis done, that commands and it stands fast, and he that is spoken of, Ps. 65:7, "Who stilleth the noise of the seas, the noise of their waves." And Ps. 107:29, "that maketh the storm a calm; so that the waves thereof are still." And Ps. 89:8–9, "O Lord God of hosts, who is a strong lord like unto thee, or to thy faithfulness round about thee? Thou rebukest the raging of the sea: when the waves thereof arise, thou stillest them." Christ by casting out devils, remarkably appeared as "the Lion of the tribe of Judah," and showed that he was stronger than the roaring lion, that seeks whom he may devour. He commanded them to come out, and they were forced to obey: they were terribly afraid of him; they fall down before him, and beseech him not to torment them: he forces a whole legion of them to forsake their old hold, by his powerful word; and they could not so much as enter into the swine without his leave. He showed the glory of his omniscience, by telling the thoughts of men; as we have often an account. Herein he appeared to be that God spoken of, Amos 4:13, "That declareth unto man what is his thought." Thus in the midst of his meanness and humiliation, his divine glory appeared in his miracles, John 2:11, "This beginning of miracles did Jesus in Cana of Galilee, and manifested forth his glory."

And though Christ ordinarily appeared without outward glory, and in great obscurity, yet at a certain time he threw off the veil, and appeared in his divine majesty, so far as it could be outwardly manifested to men in this frail state, when he was transfigured in the mount. The apostle Peter speaks of it, II Pet. 1:16–17, speaking there of himself, as one that was an "eyewitness of his majesty, when he received from God the Father, honor and glory, when there came such a voice to him, from the excellent glory, This is my beloved Son, in whom I am well pleased"; which voice that came from heaven, they heard, when they were with him in the holy mount.

And at the same time that Christ was wont to appear in such meekness, condescension, and humility, in his familiar discourses with his disciples, appearing therein as the Lamb of God, he was also wont to appear as "the Lion of the tribe of Judah," with divine authority and majesty, in his so sharply rebuking the scribes and Pharisees, and other hypocrites.

Third. This admirable conjunction of excellencies remarkably appears, in his offering up himself a sacrifice for sinners in his last sufferings. As this was the greatest thing in all the work of redemption, the greatest act of Christ in that work; so in this act especially, does there appear that admirable conjunction of excellencies, that has been spoken of. Christ never so much appeared as a lamb, as when he was slain: "He came like a lamb to the slaughter," Is. 53:7. Then he was offered up to God as a lamb without blemish, and without spot: then especially did he appear to be the antitype of the lamb of the Passover: I Cor. 5:7, "Christ our passover is sacrificed for us." And yet in that act, he did in an especial manner appear as "the Lion of the tribe of Judah"; yea, in this above all other acts, in many respects, as may appear in the following things.

1. Then was Christ in the greatest degree of his humiliation, and yet by that, above all other things, his divine glory appears. Christ's humiliation was great, in being born in such a low condition, of a poor virgin, and in a stable: his humiliation was great, in being subject to Joseph the carpenter, and Mary his mother, and afterwards in living in poverty, so as not to have where to lay his head, and in suffering such manifold and bitter reproaches as he suffered, while he went about preaching and working miracles: but his humiliation was never so great, as it was in his last sufferings, beginning with his agony in the garden, till he expired on the cross. Never was he subject to such ignominy as then; never did he suffer so much pain in his body, or so much sorrow in his soul; never was he in so great an exercise of his condescension, humility, meekness, and patience, as he was in these last sufferings; never was his divine glory and majesty covered with so thick and dark a veil; never did he so empty himself, and make himself of no reputation, as at this same time: and yet never was his divine glory so manifested, by any act of his, as in that act, of yielding himself up to these sufferings. When the fruit of it came to appear, and the mystery and ends of it to be unfolded, in the issue of it, then did the glory of it appear; then did it appear, as the most glorious act of Christ that ever he exercised towards the creature. This act of his is celebrated by the angels and hosts of heaven with peculiar praises, as that which is above all others glorious, as you may see in the context, vv. 9–12:

> And they sung a new song, saying, Thou art worthy to take the book, and to open the seals thereof, for thou wast slain, and hast redeemed us to God by thy blood, out of every kindred, and tongue, and people, and nation, and hast made us, to our God, kings, and priests, and we shall reign on earth. And I beheld, and I heard the voice of many angels, round about the throne, and the beasts, and the elders, and

> the number of them was ten thousand times ten thousand, and thousands of thousands, saying, with a loud voice, Worthy is the Lamb that was slain, to receive power, and riches, and wisdom, and strength, and honor, and glory, and blessing.

2. He never in any act gave so great a manifestation of love to God, and yet never so manifested his love to those that were enemies to God, as in that act. Christ never did anything whereby his love to the Father was so eminently manifested, as in his laying down his life, under such inexpressible sufferings, in obedience to his command, and for the vindication of the honor of his authority and majesty; nor did ever any mere creature give such a testimony of love to God as that was: and yet this was the greatest expression of all, of his love to sinful men, that were enemies to God. Rom. 5:10, "While we were enemies, we were reconciled to God, by the death of his Son." The greatness of Christ's love to such, appears in nothing so much, as in its being dying love. That blood of Christ that was sweat out, and fell in great drops to the ground, in his agony, was shed from love to God's enemies, and his own. That shame and spitting, that torment of body, and that exceeding sorrow, even unto death, that he endured in his soul, was what he underwent from love to rebels against God, to save them from hell, and to purchase for them eternal glory. Never did Christ so eminently show his regard to God's honor, as in offering up himself a victim to revenging justice, to vindicate God's honor. And yet in this above all, he manifested his love to them that dishonored God, so as to bring such guilt on themselves, that nothing less than his blood could atone for it.

3. Christ never so eminently appeared for divine justice, and yet never suffered so much from divine justice, as when he offered up himself a sacrifice for our sins. In Christ's great sufferings, did his infinite regard to the honor of God's justice distinguishingly appear; for it was from regard to that, that he thus humbled himself: and yet in these sufferings, Christ was the mark of the vindictive expressions of that very justice of God. Revenging justice then spent all its force upon him, on the account of our guilt that was laid upon him; he was not spared at all; but God spent the arrows of his vengeance upon him, which made him sweat blood, and cry

out upon the cross, and probably rent his vitals, broke his heart, the fountain of blood, or some other internal blood vessels, and by the violent fermentation turned his blood to water: for the blood and water that issued out of his side, when pierced by the spear, seems to have been extravasated blood; and so there might be a kind of literal fulfillment of that, in Ps. 22:14, "I am poured out like water, and all my bones are out of joint: my heart is like wax, it is melted in the midst of my bowels." And this was the way and means by which Christ stood up for the honor of God's justice, viz. by thus suffering its terrible executions. For when he had undertaken for sinners, and had substituted himself in their room, divine justice could have its due honor, no other way than by his suffering its revenges.

In this the diverse excellencies that met in the person of Christ appeared, viz. his infinite regard to God's justice, and such love to those that have exposed themselves to it, as induced him thus to yield himself a sacrifice to it.

4. Christ's holiness never so illustriously shone forth, as it did in his last sufferings; and yet he never was to such a degree, treated as guilty. Christ's holiness never had such a trial, as it had then; and therefore never had so great a manifestation. When it was tried in this furnace, it came forth as gold, or as silver purified seven times. His holiness then above all appeared in his steadfast pursuit of the honor of God, and in his obedience to him: for his yielding himself unto death was transcendently the greatest act of obedience, that ever was paid to God, by any one since the foundation of the world.

And yet then Christ was in the greatest degree treated as a wicked person. He was apprehended and bound as a malefactor. His accusers represented him as a most wicked wretch. In his sufferings before his crucifixion he was treated as if he had been the worst and vilest of mankind; and then, he was put to a kind of death, that none but the worst sort of malefactors were wont to suffer, those that were most abject in their persons, and guilty of the blackest crimes. And he suffered as though guilty from God himself, by reason of our guilt imputed to him; for he was made sin for us, who knew no sin; he was made subject to wrath as if he had been sinful himself: he was made a curse for us.

Christ never so greatly manifested his hatred of sin, as against God, as in his dying to take away the dishonor that sin had done to God; and yet never was he to such a degree subject to the terrible effects of God's hatred of sin, and wrath against it, as he was then. In this appears those diverse excellencies meeting in Christ, viz. love to God, and grace to sinners.

5. He never was so dealt with as unworthy as in his last sufferings, and yet it is chiefly on account of them that he is accounted worthy. He was therein dealt with as if he had not been worthy to live: they cry out, "Away with him! Away with him! Crucify him," John 19:15. And they prefer Barabbas before him. And he suffered from the Father, as one whose demerits were infinite, by reason of our demerits that were laid upon him. And yet it was especially by that act of his subjecting himself to those sufferings, that he merited, and on the account of which chiefly he was accounted worthy of, the glory of his exaltation. Philip. 2:8–9, "He humbled himself, and became obedient unto death; wherefore God hath highly exalted him." And we see that 'tis on this account chiefly, that he is extolled as worthy by saints and angels in the context; "worthy," say they, "is the Lamb that was slain." This shows an admirable conjunction in him of infinite dignity, and infinite condescension and love to the infinitely unworthy.

6. Christ in his last sufferings suffered most extremely from those that he was then in his greatest act of love to. He never suffered so much from his Father (though not from any hatred to him, but from hatred to our sins), for he then forsook him (as Christ on the cross expresses it), or took away the comforts of his presence; and then "it pleased the Lord to bruise him, and put him to grief," as Is. 53:10. And yet never gave so great a manifestation of love to God as then, as has been already observed. So Christ never suffered so much from the hands of men as he did then; and yet never was in so high an exercise of love to men. He never was so ill-treated by his disciples; who were so unconcerned about his sufferings, that they would not watch with him one hour, in his agony; and when he was apprehended, all forsook him and fled, except Peter, who denied him with oaths and curses. And yet then he was suffering, shedding his blood, and pouring out his soul unto death, for them. Yea, he probably was then shedding his blood, for some of them that shed his blood: he was dying for

some that killed him; whom he prayed for, while they were crucifying him; and were probably afterwards brought home to Christ by Peter's preaching. Compare Luke 23:34; Acts 2:23, 36–37, 41; and ch. 3:17; and ch. 4:4. This shows an admirable meeting of justice and grace in the redemption of Christ.

7. It was in Christ's last sufferings, above all, that he was delivered up to the power of his enemies; and yet by these, above all, he obtained victory over his enemies. Christ never was so in his enemies' hands, as in the time of his last sufferings. They sought his life before! But from time to time they were restrained, and Christ escaped out of their hands; and this reason is given for it, that "his time was not yet come"; but now they were suffered to work their will upon him; he was in a great degree delivered up to the malice and cruelty of both wicked men and devils: and therefore when Christ's enemies came to apprehend him, he says to them, Luke 22:53, "When I was daily with you in the temple, ye stretched forth no hand against me: but this is your hour and the power of darkness."

And yet it was principally by means of those sufferings, that he conquered and overthrew his enemies. Christ never so effectually bruised Satan's head, as when he bruised his heel. The weapon with which Christ warred against the devil, and obtained a most complete victory and glorious triumph over him, was the cross, the instrument and weapon with which he thought he had overthrown Christ, and brought on him shameful destruction. Col. 2:14–15, "Blotting out the handwriting of ordinances . . . nailing it to his cross: and having spoiled principalities and powers, he made a show of them openly, triumphing over them in it." In his last sufferings Christ sapped the very foundations of Satan's kingdom; he conquered his enemies in their own territories, and beat them with their own weapons; as David cut off Goliath's head with his own sword. The devil had as it were swallowed up Christ, as the whale did Jonah; but it was deadly poison to him; he gave him a mortal wound in his own bowels; he was soon sick of his morsel, and forced to vomit him up again; and is to this day heartsick of what he then swallowed as his prey. In those sufferings of Christ, was laid the foundation of all that glorious victory that he has already obtained over Satan, in the overthrow of his heathenish kingdom, in the Roman empire, and all the success the gospel has had since;

and also of all his future and still more glorious victory that is to be obtained in all the earth. Thus Samson's riddle is most eminently fulfilled, Judges 14:14, "Out of the eater came forth meat, and out of the strong came forth sweetness." And thus the true Samson does more towards the destruction of his enemies at his death, than in his life, in yielding up himself to death, he pulls down the temple of Dagon, and destroys many thousands of his enemies even while they are making themselves sport in his sufferings; and so he whose type was the ark, pulls down Dagon, and breaks off his head and hands in his own temple, even while he is brought in there as Dagon's captive.

Thus Christ appeared at the same time, and in the same act, as both a lion and a lamb. He appeared as a lamb in the hands of his cruel enemies; as a lamb in the paws, and between the devouring jaws of a roaring lion; yea, he was a lamb actually slain by this lion: and yet at the same time, as "the Lion of the tribe of Judah," he conquers and triumphs over Satan, destroying his own devourer; as Samson did the lion that roared upon him, when he rent him as he would a kid. And in nothing has Christ appeared so much as a lion, in glorious strength destroying his enemies, as when he was brought as a lamb to the slaughter: in his greatest weakness, he was most strong; and when he suffered most from his enemies, he brought the greatest confusion on his enemies.

Thus this admirable conjunction of diverse excellencies was manifest in Christ, in his offering up himself to God in his last sufferings.

Fourth. It is still manifest in his acts, in his present state of exaltation in heaven. Indeed in his exalted state he most eminently appears in a manifestation of those excellencies, on the account of which he is compared to a lion; but still he appears as a lamb. Rev. 14:1, "And I looked, and lo a lion stood on Mount Sion." As in his state of humiliation, he chiefly appeared as a lamb, and yet did not appear without manifestation of his divine majesty and power, as "the Lion of the tribe of Judah." Though Christ be now at the right hand of God, exalted as King of heaven, and Lord of the universe; yet as he still is in the human nature, he still excels in humility. Though the man Christ Jesus be the highest of all creatures in heaven, yet he as much excels them all in humility, as he doth in glory and dignity; for none sees so much of the distance between God and him, as he does. And though he now appears in such glorious majesty and dominion in heaven, yet he appears as a lamb in his condescending, mild and sweet treatment of his saints there; for he is a Lamb still, even amidst the throne of his exaltation; and he that is the shepherd of the whole flock, is himself a lamb, and goes before them in heaven as such. Rev. 7:17, "For the Lamb, which is in the midst of the throne, shall feed them, and shall lead them into living fountains of waters, and God shall wipe away all tears from their eyes." Though in heaven every knee bows to him, and though the angels fall down before him, adoring him, yet he treats his saints with infinite condescension, mildness and endearment. And in his acts towards the saints on earth, he still appears as a Lamb, manifesting exceeding love and tenderness, in his intercession for them, as one that has had experience of affliction and temptation: he has not forgot what these things are; nor has he forgot how to pity those that are subject to them. And he still manifests his lamb-like excellencies, in his dealings with his saints on earth, in admirable forbearance, love, gentleness, and compassions, instructing, supplying, supporting, and comforting them, often coming to them, and manifesting himself to them by his Spirit, that he may sup with them, and they with him, admitting them to sweet communion with him, enabling them with boldness and confidence to come to him, and solace their hearts in him. And in heaven Christ still appears, as it were with the marks of his wounds upon him; and so appears as a Lamb as it had been slain; as he was represented in vision to St. John, in the text, when he appeared to open the book sealed with seven seals, which is part of the glory of his exaltation.

Fifth, and lastly, this admirable conjunction of excellencies will be manifest in Christ's acts at the last judgment. He then above all other times will appear as "the Lion of the tribe of Judah," in infinite greatness and majesty, when he shall come in the glory of his Father, with all the holy angels, and the earth shall tremble before him, and the hills shall melt. This is he, spoken of, Rev. 20:11, "that shall sit on a great white throne, before whose face the earth and heaven shall flee away." He will then appear in the most dreadful and amazing manner to the wicked: the devils tremble at the thoughts of that appearance; and when it shall be, the kings, and the great men, and the rich men, and the chief captains, and the mighty men, and every bondman, and every freeman, shall hide themselves in the dens, and in the rocks of the mountains, and shall cry to the mountains and rocks to fall on them, to hide them from the face and wrath of the Lamb. And none can declare or conceive of the amazing manifestations of wrath, in which he will then appear, towards these; or the trembling and astonishment, the shrieking and gnashing of teeth, with which they shall stand before his judgment seat, and receive the terrible sentence of his wrath.

And yet he will at the same time appear as a Lamb to his saints. He will receive them as friends and brethren, treating them with infinite mildness and love: there shall be nothing in him terrible to them; but towards them, he will clothe himself wholly with sweetness and endearment. The church shall then be admitted to him as his bride: that shall be her wedding day: the saints shall all be sweetly invited to come with him, to inherit the kingdom, and reign in it with him, to all eternity.

APPLICATION.

I. From this doctrine we may learn one reason why Christ is called by such a variety of names, and held forth under such a variety of representations in Scripture. 'Tis the better to signify, and exhibit to us, that variety of excellencies that meet together, and are conjoined in him. Many appellations are mentioned together in one verse, Is. 9:6, "For unto us a child is born, unto us a Son is given, and the government shall be upon his shoulder: and his name shall be called Wonderful, Counselor, the mighty God, the everlasting Father, the Prince of Peace." It shows a wonderful conjunction of excellencies, that the same person should be a Son, born and given, and yet be the everlasting Father, without beginning or end; that he should be a child, and yet be he whose name is Counselor, and the mighty God; and well may his name, in whom such things are conjoined, be called Wonderful.

By reason of the same wonderful conjunction, Christ is represented by a great variety of sensible things, that are on some account excellent. Thus in some places he is called a sun, as Mal. 4:2, in others a star, Num. 24:17. And he is especially represented by the morning star, as being that which excels all other stars in brightness, and is the forerunner of the day, Rev.

22:16. And as in our text, he is compared to a lion, in one verse, and a lamb in the next, so sometimes he is compared to a roe or a young hart, another creature most diverse from a lion. So in some places he is called a rock, in others he is compared to a pearl: in some places he is called a man of war, and the captain of our salvation, in other places he is represented as a bridegroom. In the second chapter of Canticles, the first verse, he is compared to a rose and lily, that are sweet and beautiful flowers; in the next verse but one, he is compared to a tree, bearing sweet fruit. In Is. 53:2, he is called "a root out of a dry ground"; but elsewhere, instead of that, he is called the tree of life, that grows (not in a dry or barren ground, but) "in the midst of the paradise of God," Rev. 2:7.

II. Let the consideration of this wonderful meeting of diverse excellencies in Christ induce you to accept of him, and close with him as your Savior. As all manner of excellencies meet in him, so there are concurring in him all manner of arguments and motives, to move you to choose him for your Savior, and everything that tends to encourage poor sinners to come and put their trust in him: his fullness and all-sufficiency as a Savior, gloriously appear in that variety of excellencies that has been spoken of.

Fallen man is in a state of exceeding great misery, and is helpless in it; he is a poor weak creature, like an infant cast out in its blood, in the day that it is born: but Christ is "the Lion of the tribe of Judah"; he is strong, though we are weak; he hath prevailed to do that for us, which no creature else could do. Fallen man is a mean despicable creature, a contemptible worm; but Christ, who has undertaken for us, is infinitely honorable and worthy. Fallen man is polluted, but Christ is infinitely holy: fallen man is hateful, but Christ is infinitely lovely: fallen man is the object of God's indignation, but Christ is infinitely dear to him: we have dreadfully provoked God, but Christ has performed that righteousness that is infinitely precious in God's eyes.

And here is not only infinite strength and infinite worthiness, but infinite condescension; and love and mercy, as great as power and dignity. If you are a poor distressed sinner, whose heart is ready to sink for fear that God never will have mercy on you, you need not be afraid to go to Christ, for fear that he is either unable or unwilling to help you: here is a strong foundation, and an inexhaustible treasure, to answer the necessities of your poor soul; and here is infinite grace and gentleness to invite and embolden a poor unworthy fearful soul to come to it. If Christ accepts of you, you need not fear but that you will be safe; for he is a strong lion for your defense: and if you come, you need not fear but that you shall be accepted; for he is like a Lamb to all that come to him, and receives them with infinite grace and tenderness. 'Tis true he has awful majesty; he is the great God, and is infinitely high above you; but there is this to encourage and embolden the poor sinner, that Christ is man as well as God; he is a creature, as well as the Creator; and he is the most humble and lowly in heart of any creature in heaven or earth. This may well make the poor unworthy creature bold in coming to him. You need not hesitate one moment; but may run to him, and cast yourself upon him: you will certainly be graciously and meekly received by him. Though he be a lion, he will only be a lion to your enemies; but he will be a lamb to you. It could not have been conceived, had it not been so in the person of Christ, that there could have been so much in any Savior, that is inviting, and tending to encourage sinners to trust in him. Whatever your circumstances are, you need not be afraid to come to such a Savior as this: be you never so wicked a creature, here is worthiness enough: be you never so poor, and mean, and ignorant a creature, there is no danger of being despised; for though he be so much greater than you, he is also immensely more humble than you. Any one of you that is a father or mother, won't despise one of your own children that comes to you in distress; much less danger is there of Christ despising you, if you in your heart come to him.

Here let me a little expostulate with the poor, burdened, distressed soul.

First. What are you afraid of, that you dare not venture your soul upon Christ? Are you afraid that he can't save you, that he is not strong enough to conquer the enemies of your soul? But how can you desire one stronger than the "mighty God"? as Christ is called, Is. 9:6. Is there need of greater than infinite strength? Are you afraid that he won't be willing to stoop so low, as to take any gracious notice of you? But then look on him, as he stood in the ring of soldiers, exposing his blessed face to be buffeted and spit upon, by them! Behold him bound, with his back uncovered to those that smote him! And behold him hanging on the cross! Do you think that he that had condescension enough to stoop to these things, and that for his crucifiers, will be unwilling to accept of you if you come to him? Or, are you afraid that if he does accept of you, that God the Father won't accept of him for you? But consider, will God reject his own Son, in whom his infinite delight is, and has been, from all eternity, and that is so united to him, that if he should reject him he would reject himself?

Second. What is there that you can desire should be in a Savior, that is not in Christ? Or, wherein should you desire a Savior that should be otherwise than Christ is? What excellency is there wanting? What is there that is great or good? What is there that is venerable or winning? What is there that is adorable or endearing? Or what can you think of that would be encouraging, that is not to be found in the person of Christ? Would you have your Savior to be great and honorable, because you are not willing to be beholden to a mean person? And, is not Christ a person honorable enough to be worthy that you should be dependent on him? Is he not a person high enough to be worthy to be appointed to so honorable a work as your salvation? Would you not only have a Savior that is of high degree, but would you have him notwithstanding his exaltation and dignity, to be made also of low degree, that he might have experience of afflictions and trials, that he might learn by the things that he has suffered, to pity them that suffer and are tempted? And has not Christ been made low enough for you? And has he not suffered enough? Would you not only have him have experience of the afflictions you now suffer, but also of that amazing wrath that you fear hereafter, that he may know how to pity those that are in danger of it, and afraid of it? This Christ has had experience of, which experience gave him a greater sense of it, a thousand times, than you have, or any man living has. Would you have your Savior to be one that is near to God, that so his mediation might be prevalent with him? And can you desire him to be nearer to God than Christ is, who is his only begotten Son, of the same essence with the Father? And would you not only have him near to God, but also near to you, that you may have free access to him? And would you have him nearer to you than to be in the same nature, not only so, but united to you by a spiritual union, so close as to be fitly represented by the union of the wife to the husband, of the branch to the vine, of the member to the head, yea, so as to be one, and called one spirit? For so he will be united to you, if you accept of him. Would you have a

Savior that has given some great and extraordinary testimony of mercy and love to sinners, by something that he has done, as well as by what he says? And can you think or conceive of greater things than Christ has done? Was it not a great thing for him, who was God, to take upon him human nature, to be not only God, but man thenceforward to all eternity? But would you look upon suffering for sinners to be a yet greater testimony of love to sinners, than merely doing, though it be never so extraordinary a thing that he has done? And would you desire that a Savior should suffer more than Christ has suffered for sinners? What is there wanting, or what would you add if you could, to make him more fit to be your Savior? But further to induce you to accept of Christ as your Savior, consider two things particularly.

1. How much Christ appears as the Lamb of God, in his invitations to you, to come to him and trust in him. With what sweet grace and kindness does he from time to time, call and invite you; as Prov. 8:4, "Unto you, O men I call, and my voice is to the sons of men." And Is. 55:1–3, "Ho every one that thirsteth, come ye to the waters, and he that hath no money, come ye, buy and eat, yea, come buy wine and milk, without money, and without price." How gracious is he here in inviting every one that thirsts, and in so repeating his invitation over and over, "Come ye to the waters, come buy and eat, yea come!" And in declaring the excellency of that entertainment which he invites you to accept of, "Come buy wine and milk!" and in assuring you that your poverty, and having nothing to pay for it, shall be no objection, "Come, he that hath no money, come without money, and without price!" And in the gracious arguments and expostulations that he uses with you! As it follows, "Wherefore do ye spend money for that which is not bread, and your labor for that which satisfieth not? Hearken diligently unto me, and eat ye that which is good, and let your soul delight itself in fatness." As much as to say, "'Tis altogether needless for you to continue laboring and toiling for that which can never serve your turn, seeking rest in the world, and in your own righteousness; I have made abundant provision for you, of that which is really good, and will fully satisfy your desires, and answer your end, and stand ready to accept of you: you need not be afraid; if you will come to me, I will engage to see all your wants supplied, and you made an happy creature." As he promises in the

third verse, "Incline your ear, and come unto me; hear, and your soul shall live; and I will make an everlasting covenant with you, even the sure mercies of David." And so, Prov. 9, at the beginning. How gracious and sweet is the invitation there! "Whoso is simple, let him turn in hither"; let you be never so poor, ignorant, and blind a creature, you shall be welcome. And in the following words, Christ sets forth the provision that he has made for you, "Come eat of my bread, and drink of the wine which I have mingled." You are in a poor famishing state, and have nothing wherewith to feed your perishing soul; you have been seeking something, but yet remain destitute; hearken! how Christ calls you to eat of his bread, and to drink of the wine that he hath mingled! And how much like a lamb does Christ appear, in Matt. 11:28–30, "Come unto me all ye that labor and are heavy laden, and I will give you rest: take my yoke upon you, and learn of me, for I am meek and lowly in heart, and ye shall find rest to your souls. For my yoke is easy, and my burden is light." O thou poor distressed soul! Whoever thou art that art afraid that you never shall be saved, consider that this that Christ mentions is your very case, when he calls to them that labor and are heavy laden! And how he repeatedly promises you rest if you come to him! In the twenty-eighth verse he says, "I will give you rest." And in the twenty-ninth verse, "Ye shall find rest to your souls." This is what you want! This is the thing you have been so long in vain seeking after! Oh how sweet would rest be to you, if you could but obtain it! Come to Christ, and you shall obtain it. And hear how Christ, to encourage you, represents himself as a lamb! He tells you that he is meek and lowly in heart; and are you afraid to come [to] such an one? And again, Rev. 3:20, "Behold, I stand at the door and knock: if any man hear my voice, and open the door, I will come in to him, and I will sup with him, and he with me." Christ condescends not only to call you to him; but he comes to you; he comes to your door, and there knocks. He might send an officer, and seize you as a rebel and vile malefactor; but instead of that, he comes and knocks at your door, and seeks that you would receive him into your house, as your friend and Savior. And he not only knocks at your door, but he stands there waiting while you are backward and unwilling. And not only so, but he makes promises what he will do for you, if you will admit him, what privileges he will admit you to; he will "sup with you, and you with him." And again, Rev. 22:16–17, "I am the root, and the offspring of David, the bright and morning star. And the Spirit and the bride say, Come: and let him that heareth, say, Come; and let him that is athirst, come: and whosoever will let him come, take of the water of life freely." How does Christ here graciously set before you his own winning attractive excellency! And how does he condescend to declare to you, not only his own invitation, but the invitation of the Spirit and the bride, if by any means he might encourage you to come! And how does he invite every one that will, that they may "take of the waters of life freely," that they may take it a free gift, however precious it be, and though it be the water of life!

2. If you do come to Christ he will appear as a lion, in his glorious power and dominion, to defend you. All those excellencies of his in which he appears as a lion, shall be yours, and shall be employed for you, in your defense, for your safety, and to promote your glory; he will be as a lion to fight against your enemies: he that touches you, or offends you, will provoke his wrath, as he that stirs up a lion. Unless your enemies can conquer this lion, they shall not be able to destroy or hurt you; unless they are stronger than he, they shall not be able to hinder your happiness. Is. 31:4, "For thus hath the Lord spoken unto me, like as the lion, and the young lion, roaring on his prey, when a multitude of shepherds is called forth against him, he will not be afraid of their voice, nor abase himself for the noise of them; so shall the Lord of hosts come down to fight for Mount Zion, and for the hill thereof."

III. Let what has been said, be improved to induce you to love the Lord Jesus Christ, and choose him for your friend and portion. As there is such an admirable meeting of diverse excellencies in Christ, so there is everything in him to render him worthy of your love and choice, and to win and engage it. Whatsoever there is, or can be, that is desirable to be in a friend, is in Christ, and that to the highest degree that can be desired.

Would you choose a friend that is a person of great dignity? It is a thing taking with men to have those for their friends that are much above them; because they look upon themselves honored by the friendship of such. Thus how taking would it be with an inferior maid, to be the object of the dear love of some great and excellent prince. But Christ is infinitely above you, and above all the princes of the earth; for he is the King of kings. So honorable a person as this offers himself to you, in the nearest and dearest friendship.

And would you choose to have a friend not only great but good? In Christ infinite greatness, and infinite goodness meet together, and receive luster and glory one from another. His greatness is rendered lovely by his goodness. The greater any one is without goodness, so much the greater evil; but when infinite goodness is joined with greatness, it renders it a glorious and adorable greatness. So on the other hand, his infinite goodness receives luster from his greatness. He that is of great understanding and ability, and is withal of a good and excellent disposition, is deservedly more esteemed than a lower and lesser being, with the same kind inclination and good will. Indeed goodness is excellent in whatever subject it be found; it is beauty and excellency itself, and renders all excellent that are possessed of it; and yet more excellent when joined with greatness; as the very same excellent qualities of gold, do render the body in which they are inherent more precious, and of greater value, when joined with greater, than when with lesser dimensions. And how glorious is the sight, to see him who is the great Creator and supreme Lord of heaven and earth, full of condescension, and tender pity and mercy, towards the mean and unworthy! His almighty power, and infinite majesty and self-sufficiency render his exceeding love and grace the more surprising. And how do his condescension and compassions endear his majesty, power, and dominion, and render those attributes pleasant, that would otherwise be only terrible! Would you not desire that your friend, though great and honorable, should be of such condescension and grace, and so to have the way opened to free access to him, that his exaltation above you might not hinder your free enjoyment of his friendship?

And would you choose, not only, that the infinite greatness and majesty of your friend should be, as it were, mollified and sweetened with condescension and grace; but would you also desire to have your friend in your own nature, that he might be brought nearer to you? Would you choose a friend far above you, and yet as it were upon a level with you too? (Though it be taking with men to have a near and dear friend of superior dignity, yet there is also an inclination in them to have their friend a sharer with them in circumstances.) Thus is Christ. Though he be the great God, yet he has as it were brought himself down to be upon a level with you, so as to become man as your are, that he might not only be your Lord, but your brother, and that he might be the more fit to be a companion for such a worm of the dust. This is one end of Christ's taking upon him man's nature, that his people might be under advantages for a more familiar converse with him, than the infinite distance of the divine nature would allow of. And upon this account the church longed for Christ's incarnation. Cant. 8:1, "O thou that wert my brother, that sucked the breasts of my mother; when I should find thee without, I would kiss thee; yea, I should not be despised." One design of God in the gospel, is to bring us to make God the object of our undivided respect, that he may engross our regard every way, that whatever natural inclination there is in our souls, he may be the center of it; that God may be all in all. But there is an inclination in the creature, not only to the adoration of a Lord and sovereign, but to complacence in some one as a friend, to love and delight in some one that may be conversed with as a companion. And virtue and holiness don't destroy or weaken this inclination of our nature. But so hath God contrived in the affair of our redemption, that a divine person may be the object even of this inclination of our nature. And in order hereto, such an one is come down to us, and has taken our nature, and is become one of us, and calls himself our friend, brother, and companion. Ps. 122:8, "For my brethren and companions' sake, will I now say, Peace be within thee."

But is it not enough in order to invite and encourage you to free access to a friend so great and high, that he is one of infinite condescending grace, and also has taken your own nature, and is become man? But would you further to embolden and win you, have him a man of wonderful meekness and humility? Why such an one is Christ! He is not only become man for you, but far the meekest and most humble of all men, the greatest instance of these sweet virtues, that ever was, or will be. And besides these, he has all other human excellencies, in the highest perfection. These, indeed, are no proper addition to his divine excellencies. Christ has no more excellency in his person, since his incarnation, than he had before; for divine excellency is infinite, and can't be added to: yet his human excellencies are additional manifestations of his glory and excellency to us, and are additional recommendations of him to our esteem and love, who are of finite comprehension. Though his human excellencies are but communications and reflections of his divine; and though this light, as reflected, falls infinitely short of the divine fountain of light, in its immediate glory: yet the reflection shines, not without its proper advantages, as presented to our view and affection. As the glory of Christ appears in the qualifications of his human nature, it appears to us in excellencies that are of our own kind, and are exercised in our own way and manner, and so, in some respects, are peculiarly fitted to invite our acquaintance, and draw our affection. The glory of Christ as it appears in his divinity, though it be far brighter, yet doth it also more dazzles our eyes, and exceeds the strength or comprehension of our sight. But as it shines in the human excellencies of Christ, it is brought more to a level with our conceptions, and suitableness to our nature and manner, yet retaining a semblance of the same divine beauty, and a savor of the same divine sweetness. But as both divine and human excellencies meet together in Christ, they set off and recommend each other to us. It is what tends to endear the divine and infinite majesty and holiness of Christ to us, that these are attributes of a person that is in our nature, that is one of us, that is become our brother, and is the meekest and humblest of men; it encourages us to look upon these divine perfections, however high and great, yet as what we have some near concern in, and more of a right to, and liberty freely to enjoy. And on the other hand, how much more glorious and surprising do the meekness, the humility, obedience, and resignation, and other human excellencies of Christ appear, when we consider that they are in so great a person, as the eternal Son of God, the Lord of heaven and earth!

By your choosing Christ for your friend and portion, you will obtain these two infinite benefits.

First. Christ will give himself to you, with all those various excellencies that meet in him, to your full and everlasting enjoyment. He will ever after treat you as his dear friend; and you shall ere long be where he is, and shall behold his glory, and shall dwell with him, in most free and intimate communion and enjoyment.

When the saints get to heaven, they shall not merely see Christ, and have to do with him as subjects and servants with a glorious and gracious Lord and Sovereign, but Christ will entertain them as friends and brethren. This we may learn from the manner of Christ's conversing with his disciples here on earth: though he was their sovereign Lord, and did not refuse, but required, their supreme respect and adoration, yet he did not treat them as earthly sovereigns are wont to do their subjects; he did not keep them at an awful distance; but all along conversed with them with the most friendly familiarity, as a father amongst a company of children, yea, as with brethren. So he did with the twelve, and so he did with Mary, Martha, and Lazarus. He told his disciples, that he did not call them servants, but friends; and we read of one of them that leaned on his bosom. And doubtless he will not treat his disciples with less freedom and endearment in heaven: he won't keep them at a greater distance for his being in a state of exaltation; but he will rather take them into a state of exaltation with him. This will be the improvement Christ will make of his own glory, to make his beloved friends partakers with him, to glorify them in his glory, as he says to his Father, John 17:22–23, "And the glory which thou hast given me, have I given them, that they may be one, even as we are one; I in them," etc. We are to consider, that though Christ is greatly exalted, yet he is exalted not as a private person, for himself only, but as his people's head; he is exalted in their name, and upon their account, as the first fruits, and as representing the whole harvest. He is not exalted that he may be at a greater distance from them, but that they may be exalted with him. The exaltation and honor of the head is not to make a greater distance between the head and the members; but the members have the same relation and union with the head they had before, and are honored with the head; and instead of the distance being greater, the union shall be nearer, and more perfect. When believers get to heaven, Christ will conform them to himself; as he is set down in his Father's throne, so they shall sit down with him on his throne, and shall in their measure be made like him.

When Christ was going to heaven, he comforted his disciples with that, that after a while he would come again, and take them to himself, that they might be with him again. And we are not to suppose that when the disciples got to heaven, they found him keeping a greater distance, than he used to do. No, doubtless, he embraced them as friends, and welcomed them to his, and their, Father's house, and to his, and their, glory. They that had been his friends in this world, who had been together with him here, and had together partook of sorrows and troubles, are now welcomed by him to rest, and to partake of glory with him. He took them and led them into his chambers, and showed them all his glory; as he prayed, John 17:24, "Father, I will, that they also whom thou hast given me, be with me, that they may behold the glory which thou hast given me." And he led them to his living fountains of waters, and made them partake of his delights; as he prays, John 17:13, "That my joy may be fulfilled in themselves." And set them down with him at his table in his kingdom, and made them partake with him of his dainties, according to his promise, Luke 22:30. And led them into his banqueting house, and made them to drink new wine with him in the kingdom of his heavenly Father; as he foretold them, when he instituted the Lord's Supper; Matt. 26:29.

Yea, the saint's conversation with Christ in heaven, shall not only be as intimate, and their access to him as free, as of the disciples on earth; but in many respects, much more so: for in heaven, that vital union shall be perfect, which is exceeding imperfect here. While the saints are in this world, there are great remains of sin and darkness, to separate or disunite them from Christ, which shall then all be removed. This is not a time for that full acquaintance, and those glorious manifestations of love, which Christ designs for his people hereafter; which seems to be signified by Christ's speech to Mary Magdalene, when ready to embrace him, when she met him after his resurrection; John 20:17, "Jesus saith unto her, touch me not, for I am not yet ascended to my Father."

When the saints shall see Christ's glory and exaltation in heaven, it will indeed possess their hearts with the greater admiration and adoring respect, but will not awe them into any separation, but will serve only to heighten their surprise and joy, when they find Christ condescending to admit them to such intimate access, and so freely and fully communicating himself to them.

So that if we choose Christ for our friend and portion, we shall hereafter be so received to him, that there shall be nothing to hinder the fullest enjoyment of him, to the satisfying the utmost cravings of our souls. We may take our full swing at gratifying our spiritual appetite after these holy pleasures. Christ will then say, as in Cant. 5:1, "Eat, O friends. Drink, yea, drink abundantly, O beloved." And this shall be our entertainment to all eternity! There shall never be any end of this happiness, or anything to interrupt our enjoyment of it, or in the least to molest us in it!

Second. By your being united to Christ, you will have a more glorious union with, and enjoyment of, God the Father, than otherwise could be. For hereby the saints' relation to God becomes much nearer; they are the children of God in an higher manner, than otherwise could be. For being members of God's own natural Son, they are in a sort partakers of his relation to the Father: they are not only sons of God by regeneration, but by a kind of communion in the sonship of the eternal Son. This seems to be intended, Gal. 4:4–6, "God sent forth his Son, made of a woman, made under the law, to redeem them that are under the law, that we might receive the adoption of sons. And because ye are sons, God hath sent forth the Spirit of his Son into your hearts, crying, Abba, Father." The church is the daughter of God, not only as he hath begotten her by his Word and Spirit, but as she is the spouse of his eternal Son.

So we being members of the Son, are partakers in our measure, of the Father's love to the Son, and complacence in him. John 17:23, "I in them, and thou in me . . . Thou hast loved them, as thou hast loved me." And v. 26, "That the love wherewith thou hast loved me, may be in them." And ch. 16:27, "The Father himself loveth you, because ye loved me, and have believed that I came out from God." So we shall, according to our capacities, be partakers of the Son's enjoyment of God, and have his joy fulfilled in ourselves, John 17:13. And by this means, we shall come to an immensely higher, more intimate, and full enjoyment of God, than otherwise could have been. For there is doubtless an infinite intimacy between the Father and the Son; which is expressed by his being in the bosom of the Father. And saints being in him, shall, in their measure and manner, partake with him in it, and of the blessedness of it.

And thus is the affair of our redemption ordered, that thereby we are brought to an immensely more exalted kind of union with God, and enjoyment of him, both the Father and the Son, than otherwise could have been. For Christ being united to the human nature, we have advantage for a more free and full enjoyment of him, than we could have had if he had remained only in the divine nature. So again, we being united to a divine person, as his members, can have a more intimate union and intercourse with God the Father, who is only in the divine nature, than otherwise could be. Christ who is a divine person, by taking on him our nature, descends from the infinite distance and height above us, and is brought nigh to us; whereby we have advantage for the full enjoyment of him. And, on the other hand, we, by being in Christ a divine person, do as it were ascend up to God, through the infinite distance, and have hereby advantage for the full enjoyment of him also.

This was the design of Christ, to bring it to pass, that he, and his Father, and his people, might all be united in one. John 17:21–23, "That they all may be one; as thou Father art in me, and I in thee; that they also may be one in us; that the world may believe that thou hast sent me. And the glory which thou hast given me, I have given them, that they may be one, even as we are one; I in them, and thou in me; that they may be made perfect in one." Christ has brought it to pass, that those that the Father has given him, should be brought into the household of God; that he, and his Father, and his people, should be as it were one society, one family; that the church should be as it were admitted into the society of the blessed Trinity.

Much in Deeds of Charity (1741)

Acts 10:4–6.

And when he looked on him, he was afraid, and said, What is it, Lord? And he said unto him, Thy prayers and thine alms are come up for a memorial before God. And now send men to Joppa, and call for one Simon, whose surname is Peter: he lodgeth with one Simon a tanner, whose house is by the sea side: he shall tell thee what thou oughtest to do.

In these words I would observe two things:

1. Here are two duties mentioned that Cornelius had been much in the practice of, viz. prayer and giving of alms. "Thy prayers and thine alms are come up for a memorial before God." How he abounded in them is [more] particularly declared in the second verse. There it is said that he "gave much alms to the people, and prayed to God always."

2. I would observe the great benefits he obtained in the way of the practice of these duties. In the first place, he is peculiarly favored and honored of God by a vision of [an] angel. God sends an angel to him to appear to him and to talk with him and give him directions. And then this was in order to his being brought to a clear, saving discovery of Christ and acquaintance with the way of salvation by him. The angel directs him to send men to Joppa to call for the apostle Peter, that he might come to him and be the means of Christ's being discovered to him and [his] receiving great spiritual comfort and joy and being filled with the Holy Ghost, as we have an account in the ensuing part of the chapter of Peter's preaching Christ to Cornelius and his family, and then of the Holy Ghost descending upon them, filling their hearts with joy and their mouths with praises. Verse 44, "While Peter yet spake these words, the Holy Ghost fell on all them which heard the word."

These glorious benefits were what Cornelius obtained in the way of the practice of these two duties, praying to God and giving alms to men, for the angel gives this reason why God would bestow these benefits upon him: that his practice of those duties were come up for a memorial before

God, so that it was manifest that the blessing he obtained was in consequence of his using those means. It was not only a consequence of his praying to God—that is a duty commonly attended by those that seek spiritual discoveries—but also as a consequence of his giving much alms to the people.

DOCTRINE.

To be much in deeds of charity is the way to have spiritual discoveries.

If we would seek spiritual discoveries in a right way, we must not only abound in the duties of the first table, we must not only spend a great deal of time in the duty of prayer, crying earnestly to God for the discoveries we need and desire (though that be a great duty that must be attended). But we must also abound in second table duties, and particularly in deeds of charity or works of love. This is the way to be successful.

I. I would show how we should be much in deeds of charity.

II. I would mention some things that do confirm that this is a way to obtain spiritual discoveries.

III. [I would inquire] how it is so, or what influence the practice of this duty has to the obtaining of such a benefit.

And then make application.

I. I would show how we should be much in deeds of charity. What is intended is that we should be so according to what we have, or according to our abilities and opportunities. II Cor. 8:12, "For if there be first a willing mind, it is accepted according to what a man hath, and not according to what he hath not." That which be a very penurious gift in one may be a very bountiful one in another, according to the observation Christ makes of the gift of the poor widow. Mark 12:42–43, "And there came a certain poor widow, and she threw in two mites, which make a farthing. And he called unto him his disciples, and said unto them, Verily I say unto you, That this poor widow hath cast more in, than all they which have cast into the treasury." If we would obtain any great benefits at the hand of God for what we do in deeds of charity, we must not only do something but we must be liberal and bountiful, free-hearted and open-handed.

It was said of Cornelius that he gave much alms to the people. Persons may give so little that what they do give is more of a manifestation of covetousness than of bounty. II Cor. 9:5, "Therefore I thought it necessary to exhort the brethren, that they would go before unto you, and make up beforehand your bounty, whereof ye had notice before, that the same might be ready, as a matter of bounty, and not of covetousness." The reason why many never receive any remarkable benefit of what they give is because they give so little. But I proceed,

II. To mention some things that confirm it to be so, that to abound in deeds of charity is the way to receive spiritual discoveries.

First. This is confirmed by God's promises, as particularly in Is. 58:7–11:

> Is it not to deal thy bread to the hungry, and that thou bring the poor that are cast out to thy house? when thou seest the naked, that thou cover him; and that thou hide not thyself from thine own flesh? Then shall thy light break forth as the morning, and thine health shall spring forth speedily: and thy righteousness shall go before thee; the glory of the Lord shall be thy rearward. Then shalt thou call, and the Lord shall answer; thou shalt cry, and he shall say, Here I am. If thou take away from the midst of thee the yoke, the putting forth of the finger, and speaking vanity; and if thou draw out thy soul to the hungry, and satisfy the afflicted soul; then shall thy light rise in obscurity, and thy darkness be as the noonday: and the Lord shall guide thee continually, and satisfy thy soul in drought, and make fat thy bones: and thou shalt be like a watered garden, and like a spring of water, whose waters fail not.

In the eighth verse 'tis promised that if we deliver bread to the hungry, etc., that our light shall "break forth as the morning." And though receiving spiritual light and gracious discoveries of God's glory and mercy to the soul be not the only thing there is intended, yet it is not to be excluded, but without doubt is a principal thing by which such a promise is fulfilled.

In the tenth verse 'tis said, "then shall thy light rise in obscurity, and thy darkness be as the noonday." And spiritual blessing, the gracious influences and counsels of God's Holy Spirit, are often in Scripture signified by such like expressions as are used in the eleventh verse: "And the Lord shall guide thee continually, and satisfy thy soul in drought, and make fit thy bones: and thou shalt be like a watered garden, and like a spring of water, whose waters fail not." So it is said, Prov. 11:25, "The liberal soul shall be made fat," where the benefits that the soul receives ben't all that is intended. Yet as they are what the expression most naturally points to, so they are not to be excluded.

That this is the way to have spiritual [discoveries] appears by Ps. 112:5–7, "A good man showeth favor, and lendeth: he will guide his affairs with discretion. Surely he shall not be moved for ever: the righteous shall be in everlasting remembrance. He shall not be afraid of evil tidings: his heart is fixed, trusting in the Lord." This is the way for a man to have spiritual discoveries and the comfortable evidences of the presence of God on a sick bed, as appears by Ps. 41:1, 3, "Blessed is he that considereth the poor: the Lord will deliver him in the time of trouble . . . The Lord will strengthen him upon the bed of languishing: thou wilt make all his bed in his sickness." It is revealed that to live in love is the way to have much of the presence of God. But one thing wherein living in love does principally consist is living in deeds and fruit of love and charity.

Living in deeds of love is the way to obtain assurance, as is evident by I John 3:18–19, "My little children, let us not love in word, neither in tongue; but in deed and in truth. And hereby we know that we are of the truth, and shall assure our hearts before him." This is the way to have spiritual joy, as appears by John 15:11–12, "These things have I spoken unto you, that my joy might remain in you, and that your joy might be full. This is my commandment, That ye love one another, as I have loved you."

Second. This is confirmed in providence. We have an account in Gen. 14, [the] latter end, how Abraham had been remarkably charitable to his brother Lot and to the people that he had redeemed out of captivity with him by exposing his life to rescue them, and had retaken not only the persons but all the goods, the spoil that had been taken by Chedorlaomer and the kings that were with him. And the king of Sodom offered him that, if he would give him the persons, he might take the goods to himself. Abraham refused to take anything, even a thread or a shoe latchet, but returned all. He might have greatly enriched himself if he had taken the spoils to him, for it was the spoils of five kings and their kingdoms. Yet he coveted it not. The king and people of Sodom were now become objects of charity, having been stripped of all by their enemies. Therefore Abraham generously bestowed the booty upon them. And he was soon rewarded for it by a blessed discovery that God made of himself to him, as it follows in the next words in the beginning of the next chapter:

> After these things the word of the Lord came unto Abram in a vision, saying, Fear not, Abram: I am thy shield, and thy exceeding great reward. And Abram said, Lord God, what wilt thou give me, seeing I go childless, and the steward of my house is this Eliezer of Damascus? And Abram said, Behold, to me thou hast given no seed: and, lo, one born in my house is mine heir. And, behold, the word of the Lord came unto him, saying, This shall not be thine heir; but he that shall come forth out of thine own bowels shall be thine heir. And he brought him forth abroad, and said, Look now toward heaven, and tell the stars, if thou be able to number them: and he said unto him, So shall thy seed be. And he believed in the Lord; and he counted it to him for righteousness. And he said unto him, I am the Lord that brought thee out of Ur of the Chaldees, to give thee this land to inherit it [Gen. 15:1–7].

In these words God seems manifestly to have respect to the good deed Abraham had done in rescuing Lot and the people of Sodom by overcoming their enemies and in refusing to take the spoil for his reward: [as much as to say,] "Fear not, I am thy shield to defend thee in battle, as I have now done {against Chedorlaomer and the kings that were with him}, and thine exceeding great reward, to reward thee for the good deeds thou dost, so that thou shalt not need that reward of the spoils, which thou hast refused and freely resigned up."

When Christ was upon earth he was poor. He was an object of charity. And during the time of his public ministry he was supported by the [charity] of some of his followers, and particularly certain women, as we read, Luke 8:2–3, "And certain women, which had been healed of evil spirits and infirmities, Mary called Magdalene, out of whom went seven devils, And Joanna the wife of Chuza Herod's steward, and Susanna, and many others, which ministered unto him of their substance." And these women were rewarded by being peculiarly favored with gracious manifestations, which Christ made of himself to them. He discovered himself first to them after his resurrection, before any of the twelve disciples. They first saw a vision of glorious angels who spoke comfortably to them, and then Christ appeared to them and spake peace to them, saying, "All hail [. . . .] Be not afraid." And they were admitted to come and hold him by the feet and worship him (Matt. 28:9).

So Mary and Martha and Lazarus were a family that were charitable to Christ, used joyfully to entertain him at their house and make the best provision for him that they could. And they were a family remarkably distinguished by Christ's presence and the manifestations of his love.

And though we can't now be charitable to Christ in person as they were, because he is not here, nor does he now stand in need, yet we may be charitable to Christ now as well as they then. For though Christ is not here, he has left others in his room to be his receivers, and they are the poor, and has told us that he shall look upon what is done to them as done to him; so that Christ is poor yet in his members, and we may relieve him and be in a way to receive the same benefit by it that those did that were charitable to him when he was on earth.

I come now, in the

III. [Third] place, [to inquire] how a being much in deeds of charity is the way to receive spiritual discoveries, or what influence it has to [that] end.

Answer

First, negatively. It has no influence as any price paid to God to purchase such a benefit of him. 'Tis true, what is given in this way is given to God, and God is often in consequence of it wont to grant spiritual blessings—even gracious discoveries—of himself, but not because they are at all merited by it. For of our own righteousness, what do we unto him or what receives he at our hands? We have no money or price to offer for any mercy we need. Luke 17:10, "when ye have done all [. . .] say, We are unprofitable servants: we have done that which was our duty to do." Yea, and we do but a little part of that which is our duty. The blessing of a spiritual discovery and manifestation of God to the soul is infinitely too great to be purchased by anything we have to give. If we should give all our goods to feed the poor, it would in no wise be equivalent to such a reward. But,

Second, affirmatively, in two things:

1. When such deeds are done from right principles, God will give spiritual discoveries as a free reward. Though the goodness and excellency of the reward be infinitely greater than the worth of what is given in charity, yet for Christ's sake it shall be accepted and shall receive such an exceeding great reward. For there is no man that gives a cup of [water in Christ's name who loses his reward] (Mark 9:41). For God rewards good persons—pressed down, {and shaken together, and running over} [Luke 6:38]. Yea, he rewards an hundredfold; yea, and much more than so. When we give to others earthly good things, God will reward us with heavenly good things. This Christ promises, Luke 14:[13–]14, "when thou makest a feast, invite the poor, the maimed, the lame, the blind: and thou shalt be blessed; for they cannot recompense thee: but thou shalt be recompensed at the resurrection of the just." And God often gives persons foretastes of those future rewards while here. Treasure is this way laid up in heaven and, therefore, heavenly blessings shall flow down from heaven upon them while they are here.

If we will be kind to Christ and entertain him well, and when we see him hungry will feed him and thirsty will give him drink, that is the way to be rewarded with much of his company. If we will feed Christ with the food of our houses, even outward food, Christ will reward us by feeding us with the food of his house, which is spiritual food. He will feed us with the angels' food, the food of spiritual discoveries and divine comforts. If we will bring the poor and those that are cast out into our houses to refresh their bodies, Christ will bring us into his banqueting house.

2. This is a part of that way of duty, which is the appointed way, in which we are to seek those spiritual discoveries that we stand in need of. 'Tis the way of God's appointment both for saints and sinners to seek his face. The way in which God has directed us to seek him is the way of attending on all commanded duties. It is not only to read and to pray and to go to meeting and to meditate, but is to attend all the duties which God has required of us, both towards God and towards our neighbor. Some

that are concerned for their salvation seem not to think much of any other but only first table duties. They think if they would obtain spiritual discoveries they must read {and pray and go to meeting and meditate}, but don't seem to think of second table duties as what belong to seeking conversion.

John the Baptist was of another mind when he preached the baptism of repentance, and there was a great outpouring of the Spirit and a general awakening among the people, and one and another came to him with that question: "What shall we do?" He directed 'em to moral duties, second table duties, and particularly to this duty of charity, as you may see, Luke 3:9–11, "And now also the ax is laid unto the root of the trees: every tree therefore which bringeth not forth good fruit is hewn down, and cast into the fire. And the people asked him, saying, What shall we do then? He answereth and saith unto them, He that hath two coats, let him impart to him that hath none; and he that hath meat, let him do likewise."

Natural men can't do this duty in sincerity. But yet they can be in the way of God's appointment in attendance on this part of their duty, as [in] other things. For they can only do the external part in other things, and their attending this duty has as much a tendency to the blessing sought as their other external performances.

This very duty is one of the duties Christ had respect to when he said, Matt. 7:13[–14], "Enter ye in at the strait gate [. . .] Because strait is the gate, and narrow is the way, which leadeth unto life, and few there be that find it." For 'tis to be observed that those words of Christ are part of the conclusion of his Sermon on the Mount, and are to enforce the rules that he had been laying down in his foregoing discourse. Christ was aware that many of his hearers would think that many of his rules were very strait and hard. They had not been used to such kind of doctrine. And therefore Christ, when he had done laying down these strait rules, intimates to 'em that, as strait as they were, they must be attended if they would enter into the kingdom of heaven. For, says he, "strait is the gate, and narrow is the way, which leadeth unto life, and few there be that find it"; as much as to say, "You think those rules that I have been giving you {are very strait and hard but, as strait as they are, they must be attended if you would enter into the kingdom of heaven}."

But this [duty] of giving liberally in a way of charity is one of those rules, as ch. 5:42, "Give to him that asketh of you, and from him that would borrow of thee turn not thou away." And so, ch. 6, at the beginning: "Take heed that ye do not your alms before men, to be seen of them: otherwise ye have no reward of your Father which is in heaven" [v. 1]. And so, vv. 19–20: "Lay not up for yourselves treasures upon earth, where moth and rust doth corrupt, and where thieves break through and steal: but lay up for yourselves treasure in heaven, where neither moth nor rust doth corrupt, and where thieves do not break through nor steal."

The way of the practice of all duty is the way in which persons should seek the grace of God, and especially the more important duties. But this duty of charity to the poor is in God's account a very important duty, as appears by its being so much insisted on in the Word of God. 'Tis more important than outward acts of worship, as appears by Matt. 9:13, "I will have mercy, and not sacrifice." God has appointed this as a way wherein we should seek his grace: from his goodness. The duty of charity or almsgiving is in a peculiar manner agreeable to the attribute of his goodness and, therefore, he especially encourages persons to seek him in this way.

That which we seek of God when we ask the influences of his Spirit and spiritual discoveries is a free gift of God. If God bestows it upon us, it will be out of pity to our poverty and necessity, and without any money or price. But how can we expect that God should be thus liberal to us in our poverty when at the same time we are strait-handed to our fellow creatures in their indigent circumstances? 'Tis as needful that we should part with the world in our hearts in order to our being fitted for spiritual comforts as that we should part with our own righteousness. But a freeness to give away of our worldly possession to the poor is an expression of our weanedness from the world and the looseness of our affections to these things and, therefore, fits persons for spiritual discoveries and comforts.

APPLICATION.

The *Use* is of *Exhortation*, to exhort to be much in deeds of charity. Many of you seem to value spiritual discoveries. There are some that never had any such discoveries in their lives, but yet surely they would not be willing always to live and at last to die without [them]. And there are many that hope they have had some spiritual discoveries made to their souls in times past that yet now very much complain of their dullness and darkness. They seem to be unwilling to remain so destitute of light as they are now. They complain that it is very uncomfortable living so. They seem to wish that it was with them as in months past, and that it is with them as it is with some of their neighbors. They want to see more clearly, to have a more lively sense of things and to have much of the presence of God and sweet communion with the Lord Jesus Christ.

You have now heard of one thing that you should do in order to it, one likely means of obtaining it. If you would seek spiritual discoveries in the use of all appointed means and in all likely ways, don't neglect this. Don't only pray to God always, as Cornelius did, but also give much alms to the people according to your ability, as Cornelius did. And see if you han't the like success that he had. See if the Holy Ghost don't fall on you as he did on him, and if Christ ben't revealed to you as he was to him, that you may be enabled to magnify God as he did. Here,

First. This would be a likely way for particular persons to have the Holy Spirit come down into their souls in his divine, sweet influences.

Second. This would be a likely way to have the Holy Ghost poured out upon families, if parents and heads of families would thus improve the substance that they have in their houses this way.

[*Third.* It would be the way to have much of the Holy Spirit poured out upon a people, for them to be much in deeds of charity.]

First. It is spoken of as very reasonable that we should be ready to communicate of our carnal things to those of whom we have received spiritual things (Rom. 15:24). Certainly therefore, as we receive all spiritual things from Christ or depend upon him for all we hope for, we should be ready to give him our carnal things; otherwise, how justly might he for the time to come withhold spiritual things from us.

The instance of Cornelius should have the more influence upon us because he was the firstfruits of the Gentiles. We are Gentiles. We are some of them that have benefit of that great dispensation of providence and grace: the calling of the Gentiles. But the beginning of the calling of the Gentiles was in those spiritual discoveries that Cornelius and his family received in consequence of his prayers and his giving much alms to the people. As he was the first of the Gentiles that was called, so we may look upon him as an instance set forth in the holy Scriptures, as a pattern to other Gentiles that should be called after him, and as an encouragement to them that they may obtain the like blessings in the like way.

Be therefore exhorted to seek divine discoveries and gracious influences this way, together with the use of other means. You should seek the grace and presence of God in an attendance on all duties, and this that is so much insisted on in Scripture surely should not be neglected. Let all be exhorted to try this method, and don't think you have made sufficient trial by only doing a little matter, or by continuing in the practice of this duty a little while. The husbandman don't expect to reap as soon as he sows, but with patience waits for the precious fruits of his seed. So continue in this way of well doing and then you shall reap. Gal. 6:9, "And let us not be weary in well doing: for in due season we shall reap, if we faint not." Therefore if things seem to go contrary for a little while, you seem for the present to have no help, to receive no light or divine discovery, but darkness, this may be for your trial, and is no sign that God won't richly reward you in his own time, as it sometimes is with respect to the reward for other duties. So it was with Joseph . . . [Gen. 37–50].

Here,

1. Let me exhort sinners that are concerned for their salvation and never had any divine discoveries, to seek 'em in the practice of this as well as other duties. Isaac was a type of Christ. He was the promised seed of Abraham. He was as it were offered up to God in sacrifice, was as it were raised from the dead, whence Abraham received [him]. Rebekah's marriage with Isaac did in many things represent the church's espousal to Christ and the spiritual marriage of the soul to him in conversion. She was an alien and stranger. She was far off, in a far country, at a great distance from Canaan, the land of promise. But she forgot her own people and her father's house and forsook all for Isaac, and so was espoused to that promised seed, and was received into the line of the covenant, and became a sharer with her husband of the great spiritual blessings that were entailed

to her family, and became the mother of Christ, for Christ came of her. And this great privilege she obtained in a way of doing deeds of charity, by her showing a bountiful spirit to strangers, Abraham's servants and his company, when she knew not who they were, as you may see, Gen. 24:13–20,

> Behold, I stand here by the well of water; and the daughters of the men of the city come out to draw water: and let it come to pass, that the damsel to whom I shall say, Let down thy pitcher, I pray thee, that I may drink; and she shall say, Drink, and I will give thy camels drink also: let the same be she that thou hast appointed for thy servant Isaac; and thereby shall I know that thou hast shown kindness unto my master. And it came to pass, before he had done speaking, that, behold, Rebekah came out, who was born to Bethuel, son of Milcah, the wife of Nahor, Abraham's brother, with her pitcher upon her shoulder. And the damsel was very fair to look upon, a virgin, neither had any man known her: and she went down to the well, and filled her pitcher, and came up. And the servant ran to meet her, and said, Let me, I pray thee, drink a little water of thy pitcher. And she said, Drink, my lord: and she hasted, and let down her pitcher upon her hand, and gave him drink. And when she had done giving him drink, she said, I will draw water for thy camels also, until they have done drinking. And she hasted, and emptied her pitcher into the trough, and ran again unto the well to draw water, and drew for all his camels.

So David was another eminent type of Christ, and Abigail's marriage with him did also represent the espousals of the church and believing souls in conversion. She also obtained that privilege in the same way {of doing deeds of charity} [I Sam. 25].

There are some now that are ready to come with the same question that the people did to John the Baptist: "What shall we do then?"

Obj. This will be the way for me to trust in my own righteousness. I shall think I do something to purchase {my spiritual discoveries}.

Ans. You may make the same objection against any duty whatsoever. Doing first table duties have as direct a tendency to raise in natural men expectations of receiving something from God on the account of them as second table duties, and on some accounts more. For those duties are more immediately offered to God than second table duties and, therefore, persons are the more ready to look for something from God for them. No duty is to be neglected for fear of making a righteousness {of works out of it}. A partial doing [of one's] duty [is what is] most likely to excite self-righteousness.

2. Let godly persons be hence exhorted to abound in deeds of charity. They who are the subject of so much of the free mercy and kindness of God are above all persons obliged to this duty and, if they neglect it, will in a peculiar manner act beside their character. For in Scripture language the merciful man and the good man are the same thing. This would be a very likely way for them to be rewarded—as Abraham and Mary Magdalene and Cornelius and other saints have been—for their charity, with several manifestations that Christ has made of himself to them, and the way to grow in grace and to have the fruits of their righteousness increased. II Cor. 9:9–10, "As it is written, He hath dispersed abroad; he hath given to the poor; his righteousness remaineth for ever. Now he that ministereth seed to the sower both minister bread for your food, and multiply your seed sown, and increase the fruits of your righteousness."

If the children of this world were not wiser in their generation than the children of light, God's people would be as much in earnest to grow rich in spirituals in this way as the men of this world are to enrich themselves by putting out their money to use or to improve in trade, or the husbandman to enrich himself by sowing his field.

Second. This would be a likely way to have the Spirit of God poured out upon families, if parents and heads of families would thus improve the substance they have in their houses. It may [be] the way for parents to have such a blessing bestowed upon their children. This is said in the thirty-seventh Psalm to be the way for a man to have his seed blessed. Verse 26, "He is ever merciful, and lendeth; and his seed is blessed." And the instance in the text here is very apposite, for Cornelius' prayers and his alms came up for a memorial before God. And the consequences: the pouring out of the Holy Ghost on him and all his family. Verse 44, "While Peter yet spake these words, the Holy Ghost fell on all them which heard the word." So that he was rewarded with the salvation of himself and all his family, as in the next chapter, [vv.] 13–14: "And he showed me how that he had seen an angel in his house, which stood and said unto him, Send men to Joppa, and call for Simon, whose surname is Peter; who shall tell thee words, whereby thee and all thy house shall be saved."

Third. It would be the way to have much of the Holy Spirit poured out upon a people, for them to be much in deeds of charity. Remarkable outpourings of the Spirit of God and an abounding in the practice of the duty have been wont to accompany one another. So did that remarkable outpouring of the Spirit of God that was at Jerusalem in the apostles' times, {when those who received the Holy Spirit "sold their possessions and goods, and parted them to all men, as every man had need"} [Acts 2:45].

So of late, a remarkable reviving of religion [has] begun by the labors of a certain divine in Saxony named [August] Hermann Francke.[1] It began after this manner, and has now been wonderfully carried on for above thirty years, and has spread in the happy influences of it into many parts of the world (I have heretofore told you of it). It began with setting on foot a charitable design for the relief of poor orphans, and was carried on in that way in the building of an orphan house by deeds of charity, where many hundreds of orphans have been for many years supported and instructed by the charity of others. God has wonderfully [smiled upon it].

The Reverend Mr. Whitefield took pattern by this, as he declares in his printed letter of his.[2] And God has likewise wonderfully smiled upon his charitable designs. 'Tis in some public accounts that not only he but his followers in England do abound in deeds of charity.

And there would be no more likely way for us to have the outpouring of the Spirit of God continued here. In Germany, God did not only pour out his Spirit for a little while, but has continued it, as I said before, for above thirty years, {and it has spread in the happy influences of it into many parts of the world}.

1. August Hermann Francke (1665–1727) was a German pietistic theologian, educator and philanthropist who in 1704 founded a charitable center (including an orphan school) at Halle in Saxony.

2. Probably a reference to George Whitefield's letter in the *Pennsylvania Gazette*, Nov. 8, 1739, in which he announced an auction, the profits from which would go toward building an orphanage in Georgia.

This would show our thankfulness {to God for the blessings we have already received}. What does it signify to pretend to be thankful {and yet to neglect our second table duties}? There is nothing seems to be more inviting, as it were, to the God of love to dwell among a people, than the prevailing of such a spirit and practice: their abounding in deeds of love.

And so it will be in that great outpouring of the Spirit of God that shall be in the latter days, in those glorious times that we are expecting. 'Tis particularly prophesied that then professors shall abound in deeds of charity. Is. 32:1, 5, 8, "Behold, A king shall reign in righteousness, and princes shall rule in judgment. . . . The vile person shall be no more called liberal, nor the churl said to be bountiful. . . . But the liberal deviseth liberal things; and by liberal things shall he stand."

Let us, therefore, as we desire the continuance of the outpouring of the Spirit of God upon us, abound in such deeds. You see how God is not behind hand with you, but has smiled upon the charitable spirit when the Rev. Mr. Whitefield was here. Let us go on and God will go on. God won't be behind handwith us if we give him our carnal things. He will continue with a liberal hand to bestow spiritual things.

A Farewell Sermon Preached at the First Precinct in Northampton, After the People's Public Rejection of Their Minister . . . on June 22, 1750

II Corinthians 1:14.

As also ye have acknowledged us in part, that we are your rejoicing, even as ye also are ours, in the day of the Lord Jesus.

The Apostle, in the preceding part of the chapter, declares what great troubles he met with in the course of his ministry. In the text, and two foregoing verses, he declares what were his comforts and supports under the troubles he met with. There are four things in particular.

1. That he had approved himself to his own conscience. Verse 12, "For our rejoicing is this, the testimony of our conscience, that in simplicity and godly sincerity, not with fleshly wisdom, but by the grace of God, we have had our conversation in the world, and more abundantly to you-wards.

2. Another thing he speaks of as matter of comfort, is, that as he had approved himself to his own conscience, so he had also to the consciences of his hearers, the Corinthians whom he now wrote to, and that they should approve of him at the day of judgment.

3. The hope he had of seeing the blessed fruit of his labors and sufferings in the ministry, in their happiness and glory, in that great day of accounts.

4. That in his ministry among the Corinthians, he had approved himself to his Judge, who would approve and reward his faithfulness in that day.

These three last particulars are signified in my text and the preceding verse; and indeed all the four are implied in the text: 'tis implied, that the Corinthians had acknowledged him as their spiritual father, and as one that had been faithful among them, and as the means of their future joy and glory at the day of judgment, and one whom they should then see, and have a joyful meeting with as such. 'Tis implied, that the Apostle expected at that time to have a joyful meeting with *them* before the Judge, and with joy to behold their glory, as the fruit of his labors; and so they would be *his rejoicing*. 'Tis implied also, that he then expected to be approved of the great Judge, when he and they should meet together before him; and that he would then acknowledge his fidelity, and that this had been the means of their glory; and that thus he would as it were give them to him as his crown of rejoicing. But this the Apostle could not hope for, unless he had the testimony of his own conscience in his favor. And therefore the words do imply in the strongest manner, that he had approved himself to his own conscience.

There is one thing implied in each of these particulars, and in every part of the text, which is that point I shall make the subject of my present discourse, viz.

DOCTRINE.

Ministers and the people that have been under their care, must meet one another, before Christ's tribunal, at the day of judgment.

Ministers and the people that have been under their care, must be parted in this world, how well soever they have been united: if they are not separated before, they must be parted by death: and they may be separated while life is continued. We live in a world of change, where nothing is certain or stable; and where a little time, a few revolutions of the sun, brings to pass strange things, surprising alterations, in particular persons, in families, in towns and churches, in countries and nations. It often happens, that those who seem most united, in a little time are most disunited, and at the greatest distance. Thus ministers and people, between whom there has been the greatest mutual regard and strictest union, may not only differ in their judgments, and be alienated in affection: but one may rend from the other, and all relation between them be dissolved; the minister may be removed to a distant place, and they may never have any more to do one with another in this world. But if it be so, there is one meeting more that they must have, and that is in the last great day of accounts.

Here I would show,

I. In what manner, ministers and the people which have been under their care, shall meet one another at the day of judgment.

II. For what purposes.

III. For what reasons God has so ordered it, that ministers and their people shall then meet together in such a manner, and for such purposes.

I. I would show, in some particulars, in what manner ministers and the people which have been under their care, shall meet one another at the day of judgment. Concerning this I would observe two things in general.

First. That they shall not then meet only as all mankind must then meet, but there will be something peculiar in the manner of their meeting.

Second. That their meeting together, at that time, shall be very different from what used to be in the house of God in this world.

First. They shall not meet at that day merely as all the world must then meet together. I would observe a difference in two things.

1. As to the clear actual view, and distinct knowledge and notice of each other.

Although the whole world will be then present, all mankind of all generations gathered in one vast assembly, with all of the angelic nature, both elect and fallen angels; yet we need not suppose, that everyone will have a distinct and particular knowledge of each individual of the whole assembled multitude, which will undoubtedly consist of many millions of millions. Though 'tis probable that men's capacities will be much greater than in their present state, yet they will not be infinite: though their understanding and comprehension will be vastly extended, yet men will not be deified. There will probably be a very enlarged view, that particular persons will have of the various parts and members of that vast assembly, and so of the proceedings of that great day: but yet it must needs be, that according to the nature of finite minds, some persons and some things, at that day shall fall more under the notice of particular persons, than others;

and this (as we may well suppose) according as they shall have a nearer concern with some than others, in the transactions of that day. There will be special reason, why those who have had special concerns together in this world, in their state of probation, and whose mutual affairs will be then to be tried and judged, should especially be set in one another's view. Thus we may suppose, that rulers and subjects, earthly judges and those whom they have judged, neighbors who have had mutual converse, dealings and contests, heads of families and their children and servants, shall then meet, and in a peculiar distinction be set together. And especially will it be thus with ministers and their people. 'Tis evident by the text that these shall be in each others' view, shall distinctly know each other, and shall have particular notice one of another at that time.

2. They shall meet together, as having special concern one with another in the great transactions of that day.

Although they shall meet the whole world at that time, yet they will not have any immediate and particular concern with all. Yea, the far greater part of those who shall then be gathered together, will be such as they have had no intercourse with in their state of probation, and so will have no mutual concerns to be judged of. But as to ministers, and the people that have been under their care, they will be such as have had much immediate concern one with another, in matters of the greatest moment, that ever mankind have to do one with another in. Therefore they especially must meet, and be brought together before the Judge, as having special concern one with another in the design and business of that great day of accounts.

[*Second.*] Thus their meeting, as to the manner of it, will be diverse from the meeting of mankind in general. Their meeting will be very diverse from their meetings one with another in this world.

Ministers and their people, while their relation continues, often meet together in this world: they are wont to meet from sabbath to sabbath, and at other times, for the public worship of God, and administration of ordinances, and the solemn services of God's house: and beside these meetings, they have also occasions to meet for the determining and managing their ecclesiastical affairs, for the exercise of church discipline, and the settling and adjusting those things which concern the purity and good order of public administrations. But their meeting at the day of judgment will be exceeding diverse, in its manner and circumstances, from any such meetings and interviews as they have one with another in the present state. I would observe, how, in a few particulars.

1. Now they meet together in a preparatory, mutable state, but then in an unchangeable state.

Now sinners in the congregation meet their minister in a state wherein they are capable of a saving change, capable of being turned, through God's blessing on the ministrations and labors of their pastor, from the power of Satan unto God, and being brought out of a state of guilt, condemnation and wrath, to a state of peace and favor with God, to the enjoyment of the privileges of his children, and a title to their eternal inheritance. And saints now meet their ministers with great remains of corruption, and sometimes under great spiritual difficulties and affliction: and therefore are yet the proper subjects of means of an happy alteration of their state, consisting in a greater freedom from these things; which they have reason to hope for in the way of attendance on ordinances; and of which God is pleased commonly to make his ministers the instruments. And ministers and their people now meet in order to the bringing to pass such happy changes; they are the great benefits sought in their solemn meetings in this world.

But when they shall meet together at the day of judgment, it will be far otherwise. They will not then meet in order to the use of means for the bringing to effect any such changes; for they will all meet in an unchangeable state. Sinners will be in an unchangeable state: they who then shall be under the guilt and power of sin, and have the wrath of God abiding on them, shall be beyond all remedy or possibility of change, and shall meet their ministers without any hopes of relief or remedy, or getting any good by their means. And as for the saints, they will be already perfectly delivered from all their before-remaining corruption, temptation and calamities of every kind, and set forever out of their reach; and no deliverance, no happy alteration will remain to be accomplished in the way of the use of means of grace, under the administration of ministers. It will then be pronounced, "He that is unjust, let him be unjust still; and he that is filthy, let him be filthy still; and he that is righteous, let him be righteous still; and he that is holy, let him be holy still" [Rev. 22:11].

2. Then shall they meet together in a state of clear, certain and infallible light.

Ministers are set as guides and teachers, and are represented in Scripture as lights set up in the churches; and in the present state meet their people from time to time in order to instruct and enlighten them, to correct their mistakes, and to be a voice behind them, when they turn aside to the right hand or the left, saying, "This is the way, walk in it" [Is. 30:21]; to evince and confirm the truth by exhibiting the proper evidences of it, and to refute errors and corrupt opinions, to convince the erroneous and establish the doubting. But when Christ shall come to judgment, every error and false opinion shall be detected; all deceit and delusion shall vanish away before the light of that day, as the darkness of the night vanishes at the appearance of the rising sun; and every doctrine of the Word of God shall then appear in full evidence, and none shall remain unconvinced; all shall know the truth with the greatest certainty, and there shall be no mistakes to rectify.

Now ministers and their people may disagree in their judgments concerning some matters of religion, and may sometimes meet to confer together concerning those things wherein they differ, and to hear the reasons that may be offered on one side and the other; and all may be ineffectual, as to any conviction of the truth; they may meet and part again no more agreed than before; and that side which was in the wrong, may remain so still: sometimes the meetings of ministers with their people, in such a case of disagreeing sentiments, are attended with unhappy debate and controversy, managed with much prejudice, and want of candor; not tending to light and conviction, but rather to confirm and increase darkness, and establish opposition to the truth, and alienation of affection one from another. But when they shall hereafter meet together, at the day of judgment, before the tribunal of the Great Judge, the mind and will of Christ will be made known; and there shall no longer be any debate, or difference of opinions; the evidence of the truth shall appear beyond all dispute, and all controversies shall be finally and forever decided.

Now ministers meet their people, in order to enlighten and awaken the consciences of sinners; setting before them the great evil and danger of sin, the strictness of God's law, their own wickedness of heart and practice, the great guilt they are under, the wrath that abides upon them, and their impotence, blindness, poverty and helpless and undone condition: but all is often in vain; they remain still, notwithstanding all their ministers can say, stupid and unawakened, and their consciences unconvinced. But it will not be so at their last meeting at the day of judgment; sinners, when they shall meet their minister before their great Judge, will not meet him with a stupid conscience: they will then be fully convinced of the truth of those things which they formerly heard from him, concerning the greatness and terrible majesty of God, his holiness and hatred of sin, and his awful justice in punishing of it, the strictness of his law, and the dreadfulness and truth of his threatenings, and their own unspeakable guilt and misery: and they shall never more be insensible of these things: the eyes of conscience will now be fully enlightened, and never shall be blinded again: the mouth of conscience shall now be opened, and never shall be shut anymore.

Now ministers meet with their people, in public and private, in order to enlighten them concerning the state of their souls; to open and apply the rules of God's Word to them, in order to their searching their own hearts, and discerning the state that they are in: but now ministers have no infallible discerning the state of the souls of their people; and the most skillful of them are liable to mistakes, and often are mistaken in things of this nature; nor are the people able certainly to know the state of their minister, or one another's state; very often those pass among them for saints, and it may be eminent saints, that are grand hypocrites: and on the other hand, those are sometimes censured, or hardly received into their charity, that are indeed some of God's jewels. And nothing is more common than for men to be mistaken concerning their own state: many that are abominable to God, and the children of his wrath, think highly of themselves, as his precious saints and dear children. Yea, there is reason to think, that often some that are most bold in their confidence of their safe and happy state, and think themselves not only true saints, but the most eminent saints in the congregation, are in a peculiar manner a smoke in God's nose. And thus it undoubtedly often is in those congregations where the Word of God is most faithfully dispensed; notwithstanding all that ministers can say in their clearest explications, and most searching applications of the doctrines and rules of God's Word to the souls of their hearers, in their meetings one with another. But in the day of judgment they shall have another sort of meeting; then the secrets of every heart shall be made manifest, and every man's state shall be perfectly known. I Cor. 4:5, "Therefore judge nothing before the time, until the Lord come; who both will bring to light the hidden things of darkness, and will make manifest the counsels of the heart: and then shall every man have praise of God." Then none shall be deceived concerning his own state, nor shall be any more in doubt about it. There shall be an eternal end to all the self-conceit and vain hopes of deluded hypocrites, and all the doubts and fears of sincere Christians. And then shall all know the state of one another's souls: the people shall know whether their minister has been sincere and faithful, and the minister shall know the state of everyone of their people, and to whom the Word and ordinances of God have been a savor of life unto life, and to whom a savor of death unto death.

Now in this present state, it often happens that when ministers and people meet together to debate and manage their ecclesiastical affairs, especially in a state of controversy, they are ready to judge and censure one another, with regard to each other's views and designs, and the principles and ends that each is influenced by; and are greatly mistaken in their judgment, and wrong one another in their censures: but at that future meeting, things will be set in a true and perfect light, and the principles and aims that everyone has acted from, shall be certainly known; and there will be an end to all errors of this kind, and all unrighteous censures.

3. In this world, ministers and their people often meet together to hear of and wait upon an unseen Lord; but at the day of judgment, they shall meet in his most immediate and visible presence.

Ministers, who now often meet their people to preach to 'em the King eternal, immortal and invisible, to convince 'em that there is a God, and declare to 'em what manner of being he is, and to convince 'em that he governs, and will judge the world, and that there is a future state of rewards and punishments, and to preach to 'em a Christ in heaven, at the right hand of God, in an unseen world, shall then meet their people in the most immediate sensible presence of this great God, Savior and Judge, appearing in the most plain, visible and open manner, with great glory, with all his holy angels, before them and the whole world. They shall not meet them to hear about an absent Christ, an unseen Lord, and future Judge; but to appear before that Judge, and as being set together in the presence of that Supreme Lord, in his immense glory and awful majesty, whom they have heard of so often in their meetings together on earth.

4. The meeting, at the last day, of ministers and the people that have been under their care, will not be attended, by anyone, with a careless heedless heart.

With such an heart are their meetings often attended in this world, by many persons, having little regard to him whom they pretend unitedly to adore in the solemn duties of his public worship, taking little heed to their own thoughts or the frame of their minds, not attending to the business they are engaged in, or considering the end for which they are come together: but the meeting at that great day will be very different; there will not be one careless heart, no sleeping, no wandering of mind from the great concern of the meeting, no inattentiveness to the business of the day, no regardlessness of the presence they are in, or of those great things which they shall hear from Christ at that meeting, or that they formerly heard from him, and of him by their ministers, in their meetings in a state of trial, or which they shall now hear their ministers declaring concerning them before their Judge.

Having observed these things, concerning the manner and circumstances of this future meeting of ministers and the people that have been under their care, before the tribunal of Christ at the day of judgment, I now proceed,

II. To observe, to what purposes they shall then meet.

First. To give an account before the Great Judge, of their behavior one to another, in the relation they stood in to each other in this world.

Ministers are sent forth by Christ to their people on his business, are his servants and messengers; and when they have finished their service, they must return to their master to give him an account of what they have done, and of the entertainment they have had in performing their ministry. Thus we find in Luke 14:16–21 that when the servant who was sent forth to call the guests to the great supper, had done his errand, and finished his appointed service, he returned to his master and gave him an account of what he had done, and of the entertainment he had received. And when the master, being angry, sent his servant to others, he returns again, and gives his master an account of his conduct and success. So we read in Heb. 13:17 of ministers or rulers in the house of God, "That watch for souls, as those that must give account." And we see by the forementioned Luke 14 that ministers must give an account to their master, not only of their own behavior in the discharge of their office, but also of their people's reception of them, and of the treatment they have met with among them.

And therefore as they will be called to give an account of both, they shall give an account at the great day of accounts, in the presence of their people; they and their people being both present before their Judge.

Faithful ministers will then give an account with joy, concerning those who have received them well, and made a good improvement of their ministry; and these will be given 'em, at that day, as their crown of rejoicing. And at the same time they will give an account of the ill-treatment, of such as have not well received them and their messages from Christ: they will meet these, not as they used to do in this world, to counsel and warn them, but to bear witness against them, and as their judges, and assessors with Christ, to condemn them. And on the other hand, the people will at that day rise up in judgment against wicked and unfaithful ministers, who have sought their own temporal interest, more than the good of the souls of their flock.

Second. At that time ministers and the people who have been under their care, shall meet together before Christ, that he may judge between them, as to any controversies which have subsisted between them in this world.

So it very often comes to pass in this evil world, that great differences and controversies arise between ministers and the people that are under their pastoral care. Though they are under the greatest obligations to live in peace, above persons in almost any relation whatever; and although contests and dissensions between persons so related, are the most unhappy and terrible in their consequences, on many accounts, of any sort of contentions; yet how frequent have such contentions been? Sometimes a people contest with their ministers about their doctrine, sometimes about their administrations and conduct, and sometimes about their maintenance; and sometimes such contests continue a long time; and sometimes they are decided in this world, according to the prevailing interest of one party or the other, rather than by the Word of God, and the reason of things; and sometimes such controversies never have any proper determination in this world.

But at the day of judgment there will be a full, perfect and everlasting decision of them: the infallible Judge, the infinite fountain of light, truth and justice, will judge between the contending parties, and will declare what is the truth, who is in the right, and what is agreeable to his mind and will. And in order hereto, the parties must stand together before him at the last day; which will be the great day of finishing and determining all controversies, rectifying all mistakes, and abolishing all unrighteous judgments, errors and confusions, which have before subsisted in the world of mankind.

Third. Ministers and the people that have been under their care, must meet together at that time, to receive an eternal sentence and retribution from the Judge, in the presence of each other, according to their behavior in the relation they stood in one to another in the present state.

The Judge will not only declare justice, but he will do justice between ministers and their people. He will declare what is right between them, approving him that has been just and faithful, and condemning the unjust; and perfect truth and equity shall take place in the sentence which he passes, in the rewards he bestows, and the punishments which he inflicts. There shall be a glorious reward to faithful ministers. To those who have been successful, Dan. 12:3, "And they that be wise shall shine as the brightness of the firmament, and they that turn many to righteousness, as the stars forever and ever"; and also to those who have been faithful, and yet not successful, Is. 49:4, "Then I said, I have labored in vain, I have spent my strength for naught; yet surely my judgment is with the Lord, and my reward with my God." And those who have well received and entertained them shall be gloriously rewarded, Matt. 10:40–41, "He that receiveth you, receiveth me, and he that receiveth me, receiveth him that sent me. He that receiveth a prophet, in the name of a prophet, shall receive a prophet's reward; and he that receiveth a righteous man, in the name of a righteous man, shall receive a righteous man's reward." Such people and their faithful ministers shall be each other's crown of rejoicing. I Thess. 2:19–20, "For what is our hope, or joy, or crown of rejoicing? Are not even ye, in the presence of our Lord Jesus Christ at his coming? For ye are our glory and joy." And in the text, "We are your rejoicing, as ye also are ours, in the day of the Lord Jesus." But they that evil entreat Christ's faithful ministers, especially in that wherein they are faithful, shall be severely punished. Matt. 10:14–15, "And whosoever shall not receive you, nor hear your words, when ye depart out of that house or city, shake off the dust of your feet. Verily, I say unto you, It shall be more tolerable for the sinners of Sodom and Gomorrah, in the day of judgment, than for that city." Deut. 33:8–11, "And of Levi he said, Let thy Thummim and thy Urim be with thy holy one . . . They shall teach Jacob thy judgments, and Israel thy law . . . Bless, Lord, his substance, and accept the work of his hands: smite through the loins of them that rise up against him, and of them that hate him, that they rise not again." On the other hand, those ministers who are found to have been unfaithful, shall have a most terrible punishment. See Ezek. 33:6, Matt. 23:1–33.

Thus justice shall be administered at the great day to ministers and their people: and to that end they shall meet together, that they may not only receive justice to themselves, but see justice done to the other party: for this is the end of that great day, to *reveal*, or declare "the righteous judgment of God"; Rom. 2:5. Ministers shall have justice done them, and they shall see justice done to their people: and the people shall receive justice themselves from their Judge, and shall see justice done to their minister. And so all things will be adjusted and settled forever between them; everyone being sentenced and recompensed according to his works; either in receiving and wearing a crown of eternal joy and glory, or in suffering everlasting shame and pain.

I come now to the next thing proposed, viz.

III. To give some reasons, why we may suppose God has so ordered it, that ministers, and the people that have been under their care, shall meet together at the day of judgment, in such a manner and for such purposes.

There are two things which I would now observe.

First. The mutual concerns of ministers and their people are of the greatest importance.

The Scripture declares, that God will bring *every work* into judgment, with every secret thing, whether it be good, or whether it be evil. 'Tis fit that all the concerns, and all the behavior of mankind, both public and private, should be brought at last before God's tribunal, and finally determined by an infallible Judge: but 'tis especially requisite that it should be thus, as to affairs of very great importance.

Now the mutual concerns of a Christian minister, and his church and congregation, are of the vastest importance; in many respects, of much greater moment than the temporal concerns of the greatest earthly monarchs, and their kingdoms or empires. It is of vast consequence how ministers discharge their office, and conduct themselves towards their people in the work of the ministry, and in affairs appertaining to it. 'Tis also a matter of vast importance how a people receive and entertain a faithful minister of Christ, and what improvement they make of his ministry. These things have a more immediate and direct respect to the great and last end for which man was made, and the eternal welfare of mankind, than any of the temporal concerns of men, whether public or private. And therefore 'tis especially fit that these affairs should be brought into judgment, and openly determined and settled in truth and righteousness; and that, to this end, ministers and their people should meet together before the omniscient and infallible Judge.

Second. The mutual concerns of ministers and their people have a special relation to the main things appertaining to the day of judgment.

They have a special relation to that great and divine person who will then appear as Judge. Ministers are his messengers, sent forth by him; and in their office and administrations among their people, represent his person, stand in his stead, as those that are sent to declare his mind, to do his work, and to speak and act in his name: and therefore 'tis especially fit that they should return to him, to give an account of their work and success. The king is judge of *all* his subjects, they are all accountable to him: but 'tis more especially requisite that the king's ministers, who are especially entrusted with the administrations of his kingdom, and that are sent forth on some special negotiation, should return to him, to give an account of themselves, and their discharge of their trust, and the reception they have met with.

Ministers are not only messengers of the person who at the last day will appear as judge, but the errand they are sent upon, and the affairs they have committed to them as his ministers, do most immediately concern his honor, and the interest of his kingdom: the work they are sent upon, is to promote the designs of his administration and government; and therefore their business with their people has a near relation to the day of judgment; for the great end of that day is completely to settle and establish the affairs of his kingdom, to adjust all things that pertain to it, that everything that is opposite to the interests of his kingdom may be removed, and that everything which contributes to the completeness and glory of it, may be perfected and confirmed, that this great king may receive his due honor and glory.

Again, the mutual concerns of ministers and their people have a direct relation to the concerns of the day of judgment, as the business of ministers with their people is to promote the eternal salvation of the souls of men, and their escape from eternal damnation; and the day of judgment is the day appointed for that end, openly to decide and settle man's eternal state, to fix some in a state of eternal salvation, and to bring their salvation to its utmost consummation, and to fix others in a state of everlasting damnation and most perfect misery. The mutual concerns of ministers and people have a most direct relation to the day of judgment, as the very design of the work of the ministry is the people's preparation for that day: ministers are sent to warn them of the approach of that day, to forewarn them of the dreadful sentence then to be pronounced on the wicked, and declare to them the blessed sentence then to be pronounced on the righteous, and to use means with them that they may escape the wrath which is then to come on the ungodly, and obtain the reward then to be bestowed on the saints.

And as the mutual concerns of ministers and their people have so near and direct a relation to that day, 'tis especially fit that those concerns should be brought into that day, and there settled and issued; and that in order to this, ministers and their people should meet and appear together before the great Judge at that day.

APPLICATION.

The improvement I would make of the things which have been observed, is to lead the people here present, who have been under my pastoral care, to some reflections, and give them some advice suitable to our present circumstances; relating to what has been lately done in order to our being separated, as to the relation we have heretofore stood in one to another; but expecting to meet each other before the great tribunal at the day of judgment.

The deep and serious consideration of that our future most solemn meeting, is certainly most suitable at such a time as this; there having so lately been that done, which, in all probability, will (as to the relation we have heretofore stood in) be followed with an everlasting separation.

How often have we met together in the house of God, in this relation? How often have I spoke to you, instructed, counseled, warned, directed and fed you, and administered ordinances among you, as the people which were committed to my care, and whose precious souls I had the charge of? But in all probability, this never will be again.

The prophet Jeremiah (ch. 25:3) puts the people in mind how long he had labored among them in the work of the ministry; "From the thirteenth year of Josiah, the son of Amon, king of Judah, even unto this day (that is, the three and twentieth year), the word of the Lord came unto me, and I have spoken unto you, rising early and speaking." I am not about to compare myself with the prophet Jeremiah; but in this respect I can say as he did, that "I have spoken the word of God to you, unto the three and twentieth year, rising early and speaking." It was three and twenty years, the fifteenth day of late February, since I have labored in the work of the ministry, in the relation of a pastor to this church and congregation. And though my strength has been weakness, having always labored under great infirmity of body, besides my insufficiency for so great a charge in other respects, yet I have not spared my feeble strength, but have exerted it for the good of your souls. I can appeal to you, as the Apostle does to his hearers, Gal. 4:13, "Ye know how through infirmity of the flesh, I preached the gospel unto you." I have spent the prime of my life and strength in labors for your eternal welfare. You are my witnesses, that what strength I have had, I have not neglected in idleness, nor laid out in prosecuting worldly schemes, and managing temporal affairs, for the advancement of my outward estate, and aggrandizing myself and family; but have given myself to the work of the ministry, laboring in it night and day, rising early and applying myself to this great business to which Christ appointed me. I have found the work of the ministry among you to be a great work indeed, a work of exceeding care, labor and difficulty: many have been the heavy burdens that I have borne in it, which my strength has been very unequal to. God called me to bear these burdens, and I bless his name, that he has so supported me as to keep me from sinking under them, and that his power herein has been manifested in my weakness; so that although I have often been troubled on every side, yet I have not been distressed; perplexed, but not in despair; cast down, but not destroyed.

But now I have reason to think, my work is finished which I had to do as your minister: you have publicly rejected me, and my opportunities cease.

How highly therefore does it now become us, to consider of that time when we must meet one another before the chief Shepherd? When I must give an account of my stewardship, of the service I have done for, and the reception and treatment I have had among the people he sent me to: and you must give an account of your own conduct towards me, and the improvement you have made of these three and twenty years of my ministry. For then both you and I must appear together, and we both must give an account, in order to an infallible, righteous and eternal sentence to be passed upon us, by him who will judge us with respect to all that we have said or done in our meetings here, all our conduct one towards another, in the house of God and elsewhere, on sabbath days and on other days; who will try our hearts, and manifest our thoughts, and the principles and frames of our minds, will judge us with respect to all the controversies which have subsisted between us, with the strictest impartiality, and will examine our treatment of each other in those controversies: there is nothing covered, that shall not be revealed, nor hid, which shall not be known;

all will be examined in the searching, penetrating light of God's omniscience and glory, and by him whose eyes are as a flame of fire; and truth and right shall be made plainly to appear, being stripped of every veil; and all error, falsehood, unrighteousness and injury shall be laid open, stripped of every disguise; every specious pretense, every cavil, and all false reasoning shall vanish in a moment, as not being able to bear the light of that day. And then our hearts will be turned inside out, and the secrets of them will be made more plainly to appear than our outward actions do now. Then it shall appear what the ends are which we have aimed at, what have been the governing principles which we have acted from, and what have been the dispositions, we have exercised in our ecclesiastical disputes and contests. Then it will appear, whether I acted uprightly, and from a truly conscientious, careful regard to my duty to my great Lord and master, in some former ecclesiastical controversies, which have been attended with exceeding unhappy circumstances, and consequences: it will appear whether there was any just cause for the resentment which was manifested on those occasions. And then our late grand controversy, concerning the qualifications necessary for admission to the privileges of members, in complete standing, in the visible church of Christ, will be examined and judged, in all its parts and circumstances, and the whole set forth in a clear, certain and perfect light. Then it will appear whether the doctrine which I have preached and published concerning this matter be Christ's own doctrine, whether he won't own it as one of the precious truths which have proceeded from his own mouth, and vindicate and honor as such before the whole universe. Then it will appear what is meant by *the man that comes without the wedding garment*; for that is the day spoken of, Matt. 22:13, wherein such an one "shall be bound hand and foot, and cast into outer darkness where shall be weeping and gnashing of teeth." And then it will appear whether in declaring this doctrine, and acting agreeable to it, and in my general conduct in this affair, I have been influenced from any regard to my own temporal interest, or honor, or desire to appear wiser than others; or have acted from any sinister, secular views whatsoever; and whether what I have done has not been from a careful, strict and tender regard to the will of my Lord and master, and because I dare not offend him, being satisfied what his will was, after a long, diligent, impartial and prayerful inquiry; having this constantly in view and prospect, to engage me to great solicitude not rashly to determine truth to be on this side of the question where I am now persuaded it is, that such a determination would not be for my temporal interest, but every way against it, bringing a long series of extreme difficulties, and plunging me into an abyss of trouble and sorrow. And then it will appear whether my people have done their duty to their pastor with respect to this matter; whether they have shown a right temper and spirit on this occasion; whether they have done me justice in hearing, attending to, and considering what I had to say in evidence of what I believed and taught as part of the counsel of God; whether I have been treated with that impartiality, candor and regard which the just Judge esteemed due; and whether, in the many steps which have been taken, and the many things that have been said and done in the course of this controversy, righteousness and charity and Christian decorum have been maintained; or if otherwise, to how great a degree these things have been violated. Then every step of the conduct of each of us in this affair, from first to last, and the spirit we have exercised in all, shall be examined and manifested, and our own consciences will speak plain and loud, and each of us shall be convinced, and the world shall know; and never shall there be any more mistake, misrepresentation or misapprehension of the affair to eternity.

This controversy is now probably brought to an issue between you and me as to this world; it has issued in the event of the week before last: but it must have another decision at that great day, which certainly will come, when you and I shall meet together before the great judgment seat: and therefore I leave it to that time, and shall say no more about it at present.

But I would now proceed to address myself particularly to several sorts of persons.

I. To those who are professors of godliness amongst us.

I would now call you to a serious consideration of that great day wherein you must meet him who has heretofore been your pastor, before the Judge, whose eyes are as a flame of fire.

I have endeavored, according to my best ability, to search the Word of God, with regard to the distinguishing notes of true piety, those by which persons might best discover their state, and most surely and clearly judge of themselves. And these rules and marks I have from time to time applied to you, in the preaching of the Word, to the utmost of my skill, and in the most plain and searching manner that I have been able; in order to the detecting the deceived hypocrite, and establishing the hopes and comforts of the sincere. And yet 'tis to be feared, that after all that I have done, I now leave some of you in a deceived, deluded state; for 'tis not to be supposed that among several hundred professors, none are deceived.

Henceforward, I am like to have no more opportunity to take the care and charge of your souls, to examine and search them. But still I entreat you to remember and consider the rules which I have often laid down to you, during my ministry, with a solemn regard to the future day when you and I must meet together before our Judge; when the uses of examination you have heard from me must be rehearsed again before you, and those rules of trial must be tried, and it will appear whether they have been good or not; and it will also appear whether you have impartially heard them and tried yourselves by them; and the Judge himself who is infallible will try both you and me: and after this none will be deceived concerning the state of their souls.

I have often put you in mind, that whatever your pretenses to experiences, discoveries, comforts, and joys have been; at that day everyone will be judged according to his works: and then you will find it so.

May you have a minister of greater knowledge of the Word of God, and better acquaintance with soul cases, and of greater skill in applying himself to souls, whose discourses may be more searching and convincing; that such of you as have held fast deceit under my preaching, may have your eyes opened by his; that you may be undeceived before that great day.

What means and helps for instruction and self-examination you may hereafter have is uncertain; but one thing is certain, that the time is short, your opportunity for rectifying mistakes in so important a concern will soon come to an end. We live in a world of great changes. There is now a great change come to pass; you have withdrawn yourselves from my ministry, under which you have continued for so many years: but the time is coming, and will soon come, when you will pass out of time into eternity; and so will pass from under all means of grace whatsoever.

The greater part of you who are professors of godliness have (to use the phrase of the Apostle) "acknowledged me in part": you have heretofore acknowledged me to be your spiritual father, the instrument of the greatest good to you that ever is, or can be obtained by any of the children of men. Consider of that day, when you and I shall meet before our Judge, when it shall be examined whether you have had from me the treatment which is due to spiritual children, and whether you have treated me as you ought to have treated a spiritual father. As the relation of a natural parent brings great obligations on children, in the sight of God; so much more, in many respects, does the relation of a spiritual father bring great obligations on such, whose conversion and eternal salvation they suppose God has made them the instruments of. I Cor. 4:15, "For though you have ten thousand instructors in Christ, yet have ye not many fathers; for in Christ Jesus, I have begotten you through the gospel."

II. Now I am taking my leave of this people, I would apply myself to such among them as I leave in a Christless, graceless condition; and would call on such seriously to consider of that solemn day when they and I must meet before the Judge of the world.

My parting with you is in some respects in a peculiar manner a melancholy parting; inasmuch as I leave you in most melancholy circumstances; because I leave you in the gall of bitterness and bond of iniquity, having the wrath of God abiding on you, and remaining under condemnation to everlasting misery and destruction. Seeing I must leave you, it would have been a comfortable and happy circumstance of our parting, if I had left you in Christ, safe and blessed in that sure refuge and glorious rest of the saints. But it is otherwise, I leave you far off, aliens and strangers, wretched subjects and captives of sin and Satan, and prisoners of vindictive justice; without Christ, and without God in the world.

Your consciences bear me witness, that while I had opportunity, I have not ceased to warn you and set before you your danger. I have studied to represent the misery and necessity of your circumstances in the clearest manner possible. I have tried all ways that I could think of tending to awaken your consciences, and make you sensible of the necessity of your improving your time, and being speedy in flying from the wrath to come, and thorough in the use of means for your escape and safety. I have diligently endeavored to find out and use the most powerful motives to persuade you to take care for your own welfare and salvation. I have not only endeavored to awaken you that you might be moved with fear, but I have used my utmost endeavors to win you: I have sought out acceptable words, that if possible I might prevail upon you to forsake sin, and turn to God, and accept of Christ as your Savior and Lord. I have spent my strength very much in these things. But yet, with regard to you whom I am now speaking to, I have not been successful: but have this day reason to complain in those words, Jer. 6:29, "The bellows are burnt, the lead is consumed of the fire, the founder melteth in vain, for the wicked are not plucked away." 'Tis to be feared that all my labors as to many of you have served to no other purpose but to harden you; and that the Word which I have preached, instead of being a savor of life unto life, has been a savor of death unto death. Though I shall not have any account to give for the future, of such as have openly and resolutely renounced my ministry as of a betrustment committed to me: yet remember you must give account for yourselves, of your care of your own souls, and your improvement of all means past and future, through your whole lives. God only knows what will become of your poor perishing souls, what means you may hereafter enjoy, or what disadvantages and temptations you may be under. May God in mercy grant, that however all past means have been unsuccessful, you may have future means which may have a new effect; and that the Word of God, as it shall be hereafter dispensed to you, may prove as the fire and the hammer that breaketh the rock in pieces. However, let me now at parting exhort and beseech you not wholly to forget the warnings you have had while under my ministry. When you and I shall meet at the day of judgment, then you will remember 'em: the sight of me your former minister, on that occasion, will soon revive 'em in your memory; and that in a very affecting manner. O don't let that be the first time that they are so revived.

You and I are now parting one from another as to this world; let us labor that we may not be parted, after our meeting at the last day. If I have been your faithful pastor (which will that day appear, whether I have or no), then I shall be acquitted, and shall ascend with Christ. O do your part, that in such a case, it may not be so, that you should be forced eternally to part from me, and all that have been faithful in Christ Jesus. This is a sorrowful parting that now is between you and me; but that would be a more sorrowful parting to you than this. This you may perhaps bear without being much affected with it, if you are not glad of it; but such a parting in that day will most deeply, sensibly and dreadfully affect you.

III. I would address myself to those who are under some awakenings.

Blessed be God, that there are some such, and that (although I have reason to fear I leave multitudes in this large congregation in a Christless state) yet I don't leave 'em all in total stupidity and carelessness about their souls. Some of you, that I have reason to hope are under some awakenings, have acquainted me with your circumstances; which has a tendency to cause me, now I am leaving you, to take my leave of you with peculiar concern for you. What will be the issue of your present exercise of mind I know not: but it will be known at that day, when you and I shall meet before the judgment seat of Christ. Therefore now be much in consideration of that day.

Now I am parting with this flock, I would once more press upon you the counsels I have heretofore given, to take heed of being slighty in so great a concern, to be thorough and in good earnest in the affair, and to beware of backsliding, to hold on and hold out to the end. And cry mightily to God that these great changes that pass over this church and congregation don't prove your overthrow. There is great temptation in them; and the devil will undoubtedly seek to make his advantage of them, if possible to cause your present convictions and endeavors to be abortive. You had need to double your diligence, and watch and pray lest you be overcome by temptation.

Whoever may hereafter stand related to you as your spiritual guide, my desire and prayer is, that the great Shepherd of the sheep would have a special respect to you, and be your guide (for there is none teacheth like him), and that he who is the infinite fountain of light, would "open your eyes, and turn you from darkness unto light, and from the power of Satan unto God, that you may receive forgiveness of sins, and inheritance among them that are sanctified through faith that is in Christ" [Acts 26:18]; that so, in that great day, when I shall meet you again before your Judge and mine, we may meet in joyful and glorious circumstances, never to be separated anymore.

IV. I would apply myself to the young people of the congregation.

Since I have been settled in the work of the ministry in this place, I have ever had a peculiar concern for the souls of the young people, and a desire that religion might flourish among them; and have especially exerted myself in order to it; because I knew the special opportunity they had beyond others, and that ordinarily those whom God intended mercy for were brought to fear and love him in their youth. And it has ever appeared to me a peculiarly amiable thing to see young people walking in the ways of virtue and Christian piety, having their hearts purified and sweetened with a principle of divine love. And it has appeared a thing exceeding beautiful, and what would be much to the adorning and happiness of the town, if the young people could be persuaded, when they meet together, to converse as Christians, and as the children of God; avoiding impurity, levity and extravagance; keeping strictly to the rules of virtue, and conversing together of the things of God and Christ and heaven. This is what I have longed for: and it has been exceedingly grievous to me when I have heard of vice, vanity and disorder among our youth. And so far as I know my heart, it was from hence that I formerly led this church to some measures, for the suppressing vice among our young people, which gave so great offense, and by which I became so obnoxious. I have sought the good and not the hurt of our young people. I have desired their truest honor and happiness, and not their reproach; knowing that true virtue and religion tended, not only to the glory and felicity of young people in another world, but their greatest peace and prosperity, and highest dignity and honor in this world, and above all things to sweeten and render pleasant and delightful even the days of youth.

But whether I have loved you and sought your good more or less, yet God in his providence, now calling me to part with you, committing your souls to him who once committed the pastoral care of them to me, nothing remains, but only (as I am now taking my leave of you) earnestly to beseech you, from love to yourselves, if you have none to me, not to despise and forget the warnings and counsels I have so often given you; remembering the day when you and I must meet again before the great Judge of quick and dead; when it will appear whether the things I have taught you were true, whether the counsels I have given you were good, and whether I truly sought your good, and whether you have well improved my endeavors.

I have, from time to time, earnestly warned you against frolicking (as it is called) and some other liberties commonly taken by young people in the land. And whatever some may say in justification of such liberties and customs, and may laugh at warnings against them, I now leave you my parting testimony against such things; not doubting but God will approve and confirm it in that day when we shall meet before him.

V. I would apply myself to the children of the congregation, the lambs of this flock, who have been so long under my care.

I have just now said that I have had a peculiar concern for the young people: and in so saying, I did not intend to exclude you. You are in youth, and in the most early youth: and therefore I have been sensible, that if those that were young had a precious opportunity for their souls' good, you who are very young had in many respects a peculiarly precious opportunity. And accordingly I have not neglected you: I have endeavored to do the part of a faithful shepherd, in feeding the lambs as well as the sheep. Christ did once commit the care of your souls to me as your minister; and you know, dear children, how I have instructed you, and warned you from time to time: you know how I have often called you together for that end: and some of you, sometimes, have seemed to be affected with what I have said to you. But I am afraid it has had no saving effect as to many of you; but that you remain still in an unconverted condition, without any real saving work wrought in your souls, convincing you thoroughly of your sin and misery, causing you to see the great evil of sin, and to mourn for it, and hate it above all things; and giving you a sense of the excellency of the Lord Jesus Christ, bringing you with all your hearts to cleave to him as your Savior; weaning your hearts from the world; and causing you to love God above all, and to delight in holiness more than in all the pleasant things of this earth: and so that I now leave you in a miserable condition, having no interest in Christ, and so under the awful displeasure and anger of God, and in danger of going down to the pit of eternal misery.

But now I must bid you farewell: I must leave you in the hands of God: I can do no more for you than to pray for you. Only I desire you not to forget, but often think of the counsels and warnings I have given you, and the endeavors I have used, that your souls might be saved from everlasting destruction.

Dear children, I leave you in an evil world, that is full of snares and temptations. God only knows what will become of you. This the Scripture has told us, that there are but few saved: and we have abundant confirmation of it from what we see. This we see, that children die as well as others: multitudes die before they grow up; and of those that grow up, comparatively few ever give good evidence of saving conversion to God. I pray God to pity you, and take care of you, and provide for you the best means for the good of your souls; and that God himself would undertake for you, to be your heavenly Father, and the mighty Redeemer of your immortal souls. Don't neglect to pray for yourselves: take heed you ben't of the number of those, who cast off fear, and restrain prayer before God. Constantly pray to God in secret; and often remember that great day when you must appear before the judgment seat of Christ, and meet your minister there, who has so often counseled and warned you.

I conclude with a few words of advice to all in general, in some particulars, which are of great importance in order to the future welfare and prosperity of this church and congregation.

[*Dir.*] I. One thing that greatly concerns you, as you would be an happy people, is the maintaining of family order.

We have had great disputes how the church ought to be regulated; and indeed the subject of these disputes was of great importance: but the due regulation of your families is of no less, and in some respects, of much greater importance. Every Christian family ought to be as it were a little church, consecrated to Christ, and wholly influenced and governed by his rules. And family education and order are some of the chief of the means of grace. If these fail, all other means are like to prove ineffectual. If these are duly maintained, all the means of grace will be like to prosper and be successful.

Let me now therefore, once more, before I finally cease to speak to this congregation, repeat and earnestly press the counsel, which I have often urged on heads of families here, while I was their pastor, to great painfulness, in teaching, warning and directing their children; bringing them up in the nurture and admonition of the Lord; beginning early, where there is yet opportunity; and maintaining a constant diligence in labors of this kind: remembering that, as you would not have all your instructions and counsels ineffectual, there must be government as well as instructions, which must be maintained with an even hand, and steady resolution; as a guard to the religion and morals of the family, and the support of its good order. Take heed that it ben't with any of you as it was with Eli of old, who reproved his children, but restrained them not; and that by this means you do not bring the like curse on your families, as he did on his.

And let children obey their parents, and yield to their instructions, and submit to their orders, as they would inherit a blessing, and not a curse. For we have reason to think from many things in the Word of God, that nothing has a greater tendency to bring a curse on persons, in this world, and on all their temporal concerns, than an undutiful, unsubmissive, disorderly behavior in children towards their parents.

[*Dir.*] II. As you would seek the future prosperity of this society, 'tis of vast importance that you should avoid contention.

A contentious people will be a miserable people. The contentions which have been among you, since I first became your pastor, have been one of the greatest burdens I have labored under in the course of my ministry: not only the contentions you have had with me, but those which you have had one with another, about your lands, and other concerns. Because I knew that contention, heat of spirit, evil speaking, and things of the like nature, were directly contrary to the spirit of Christianity, and did in a peculiar manner tend to drive away God's Spirit from a people, and to render all means of grace ineffectual, as well as to destroy a people's outward comfort and welfare.

Let me therefore earnestly exhort you, as you would seek your own future good, hereafter to watch against a contentious spirit. "If you would see good days, seek peace and ensue it," I Pet. 3:10–11. Let the contention which has lately been about the terms of Christian communion, as it has been the greatest of your contention, so be the last of them. I would, now I am preaching my farewell sermon, say to you as the Apostle to the Corinthians, II Cor. 13:11, "Finally, brethren, farewell. Be perfect: be of one mind: live in peace; and the God of love and peace shall be with you."

And here I would particularly advise those, that have adhered to me in the late controversy, to watch over their spirits, and avoid all bitterness towards others. Your temptations are in some respects the greatest; because what has been lately done, is grievous to you. But however wrong you may think others have done, maintain, with great diligence and watchfulness, a Christian meekness and sedateness of spirit: and labor, in this respect, to excel others who are of the contrary part: and this will the best victory: for "he that rules his spirit, is better than he that takes a city." Therefore let nothing be done through strife or vainglory: indulge no revengeful spirit in any wise; but watch and pray against it: and by all means in your power, seek the prosperity of this town: and never think you behave yourselves as becomes Christians, but when you sincerely, sensibly and fervently love all men of whatever party or opinion, and whether friendly or unkind, just or injurious, to you, or your friends, or to the cause and kingdom of Christ.

[*Dir.*] III. Another thing that vastly concerns the future prosperity of the town, is that you should watch against the encroachments of error; and particularly Arminianism, and doctrines of like tendency.

You were many of you, as I well remember, much alarmed with the apprehension of the danger of the prevailing of these corrupt principles, near 16 years ago. But the danger then was small in comparison of what appears now: these doctrines at this day are much more prevalent than they were then: the progress they have made in the land, within this seven years, seems to have been vastly greater than at any time in the like space before: and they are still prevailing and creeping into almost all parts of the land, threatening the utter ruin of the credit of those doctrines, which are the peculiar glory of the gospel, and the interests of vital piety. And I have of late perceived some things among yourselves, that show that you are far from being out of danger, but on the contrary remarkably exposed. The elder people may perhaps think themselves sufficiently fortified against infection: but 'tis fit that all should beware of self-confidence and carnal security, and should remember those needful warnings of Sacred Writ, "Be not high-minded, but fear" [Rom. 11:20], and "let him that stands take heed lest he fall" [I Cor. 10:12]. But let the case of the elder people be as it will, the rising generations are doubtless greatly exposed. These principles are exceedingly taking with corrupt nature, and are what young people, at least such as have not their hearts established with grace, are easily led away with.

And if these principles should greatly prevail in this town, as they very lately have done in another large town I could name, formerly greatly noted for religion, and so for a long time, it will threaten the spiritual and eternal ruin of this people, in the present and future generations. Therefore you have need of the greatest and most diligent care and watchfulness with respect to this matter.

[*Dir.*] IV. Another thing which I would advise to, that you may hereafter be a prosperous people, is that you would give yourselves much to prayer.

God is the fountain of all blessing and prosperity, and he will be sought to for his blessing. I would therefore advise you not only to be constant in secret and family prayer, and in the public worship of God in his house, but also often to assemble yourselves in private praying societies. I would advise all such as are grieved for the afflictions of Joseph, and sensibly affected with the calamities of this town, of whatever opinion they be with relation to the subject of our late controversy, often to meet together for prayer, and to cry to God for his mercy to themselves, and mercy to this town, and mercy to Zion and the people of God in general through the world.

[*Dir.*] V. The last article of advice I would give (which doubtless does greatly concern your prosperity) is, that you would take great care with regard to the settlement of a minister, to see to it who, or what manner of person he is that you settle; and particularly in these two respects.

First. That he be a man of thoroughly sound principles, in the scheme of doctrine which he maintains.

This you will stand in the greatest need of, especially at such a day of corruption as this is. And, in order to obtain such a one, you had need to exercise extraordinary care and prudence. I know the danger. I know the manner of many young gentlemen of corrupt principles, their ways of concealing themselves, the fair specious disguises they are wont to put on, by which they deceive others, to maintain their own credit, and get themselves into others' confidence and improvement, and secure and establish their own interest, till they see a convenient opportunity to begin more openly to broach and propagate their corrupt tenets.

Second. Labor to obtain a man who has an established character, as a person of serious religion, and fervent piety.

'Tis of vast importance that those who are settled in this work should be men of true piety, at all times, and in all places; but more especially at some times, and in some towns and churches. And this present time, which is a time wherein religion is in danger, by so many corruptions in doctrine and practice, is in a peculiar manner a day wherein such ministers are necessary. Nothing else but sincere piety of heart, is at all to be depended on, at such a time as this, as a security to a young man, just coming into the world, from the prevailing infection, or thoroughly to engage him in proper and successful endeavors to withstand and oppose the torrent of error, and prejudice, against the high, mysterious, evangelical doctrines of the religion of Jesus Christ, and their genuine effects in true experimental religion. And *this place* is a place that does peculiarly need such a minister, for reasons obvious to all.

If you should happen to settle a minister, who knows nothing truly of Christ, and the way to salvation by him, nothing experimentally of the nature of vital religion; alas, how will you be exposed as sheep without a shepherd! Here is need of one in this place, who shall be eminently fit to stand in the gap, and make up the hedge, and who shall be as the chariots of Israel, and the horsemen thereof. You need one that shall stand as a champion in the cause of truth and the power of godliness.

Having briefly mentioned these important articles of advice, nothing remains; but that I now take my leave of you, and bid you all farewell; wishing and praying for your best prosperity. I would now commend your immortal souls to him, who formerly committed them to me; expecting the day, when I must meet you again before him, who is the Judge of quick and dead. I desire that I may never forget this people, who have been so long my special charge, and that I may never cease fervently to pray for your prosperity. May God bless you with a faithful pastor, one that is well acquainted with his mind and will, thoroughly warning sinners, wisely and skillfully searching professors, and conducting you in the way to eternal blessedness. May you have truly a burning and shining light set up in this candlestick; and may you, not only for a season, but during his whole life, and that a long life, be willing to rejoice in his light.

And let me be remembered in the prayers of all God's people that are of a calm spirit, and are peaceable and faithful in Israel, of whatever opinion they may be, with respect to terms of church communion.

And let us all remember, and never forget our future solemn meeting, on that great day of the Lord; the day of infallible decision, and of the everlasting and unalterable sentence, Amen.

Heaven Is a World of Love (*Charity and Its Fruits*, Sermon Fifteen, 1738)

I Corinthians 13:8–10.
Charity never faileth; but whether there be prophecies, they shall fail; whether there be tongues, they shall cease; whether there be knowledge, it shall vanish away. For we know in part, and we prophesy in part. But when that which is perfect is come, then that which is in part shall be done away.

I have already insisted on the first of these verses singly from the doctrine that the great fruit of the Spirit in which the Holy Ghost shall not only for a season but everlastingly be communicated to the church of Christ is divine love. I would now take a view of this verse together with the two following verses in order to a further instruction. And to that end, I would observe two things in these verses. First, something, which will hereafter be, which will show the great worth and excellence of charity; viz. that charity shall remain when other fruits of the Spirit have failed. And second, in what state of the church this will come to pass, viz. in its perfect state, when that which is in part shall be done away.

There is a twofold imperfect, and so a twofold perfect state of the Christian church. The Christian church in its beginning, in its first age before it was thoroughly established in the world, and settled in its New Testament state, and before the canon of the Scripture was completed, was in an imperfect state, a kind of a state of childhood in comparison with what it will be in the elder and latter ages of the church, when it will be in a state of manhood, or a perfect state in comparison with what it was in the first ages. Again, the church of Christ, as long as it remains in its militant state, and to the end of time is in an imperfect state, a state of childhood, and as the Apostle says in the eleventh verse, thinks and speaks as a child, in comparison with what it will be in the heavenly state, when it comes to a state of manhood and perfection, and to the measure of the stature of the fullness of Christ.

And so there is a twofold failing of those other gifts of the Spirit here mentioned. One is at the end of the first and infant age of the Christian church when the canon of Scripture is complete; and so there are none of them remaining in the church in its later ages, when it shall put away childish things and be in a state of manhood before the end of the world, when the Spirit of God shall be most gloriously poured out and manifested in that love and charity, which is its greatest and everlasting fruit. And again, all common fruits of the Spirit cease at the end of the militant state of the church with respect to particular persons at death, and with respect to the whole church at the end of the world. But charity remains in heaven. There the Spirit shall be poured forth in perfect love into every heart.

The Apostle seems to have respect to both these; but especially the latter. For though the glorious state of the church in its latter age be perfect in comparison with its former state, yet its state in heaven is that state of the church to which the things which the Apostle here says are most applicable, when he says, "when that which is perfect is come, that which is in part shall be done away." "Now we see through a glass darkly; but then face to face; now I know in part; but then shall I know, even as also I am known."

DOCTRINE.

Heaven is a world of love.

The Apostle in the text speaks of a state of the church which is perfect, and therefore a state in which the Holy Spirit shall more perfectly and abundantly be given to the church than it now is. But the way in which it shall be given, when it is so abundantly poured forth, will be in that great fruit of the Spirit, holy and divine love in the hearts of all the blessed inhabitants of that world. So that the heavenly state of the church is a state which is distinguished from its earthly state, as it is that state which God has designed especially for such a communication of his Holy Spirit, and in which it shall be given perfectly; whereas in the present state of the church, it is given with such great imperfection; and also a state in which this shall be, as it were, the only gift or fruit of the Spirit, as being the most perfect and glorious, and which being brought to perfection renders others, which God was wont to communicate to his church on earth, needless.

That we may the better see how heaven is a world of love, I would take the following method in considering this subject.

I. I would consider the great cause and fountain of love which is there.

II. I would consider heaven with regard to the objects of love which it contains.

III. I would consider the love which is there with regard to the subject.

IV. I would consider the principle, or the love itself, which there is in heaven.

V. I would consider the excellent circumstances in which love is there enjoyed and expressed.

VI. The happy effect and fruits of all this.

I. And here the place with respect to the cause and fountain of love which is there. What I shall say may be comprised in this proposition; viz. that the God of love dwells in heaven. Heaven is the palace, or presence-chamber, of the Supreme Being who is both the cause and source of all holy love. God, indeed, with respect to his essence is everywhere. He fills heaven and earth. But yet he is said on some accounts more especially to be in some places rather than others. He was said of old to dwell in the land of Israel above all other lands, and in Jerusalem above all other cities in that land, and in the temple above all other houses in that city, and in the Holy of Holies above all other apartments in that temple, and on the mercy seat over the ark above all other places in the Holy of Holies. But heaven is his dwelling place above all other places in the universe.

Those places in which he was said to dwell of old were all but types of this. Heaven is a part of the creation which God has built for this end, to be the place of his glorious presence. And it is his abode forever. Here he will dwell and gloriously manifest himself to eternity. And this renders heaven a world of love; for God is the fountain of love, as the sun is the fountain of light. And therefore the glorious presence of God in heaven fills heaven with love, as the sun placed in the midst of the hemisphere in a clear day fills the world with light. The Apostle tells us that God is love, I John 4:8. And therefore seeing he is an infinite Being, it follows that he is an infinite fountain of love. Seeing he is an all-sufficient Being, it follows that he is a full and overflowing and an inexhaustible fountain of love. Seeing he is an unchangeable and eternal Being, he is an unchangeable and eternal source of love. There even in heaven dwells that God from whom every stream of holy love, yea, every drop that is or ever was proceeds.

There dwells God the Father, and so the Son, who are united in infinitely dear and incomprehensible mutual love. There dwells God the Father, who is the Father of mercies, and so the Father of love, who so loved the world that he gave his only begotten Son, that whosoever believeth in him should not perish, but have everlasting life [John 3:16]. There dwells Jesus Christ, the Lamb of God, the Prince of peace and love, who so loved the world that he shed his blood, and poured out his soul unto death for it. There dwells the Mediator, by whom all God's love is expressed to the saints, by whom the fruits of it have been purchased, and through whom they are communicated, and through whom love is imparted to the hearts of all the church. There Christ dwells in both his natures, his human and divine, sitting with the Father in the same throne. There is the Holy Spirit, the spirit of divine love, in whom the very essence of God, as it were, all flows out or is breathed forth in love, and by whose immediate influence all holy love is shed abroad in the hearts of all the church [cf. Rom. 5:5]. There in heaven this fountain of love, this eternal three in one, is set open without any obstacle to hinder access to it. There this glorious God is manifested and shines forth in full glory, in beams of love; there the fountain overflows in streams and rivers of love and delight, enough for all to drink at, and to swim in, yea, so as to overflow the world as it were with a deluge of love. I proceed now

II. To consider heaven with regard to the objects of love which it contains. And under this head I would observe three things.

First. There are none but lovely objects in heaven. There is no odious or polluted person or thing to be seen there. There is nothing wicked and unholy. Rev. 21:27, "And there shall in no wise enter into it anything that defileth, neither whatsoever worketh abomination, or maketh a lie." There is nothing which is deformed either in natural or moral deformity. Everything which is to be beheld there is amiable. The God, who dwells and gloriously manifests himself there, is infinitely lovely. There is to be seen a glorious heavenly Father, a glorious Redeemer; there is to be felt and possessed a glorious Sanctifier. All the persons who belong to that blessed society are lovely. The Father of the family is so, and so are all his children. The Head of the body is so, and so are all the members. Concerning the angels, there are none who are unlovely. There are no evil angels suffered to infest heaven as they do this world. They are not suffered to come near, but are kept at a distance with a great gulf between them. In the church of saints there are no unlovely persons; there are no false professors, none who pretend to be saints, who are persons of an unchristian, hateful spirit and behavior, as is often the case in this world. There is no one object there to give offense, or at any time to give any occasion for any passion or motion of hatred; but every object shall draw forth love.

Second. Not only shall all objects there be lovely, but each shall be perfectly lovely. There are many things in this world which in general are lovely, but yet are not perfectly free from that which is the contrary. Many men are amiable and worthy to be loved, but yet they are not without those things which are very disagreeable. But it is not so in heaven. There shall be no pollution or deformity of any kind seen in any one person or thing. Everyone is perfectly pure, all over lovely; everything shall be perfectly pleasant. That world is perfectly bright without darkness, perfectly clear without spot. There shall be none appearing with any defects, either natural or moral. There is nothing seen there which is sinful, nothing weak or foolish. Nothing shall appear to which nature is averse, nothing which shall offend the most delicate eye. There shall be no string out of tune to cause any jar in the harmony of that world, no unpleasant note to cause any discord.

That God who so fully manifests himself there is perfect with an absolute and infinite perfection. That Son of God who is the brightness of his Father's glory appears there in his glory, without that veil of outward meanness in which he appeared in this world, as a root out of dry ground destitute of outward glory. There the Holy Spirit shall be poured forth with perfect sweetness, as a pure river of water of life, clear as crystal, Rev. 22 at the beginning; a river whose waters are without any manner of pollution. And every member of that glorious society shall be without blemish of sin or imprudence or any kind of failure. The whole church shall then be presented to Christ as a bride clothed in fine linen, clean and white, without spot or wrinkle. Eph. 5:25–27, "Christ loved the church, and gave himself for it, that he might sanctify and cleanse it with the washing of water by the word. That he might present it to himself a glorious church, not having spot, or wrinkle, or any such thing, but that it should be holy and without blemish." In that world, wherever the inhabitants turn their eyes they shall see nothing but beauty and glory. In the most stately cities on earth, however magnificent the buildings are, yet the streets are filthy and defiled, being made to be trodden under foot. But the very street of this heavenly city is represented as being as pure gold, like unto transparent glass, Rev. 21:21. That it should be like pure gold only does not sufficiently represent the purity of them; but they are also like the transparent glass or crystal.

Third. There are those objects upon which the saints have set their hearts and loved above all others while in this world. There they will find those things which appeared lovely to them while they dwelt on earth far beyond all they could see here, the things which captivated their souls, and drew them away from the most dear and pleasant of earthly objects. There they find those things which were their delight, upon which they used often to meditate, and with the sweet contemplation of which they used to entertain their minds. There they find the things which they chose for their portion, and which were so dear to them, that for the sake of them they were ready to undergo the severest sufferings, or to forsake father and mother, and wife, and children, and lands. There they shall dwell with that God whom they have loved with all their hearts, and with all their souls, and with all their minds. There they are brought to be with their beloved Savior. There they have such company as they have loved and longed for, and with which by faith they were conversant even while they dwelt on earth.

Thus having considered the objects of love in heaven, I come now

III. To consider the love which is there with regard to the subjects of it, or the hearts in which it is. And with respect to this I would observe that love resides and reigns in every heart there. The heart of God is the original seat or subject of it. Divine love is in him not as a subject which receives from another, but as its original seat, where it is of itself. Love is in God as light is in the sun, which does not shine by a reflected light as the moon and planets do; but by his own light, and as the fountain of light. And love flows out from him towards all the inhabitants of heaven. It flows out in the first place [necessarily] and infinitely towards his only begotten Son, being poured forth without measure, as to an object which is infinite, and so fully adequate to God's love in its fountain. Infinite love is infinitely exercised towards him. The fountain does not only send forth large streams towards this object as it does to every other, but the very fountain itself wholly and altogether goes out towards him. And the Son of God is not only the infinite object of love, but he is also an infinite subject of it. He is not only the infinite object of the Father's love, but he also infinitely loves the Father. The infinite essential love of God is, as it were, an infinite and eternal mutual holy energy between the Father and the Son, a pure, holy act whereby the Deity becomes nothing but an infinite and unchangeable act of love, which proceeds from both the Father and the Son. Thus divine love has its seat in the Deity as it is exercised within the Deity, or in God towards himself.

But it does not remain in such exercises only, but it flows out in innumerable streams towards all the created inhabitants of heaven; he loves all the angels and saints there. The love of God flows out towards Christ the Head, and through him to all his members, in whom they were beloved before the foundation of the world, and in whom his love was expressed towards them in time by his death and sufferings, and in their conversion and the great things God has done for them in this world, and is now fully manifested to them in heaven. And the saints and angels are secondarily the subjects of holy love, not as in whom love is as in an original seat, as light is in the sun which shines by its own light, but as it is in the planets which shine by reflecting the light of the sun. And this light is reflected in the first place and chiefly back to the sun itself. As God has given the saints and angels love, so their love is chiefly exercised towards God, the fountain of it, as is most reasonable. They all love God with a supreme love. There is no enemy of God in heaven, but all love him as his children. They all are united with one mind to breathe forth their whole souls in love to their eternal Father, and to Jesus Christ, their common Head. Christ loves all his saints in heaven. His love flows out to his whole church there, and to every individual member of it; and they all with one heart and one soul, without any schism in the body, love their common Redeemer. Every heart is wedded to this spiritual husband. All rejoice in him, the angels concurring. And the angels and saints all love one another. All that glorious society are sincerely united. There is no secret or open enemy among them; not one heart but is full of love, nor one person who is not beloved. As they are all lovely, so all see each other's loveliness with answerable delight and complacence. Everyone there loves every other inhabitant of heaven whom he sees, and so he is mutually beloved by everyone.

Thus having spoken of the fountain and subject of this love, I proceed

IV. To say something of the principle, or the love itself, which fills the heavenly world. And of this I would take notice, first, of the nature, and second, the degree of it.

First. As to its nature. It is altogether holy and divine. Most of the love which there is in this world is of an unhallowed nature. But in heaven, the love which has place there is not carnal, but spiritual; not proceeding from corrupt principles, not from selfish motives, and to mean and vile purposes; but there love is a pure flame. The saints there love God for his own sake, and each other for God's sake, for the sake of that relation which they bear to God, and that image of God which is upon them.

Second. With respect to the degree of their love, it is perfect. The love which is in the heart of God is perfect, with an absolute, infinite and divine perfection. The love of the angels and saints to God and Christ is perfect in its kind, or with such a perfection as is proper to their nature, perfect with a sinless perfection, and perfect in that it is commensurate with the capacities of their natures. So it is said in the text, when that which is perfect is come, that which is in part shall be done away. Their love shall be without any remains of a contrary principle. Having no pride or selfishness to interrupt or hinder its exercises, their hearts shall be full of love. That which was in the heart as but a grain of mustard seed in this world shall there be as a great tree. The soul which only had a little spark of divine love in it in this world shall be, as it were, wholly turned into love; and be like the sun, not having a spot in it, but being wholly a bright, ardent flame. There shall be no remaining enmity, distaste, coldness and deadness of heart towards God and Christ; not the least remainder of any principle of envy to be exercised towards any angels or saints who are superior in glory, no contempt or slight towards any who are inferior.

Those who have a lower station in glory than others suffer no diminution of their own happiness by seeing others above them in glory. On the contrary they rejoice in it. All that whole society rejoice in each other's happiness; for the love of benevolence is perfect in them. Everyone has not only a sincere but a perfect good will to every other. Sincere and strong love is greatly gratified and delighted in the prosperity of the beloved. And if the love be perfect, the greater the prosperity of the beloved is, the more is the lover pleased and delighted. For the prosperity of the beloved is, as it were, the food of love; and therefore the greater that prosperity is, the more richly is love feasted. The love of benevolence is delighted in beholding the prosperity of another, as the love of complacence is delighted in viewing the beauty of another. So that the superior prosperity of those who are higher in glory is so far from being any damp to the happiness of saints of lower degree that it is an addition to it, or a part of it. There is undoubtedly an inconceivably pure, sweet and fervent love between the saints in glory; and their love is in proportion to the perfection and amiableness of the objects beloved. And therefore it must necessarily cause delight in them when they see others' happiness and glory to be in proportion to their amiableness, and so in proportion to their love of them. Those who are highest in glory are those who are highest in holiness, and therefore are those who are most beloved by all the saints. For they love those most who are most holy, and so they will all rejoice in it that they are most happy. And it will be a damp to none of the saints to see them who have higher degrees of holiness and likeness to God to be more loved than themselves; for all shall have as much love as they desire, and as great manifestations of love as they can bear; all shall be fully satisfied.

And when there is perfect satisfaction, there is no room for envy. And they will have no temptation to envy those who are above them in glory from their superiors being lifted up with pride. We are apt to conceive that those who are more holy, and more happy than others in heaven, will be elated and lifted up in their spirit above others. Whereas their being above them in holiness implies their being superior to them in humility; for their superior humility is part of their superior holiness. Though all are perfectly free from pride, yet as some will have greater degrees of divine knowledge than others, will have larger capacities to see more of the divine perfections, so they will see more of their own comparative littleness and nothingness, and therefore will be lowest abased in humility. And besides, the inferior in glory will have no temptation to envy those who are higher. For those who are highest will not only be more beloved by the lower saints for their higher holiness, but they will also have more of a spirit of love to others. They will love those who are below them more than other saints of less capacity. They who are in highest degrees of glory will be of largest capacity, and so of greatest knowledge, and will see most of God's loveliness, and consequently will have love to God and love to saints most abounding in their hearts. So that those who are lower in glory will not envy those who are above them. They will be most beloved of those who are highest in glory, and the superior in glory will be so far from slighting those who are inferior, that they will have more abundant love to them, greater degrees of love in proportion to their superior knowledge and happiness; the higher in glory, the more like Christ in this respect. So that they will love them more than those who are their equals. And what puts it beyond doubt that seeing the superior happiness of others will be no damp to their happiness is this, that the superior happiness which they have consists in their greater humility, and their greater love to them, and to God and Christ, whom they will look upon as themselves. Such a sweet and perfect harmony will there be in the heavenly society, and perfect love reigning in every heart towards everyone without control, and without alloy, or any interruption. And no envy, or malice, or revenge, or contempt, or selfishness shall enter there, but shall be kept as far off as earth and hell are from heaven. I come now

V. To consider some of the excellent circumstances in which love shall be expressed and enjoyed in heaven. As particularly,

First. Love there always meets with answerable returns of love. Love is always mutual, and the returns are always in due proportion. Love always seeks this. In proportion as any person is beloved, in that proportion his love is desired and prized. And in heaven this inclination or desire of love will never fail of being satisfied. No one person there will ever be grieved that he is slighted by those whom he loves, or that he has not answerable returns. As the saints will love God with an inconceivable ardor of heart, and to the utmost of their capacity; so they will know that he has loved them from eternity, and that he still loves them, and will love them to eternity. And God will then gloriously manifest himself to them, and they shall know that all that happiness and glory of which they are possessed is the fruit of his love. With the same ardor will the saints love the Lord Jesus Christ. And their love shall be accepted, and they shall know that he has loved them with a dying love. They shall then be more sensible than they are now what great love it manifested in Christ, that he should lay down his life for them. Then Christ will open to their view the great fountain of love in his heart far beyond what they ever before saw. Hereby the saints' love to God and Christ is mutual, Prov. 8:17, "I love them, that love me"; though the love of God to the saints cannot properly be called returns of love, because he loved them first. But the sight of God's love will fill the saints the more with joy and admiration.

The love of the saints to one another will always be mutual and answerable, though we cannot suppose that everyone will in all respects be equally beloved. As some of the saints are more beloved of God than others on earth, as the angel told Daniel he was a man greatly beloved [Dan. 9:23], and John is called the beloved disciple [John 19:26], so doubtless those who have been most eminent, and are highest in glory, are most beloved of Christ; and doubtless those saints who are most beloved of Christ and nearest to him in glory are most beloved of all the saints. So we may conclude such saints as the apostle Paul and apostle John are more beloved by the saints in heaven than other saints of lower rank. They are more beloved by lower saints themselves than those of equal rank. But then there are answerable returns of love. As such are more beloved by other saints, so they have more love to other saints. The heart of Christ, the Head of the society, is fullest of love. He loves all the saints far more than any of them love each other. But the nearer any saint is to him, the more is he like him in this respect, the fuller his heart is of love.

Second. The joy of heavenly love shall never be damped or interrupted by jealousy. Heavenly lovers will have no doubt of the love of each other. They shall have no fear that their professions and testimonies of love are hypocritical; they shall be perfectly satisfied of the sincerity and strength of each other's love, as much as if there were a window in all their breasts, that they could see each other's hearts. There shall be no such thing as flattery or dissimulation in heaven, but there perfect sincerity shall reign through all. Everyone will be perfectly sincere, having really all that love which they profess. All their expressions of love shall come from the bottom of their hearts. The saints shall know that God loves them, and they shall not doubt of the greatness of his love; and they shall have no doubt of the love of all their fellow heavenly inhabitants. And they shall not be jealous of the constancy of each other's love. They shall have no suspicion that their former love is abated, that they have withdrawn their love in any degree from them for the sake of any rival, or by reason of anything in themselves which they suspect is disagreeable to them, or anything they have done which is disrelished, or through the inconstancy of their hearts. Nor will they in the least be afraid that their love towards them will ever be abated. There shall be no such thing as inconstancy and unfaithfulness in heaven to molest and disturb the friendship of that blessed society. The saints shall have no fear that the love of God will ever abate towards them, or that Christ will not continue always to love them with the same immutable tenderness. And they shall have no jealousy one of another, for they shall know that by divine grace the love of all the saints is also unchangeable.

Third. They shall have nothing within themselves to clog them in the exercises and expressions of love. In this world they find much to hinder them. They have a great deal of dullness and heaviness. They carry about with them a heavy molded body, a lump of flesh and blood which is not fitted to be an organ for a soul inflamed with high exercises of divine love, but is found a great clog to the soul, so that they cannot express their love to God as they would. They cannot be so active and lively in it as they desire. Fain would they fly, but they are held down, as with a dead weight at their feet. Fain would they be active as a flame of fire, but they find themselves, as it were, hampered or chained down, that they cannot do as their love inclines them. Love disposes them to praise, but their tongues are not obedient; they want words to express the ardor of their souls, and cannot order their speech by reason of darkness, Job 37:19. And oftentimes for want of expressions they are forced to content themselves with groans that cannot be uttered, Rom. 8:26. But in heaven they shall have no such hindrance. They will have no dullness or unwieldiness, no corruption of heart to fight against divine love and hinder suitable expressions, no clog of a heavy lump of clay, or an unfit organ for an inward heavenly flame. They shall have no difficulty in expressing all their love. Their souls, which are like a flame of fire with love, shall not be like a fire pent up but shall be perfectly at liberty. The soul which is winged with love shall have no weight tied to the feet to hinder its flight. There shall be no want of strength or activity, nor any want of words to praise the object of their love. They shall find nothing to hinder them in praising or seeing God, just as their love inclines. Love naturally desires to express itself; and in heaven the love of the saints shall be at liberty to express itself as it desires, either towards God or one another.

Fourth. In heaven love will be expressed with perfect decency and wisdom. Many in this world who are sincere in their hearts, and have indeed a principle of true love to God and their neighbor, yet have not discretion to guide them in the manner and circumstances of expressing it. Their speeches are good, but not suitably adapted to the time, or discreetly ordered in the circumstances of them. There are found in them those indiscretions which greatly obscure the loveliness of grace in the eyes of others who behold them. But in heaven the amiableness of their love shall not be obscured by any such means. There shall be no indecent or indiscreet actions or speeches, no selfish fondness, no needless officiousness, no such thing as affections clouding and darkening reason, or going before reason. But wisdom and discretion shall be as perfect in them as love, and every expression of love in them shall be ordered with the most amiable and perfect decency in all the circumstances of it.

Fifth. There shall be nothing external to keep them at a distance or hinder the most perfect enjoyment of each other's love. There shall be no separation wall to keep them asunder. They shall not be hindered from the full and constant enjoyment of each other's love by distance of habitation, for they shall be together as one family in their heavenly Father's house. There shall be no want of full acquaintance to hinder the greatest possible intimacy; much less shall there be any misunderstanding between them, or wrong construction of things which are said or done; no disunion through difference of tempers and manners, or through different circumstances, or various opinions, or various interests or alliances; for they shall all be united in the same interest, and all alike allied or related to the same God, and the same Savior, and all employed in the same business, serving and glorifying the same God.

Sixth. They shall all be united together in a very near relation. Love seeks a near relation to the object beloved. And in heaven all shall be nearly related. They shall be nearly allied to God, the supreme object of their love; for they shall all be his children. And all shall be nearly related to Christ; for he shall be the Head of the whole society, and husband of the whole church of saints. All together shall constitute his spouse, and they shall be related one to another as brethren. It will all be one society, yea, one family. Eph. 2:19, "Ye are fellow citizens with the saints, and of the household of God."

Seventh. All shall have *propriety* one in another. Love seeks to have the beloved its own, and divine love rejoices in saying, "My beloved is mine, and I am his," as Cant. 2:16. And in heaven all shall not only be related one to another, but they shall be each other's. The saints shall be God's. He brings them hence to him in glory, as that part of the creation which he has chosen for his peculiar treasure. And on the other hand God shall be theirs. He made over himself to them in an everlasting covenant in this world, and now they shall be in full possession of him as their portion. And so the saints shall be Christ's, for he has bought them with a price, and he shall be *theirs*; for he who gave himself *for* them, will have given himself *to* them. Christ and the saints will have given themselves, the one to the other. And as God and Christ shall be the saints', so the angels shall be "their angels," Matt. 18:10. And the saints shall be one another's. The

Apostle in II Cor. 8:5 speaks of saints in those days as first giving themselves to the Lord, and then to one another by the will of God. But this is done much more perfectly in heaven.

Eighth. They shall enjoy each other's love in perfect and undisturbed prosperity. What oftentimes diminishes the pleasure and sweetness of earthly friendship is that though they live in love, yet they live in poverty, and meet with great difficulties and sore afflictions whereby they are grieved for themselves, and for one another. For love and friendship in such cases, though in some respects lightens each other's burdens, yet in other respects adds to persons' afflictions, because it makes them sharers in others' afflictions. So that they have not only their afflictions to bear, but also those of their afflicted friends. But there shall be no adversity in heaven to give occasion for a pitiful grief of spirit, or to molest those heavenly friends in the enjoyment of each other's friendship. But they shall enjoy one another's love in the greatest prosperity, in glorious riches, having the possession of all things. Rev. 21:7, "He that overcometh shall inherit all things; and I will be his God, and he shall be my son." And in the highest honor rejoicing together in an heavenly kingdom, sitting together on thrones, and all wearing crowns of life. Rev. 5:10, "Hath made us kings and priests." Christ and his disciples, who in this world were together in affliction, and manifested love and friendship to each other under great and sore sufferings, are now in heaven enjoying each other's love in immortal glory, all sorrow and sighing being fled away. Christ and the saints both were acquainted with sorrow and grief in this world, though Christ had the greatest share. But in another world they sit together in heavenly places. Eph. 2:6, "Hath raised us up together, and made us sit together in heavenly places in Christ Jesus." And so all the saints enjoy each other's love in glory and prosperity in comparison with which the wealth and honor of the greatest earthly princes is sordid beggary. So that as they love one another, they have not only their own but each other's prosperity to rejoice in, and are by love made partakers of each other's glory. Such is every saint's love to other saints that it, as it were, makes that glory, which he sees other saints enjoy, his own. He so rejoices in it that they enjoy such glory, that it is in some respects to him as if he, himself, enjoyed it.

Ninth. All things in that world shall conspire to promote their love, and give advantage for mutual enjoyment. There shall be none there to tempt them to hatred, no busy adversary to make misrepresentations or create misunderstandings. Everyone and everything there shall conspire to promote love, and promote the enjoyment of each other's love. Heaven itself, the place of habitation, is a garden of pleasures, a heavenly paradise fitted in all respects for an abode of heavenly lovers, a place where they may have sweet society and perfect enjoyment of each other's love. All things there, doubtless, remarkably show forth the beauty and loveliness of God and Christ, and have a luster of divine love upon them. The very light which shines in and fills that world is the light of love. It is beams of love; for it is the shining of the glory of the Lamb of God, that most wonderful influence of lamb-like meekness and love which fills the heavenly Jerusalem with light. Rev. 22:5, "And there shall be no night there; and they need no candle, neither light of the sun; for the Lord God giveth them light." The glory which is about him who reigns in heaven is compared to the beautiful sight of the rainbow for its pleasantness and sweetness, Rev. 4:3. The same which is used as a fit token of God's love and grace manifested in his covenant, Gen. 9:12–15: "And God said, This is the token of the covenant which I make between me and you and every living creature that is with you, for perpetual generations; I do set my bow in the cloud, and it shall be for a token of a covenant between me and the earth. And it shall come to pass, when I bring a cloud over the earth, that the bow shall be seen in the cloud. And I will remember my covenant, which is between me and you, and every living creature of all flesh; and the waters shall no more become a flood to destroy all flesh." The light of the New Jerusalem, which is the light of God's glory; is said to be like a jasper stone. Rev. 21:11, "Having the glory of God; and her light was like unto a stone most precious, even like a jasper stone, clear as crystal." The jasper is a precious stone of a beautiful pleasant color.

Tenth. And lastly. They shall know that they shall forever be continued in the perfect enjoyment of each other's love. They shall know that God and Christ will be forever, and that their love will be continued and be fully manifested forever, and that all their beloved fellow saints shall live forever in glory with the same love in their hearts. And they shall know that they themselves shall ever live to love God, and love the saints, and enjoy their love. They shall be in no fear of any end of this happiness, nor shall they be in any fear or danger of any abatement of it through weariness of the exercises and expressions of love, or cloyed with the enjoyment of it, or the beloved objects becoming old or decayed, or stale or tasteless. All things shall flourish there in an eternal youth. Age will not diminish anyone's beauty or vigor, and there love shall flourish in everyone's breast, as a living spring perpetually springing, or as a flame which never decays. And the holy pleasure shall be as a river which ever runs, and is always clear and full. The paradise of love shall always be continued as in a perpetual spring. There shall be no autumn or winter; every plant there shall be in perpetual bloom with the same undecaying pleasantness and fragrancy, always springing forth, always blossoming, and always bearing fruit. Ps. 1:3, "His leaf shall not wither." Rev. 22:2, "In the midst of the street of it, and on either side of the river, was there the tree of life, which bare twelve manner of fruits, and yielded her fruit every month."

Thus having taken notice of many of the blessed circumstances with which love in heaven is expressed and enjoyed, I proceed now

VI. And lastly, to speak of the blessed fruits of this love, exercised and enjoyed in these circumstances. And I shall mention only two at this time.

First. The most excellent and perfect behavior of the inhabitants of heaven towards God and one another. Divine love is the sum of all good principles, and therefore is the fountain whence proceed all amiable actions. As this love will be perfect to the perfect exclusion of all sin consisting in enmity against God and fellow creatures, so the fruit of it will be a perfect behavior. Their life in heaven shall be without the least sinful failure or error. They shall never turn aside to the right hand or left in the least degree from the way of holiness. Every action shall be perfect in all its circumstances. Every part of their behavior shall be holy and divine in matter and form and end. We know not particularly how the saints in heaven shall be employed; but in general we know they are employed in praising and serving God. Rev. 22:3, "And there shall be no more curse; but the throne of God and of the Lamb shall be in it; and his servants shall serve him." And this they do perfectly, being influenced by such a love as has been described. And we have reason to think that they are employed so as in some way to be subservient to each other's happiness under God; because they are represented in Scripture as united together as one society, which can be for no other purpose but mutual subserviency. And they are thus mutually subservient by a most excellent and perfectly amiable behavior, one towards another, as a fruit of their perfect love one to another.

Second. The other fruit of this love in heaven exercised in such circumstances is perfect tranquillity and joy. Holy, humble and divine love is a principle of wonderful power to give ineffable quietness and tranquillity to the soul. It banishes all disturbance, it sweetly composes and brings rest, it makes all things appear calm and sweet. In that soul where divine love reigns, and is in lively exercise, nothing can raise a storm. Those are principles contrary to love which make this world so much like a tempestuous sea. It is selfishness, and revenge, and envy, and such things which keep this world in a constant tumult, and make it a scene of confusion and uproar, where no quiet rest is to be enjoyed, unless it be in renouncing the world, and looking to another world. But what rest is there in that world which the God of love and peace fills with his glorious presence, where the Lamb of God lives and reigns, and fills that world with the pleasant beams of his love; where is nothing to give any offense, no object to be seen but what has perfect sweetness and amiableness; where the saints shall find and enjoy all which they love, and so be perfectly satisfied; where there is no enemy and no enmity in any heart, but perfect love in all to everyone; where there is a perfect harmony between the higher and the lower ranks of inhabitants of that world, none envying another, but everyone resting and rejoicing in the happiness of every other. All their love is holy, humble, and perfectly Christian, without the least impurity or carnality; where love is always mutual, where the love of the beloved is answerable to the love of the lovers; where there is no hypocrisy or dissembling, but perfect simplicity and sincerity; where is no treachery, unfaithfulness or inconstancy, nor any such thing as jealousy. And no clog or hindrance to the exercises and expressions of love, nor imprudence or indecency in the manner of expressing love, no instance of folly or indiscretion in any word or deed; where there is no separation wall, no misunderstanding or strangeness, but full acquaintance and perfect intimacy in all; no division through different opinions or interests, where all that glorious loving society shall be most nearly and divinely related, and all shall be one another's, having given themselves one to another. And all shall enjoy one another in perfect prosperity, riches, and honor, without any sickness, pain, or persecution, or any enemy to molest them, any talebearer, or busybody to create jealousies and misunderstandings.

And all this in a garden of love, the Paradise of God, where everything has a cast of holy love, and everything conspires to promote and stir up love, and nothing to interrupt its exercises; where everything is fitted by an all-wise God for the enjoyment of love under the greatest advantages. And all this shall be without any fading of the beauty of the objects beloved, or any decaying of love in the lover, and any satiety in the faculty which enjoys love. O! what tranquillity may we conclude there is in such a world as this! Who can express the sweetness of this peace? What a calm is this, what a heaven of rest is here to arrive at after persons have gone through a world of storms and tempests, a world of pride, and selfishness, and envy, and malice, and scorn, and contempt, and contention and war? What a Canaan of rest, a land flowing with milk and honey to come to after one has gone through a great and terrible wilderness, full of spiteful and poisonous serpents, where no rest could be found? What joy may we conclude springs up in the hearts of the saints after they have passed their wearisome pilgrimage to be brought to such a paradise? Here is joy unspeakable indeed; here is humble, holy, divine joy in its perfection. Love is a sweet principle, especially divine love. It is a spring of sweetness. But here the spring shall become a river, and an ocean. All shall stand about the God of glory, the fountain of love, as it were opening their bosoms to be filled with those effusions of love which are poured forth from thence, as the flowers on the earth in a pleasant spring day open their bosoms to the sun to be filled with his warmth and light, and to flourish in beauty and fragrancy by his rays. Every saint is as a flower in the garden of God, and holy love is the fragrancy and sweet odor which they all send forth, and with which they fill that paradise. Every saint there is as a note in a concert of music which sweetly harmonizes with every other note, and all together employed wholly in praising God and the Lamb; and so all helping one another to their utmost to express their love of the whole society to the glorious Father and Head of it, and [to pour back] love into the fountain of love, whence they are supplied and filled with love and with glory. And thus they will live and thus they will reign in love, and in that godlike joy which is the blessed fruit of it, such as eye hath not seen, nor ear heard, nor hath ever entered into the heart of any in this world to conceive [cf. I Cor. 2:9]. And thus they will live and reign forever and ever.

APPLICATION.

Use I may be of *Instruction*.

First. If heaven be such a world as we have heard, then this may lead us to see a reason why contention has such an influence as it has to darken persons' evidences for heaven. Experience teaches it to be so, in fact, when principles of malignity and ill will prevail in God's people, as they are liable to it through remains of corruption in their hearts, and they get into a contentious frame, when they are [engaged] in any strife public or private, and their spirits are engaged in opposition to their neighbors in any affair, their former evidences for heaven seem to die away, and they are in darkness about their state; they do not find that comfortable satisfying hope which they used to enjoy. So when converted persons get into ill frames in their families, the consequence commonly, if not universally, is that they live without much of a comfortable sense of heavenly things, or any lively hope of it. They do not enjoy much of that spiritual calm and sweetness which others do who live in love and peace. They have not that help from God and communion with him, and intercourse with heaven in their prayers, as others have. The Apostle seems to speak of contention in families as having this influence. I Pet. 3:7, "Likewise, ye husbands, dwell with them according to knowledge, giving honor unto the wife, as unto the weaker vessel, and as being heirs together of the grace of life; that your prayers be not hindered." The Apostle here intimates that discord in families tends to hinder Christians in their prayers. And what Christian is there, who has made the experiment, that has not done it to his sorrow; and whose experience will not witness to the truth of this?

And why it is so, that contention has such an effect, so to hinder spiritual exercises and comforts and hopes, or any sweet sense or hope of that which is heavenly, we may learn from the doctrine. For heaven being a world of love, it follows that when persons have the least exercise of love, and most of contrary principles, they have least of heaven and are farthest from it in their frames of mind. They have least of the exercise of that which consists in a conformity to heaven, or a preparation for it, or what tends to it, or has any relation to it; and so necessarily must have least evidence of their title to it, and must be farthest from partaking of the comforts of it.

Second. Hence we may learn how happy those persons are who are entitled to heaven. There are some such persons living on earth to whom the happiness of this world belongs, as much and much more than a man's estate belongs to him. They have a part and interest in this world of love; they have proper right and title to it. Rev. 22:14, "Blessed are they that do his commandments, that they may have right to the tree of life, and may enter in through the gates into the city." And doubtless there are such persons among us. How happy are they who are entitled to an inheritance in such a world as this! Surely they are the blessed of the earth.

But here some may be ready to say, without doubt they are happy persons who have a lot and portion in such a world, and so will surely have an eternal possession there. But who are those persons, what kind of persons are they, by what are such blessed ones distinguished? In answer to such an inquiry, I shall mention three things which belong to their character.

1. They are those who have had a principle or seed of the very same love implanted in their hearts in a work of regeneration. They are not those who have no other principles in their hearts but natural principles, or such principles as they have by their first birth; for that which is born of the flesh, is flesh. But they have been the subjects of a new birth; they have been born of the Spirit. A glorious work of the Spirit of God has been wrought in their hearts, renewing their hearts, as it were, by bringing down some of that light, and some of that holy pure flame, which is in the world of love, and giving it place in them. Their hearts are a soil in which this heavenly seed has been sown and in which it abides. And so they are changed, and of earthly are become heavenly in their dispositions. The love of the world is mortified, and the love of God implanted. Their hearts are drawn to God and Christ, and for their sakes flow out to the saints in

humble and spiritual love. I Pet. 1:23, "Being born not of corruptible seed, but of incorruptible." John 1:13, "Which were born not of blood, nor of the will of the flesh, nor of the will of man, but of God."

2. They are those who have freely chosen that happiness which is to be had in the exercise and enjoyment of such love as is in heaven above all other conceivable happiness. They see and understand so much of this as to know that this is the best good. They do not merely assent that it is so from rational arguments which may be offered for it, but they have seen that it is so; they know it is so from what little they have tasted. It is the happiness of love, and the happiness of a life of such love, heavenly love, holy and humble and divine love; love to God, and love to Christ, and love to saints for God's and Christ's sake, and the enjoyment of the fruits of God's love, holy communion with God and Christ and with holy persons. This is what they have a relish for. They feel within them such a nature that such a happiness suits their disposition and relish and appetite above all others; not only above what they have, but above all that they can conceive they might have. The world does not afford anything like it. They have chosen this before any other. Their souls go out after it more than any other, and their hearts are more in pursuit of it than any other. They have chosen it freely, not merely because they have met with such sorrow, and are in such low and afflicted circumstances, that they do not expect much from the world. But their hearts are so captivated by this good that they choose it for its own sake beyond all worldly good, if they had ever so much of it, and could enjoy it ever so long. Cant. 1:2, "Thy love is better than wine."

3. They are those who from that love which is in them are in heart and practice struggling after holiness. Holy love makes them long for holiness. Divine love is a principle, which thirsts after [increase]. It is in imperfection and in a state of infancy in this world, and it desires growth. It has much to struggle with in the heart in this world, many opposite principles. And it struggles after greater increase, more liberty, more free exercise, and better fruits. The spirit lusts against the flesh, Gal. 5:17. The strife and struggle of the new man is after holiness. The heart struggles after it. The heart of a good man, one who has an interest in heaven, and has an inward active, heavenly seed in him, is in a struggle with sin, as Jacob was with

Esau in Rebecca's womb. There are ardent desires, and breathings, and cryings, and strivings; and it is to be holy. And the hands struggle as well as the heart. A man strives in his practice; his life is a life of sincere and earnest endeavors to be universally holy, and to be more holy. He is not holy enough, but is very far from it. He desires to be nearer perfection, or more like those in heaven. And this is one reason why he longs to be in heaven, that he may be perfectly holy. And the principle when he thus struggles is love. It is not only fear, but it is love to God, and love to Christ, and love to holiness. Love is a holy fire in him. And fire, if it be pent up, will cause a struggling for liberty.

Use II may be of *Awakening* to sinners.

First. What has been said on this subject may put Christless persons in mind of their misery, in that they have no portion or right in this world of love. You have heard what has been said of heaven, what kind of glory and blessedness is there, how glorious and happy the saints and angels are there in a world of love. But consider, none of this belongs to you. When you hear of such things, you hear of that in which you have no interest. No such person as you, a wicked hater of God and Christ, and one who is under the power of a spirit of enmity against all that is good, shall in any wise enter in there. In the writing of the house of Israel, such an one as you are is not written, nor shall such enter into the land of Israel. It may be said to you as Peter said to Simon Magus, Acts 8:21, "Thou hast no portion or lot in this matter, for thy heart is not right in the sight of God." And as Nehemiah said to Tobiah and Sanballat, Neh. 2:20, "Ye have no portion, nor right, nor memorial in Jerusalem." If such a soul as yours should be admitted into heaven, into that world of love, how nauseous would it be to those blessed spirits whose souls are as a flame of love. How would it discompose that loving and amiable society, and put things into confusion. It would make heaven not to be heaven if such souls should be admitted there. It would turn that world from being a world of love into a world of hatred and pride, and envy, and malice, as this world is. But it shall in no wise be suffered. All such persons shall be shut out. Rev. 22:14–15, "Blessed are they that do his commandments, that they may have right to the tree of life, and may enter in through the gates into the city. For without are dogs, and sorcerers, and whoremongers, and murderers, and idolaters, and whatsoever loveth and maketh a lie." Such as you shall be shut out as dogs, as impure, vile creatures in nowise to be admitted there to defile that world.

Second. You are in danger. Hell is a world of hatred. There are three worlds. One is this present world, which is an intermediate world, a world where good and bad, love and hatred are mixed together; a sure sign that the world is not to continue. Another is heaven, a world of love where is love and no hatred. And the other is hell, a world of hatred where there is no love, to which world you, while you remain in a Christless state, do properly belong. This is a world where God manifests his hatred, as heaven is a world where he manifests his love. In hell God manifests his being and perfections only in hatred and wrath, and hatred without love. Everything in hell is hateful. There is not one object to be beheld there but what is odious and detestable. There is no person or thing to be seen there which is amiable, there is nothing pure or holy, nothing pleasant, but everything perfectly odious. No persons there but devils and wicked, damned spirits which are like devils. Hell is, as it were, a vast den of poisonous, lusting serpents. There is that old serpent who is the devil, and there is his hateful brood. And there are none there but whom God hates with a perfect and everlasting hatred. He exercises no love, no mercy to any one object there; there he pours out his wrath without mixture. All things in the whole universe which are hateful shall be gathered together in hell, as in a grand receptacle provided on purpose, that the universe which God has made may be cleansed of its filthiness by casting it all into this great sink. And it is a world prepared on purpose for the expressions of God's wrath. God has made hell for this. He has no other use for it, but there to satisfy his hatred of sin and sinners.

And there are no tokens of God's love or mercy there. Nothing is there but what shows forth God's wrath. Every object which is to be seen shows wrath. It is a world flowed with a deluge of wrath, as with a deluge of liquid fire, so as to become a lake of fire and brimstone. There are none there but what have been haters of God, and so have procured God's hatred on themselves. And they shall continue to hate him. There is no love to God in hell. Everyone there perfectly hates him, and are continually, without restraint, expressing their hatred to him, blaspheming and cursing him, and, as it were, spitting venom at him. And though they all join together in their enmity and opposition to God, yet there is no union among themselves. They agree to nothing but hatred and expressions of hatred. They hate God, and hate Christ, and hate angels and saints in heaven. And not only so, but hate one another. They will all be like a company of serpents or vipers one to another, not only spitting poison at God but at one another, biting and tormenting one another. The devils will hate damned souls. They hated them while in this world, and therefore it was that they with such indefatigable temptations and subtlety sought their ruin. They thirsted for the blood of their souls, because they hated them. They longed to get them in their power to torment them. They watched them, as a roaring lion does his prey, because they hated them. Therefore they flew upon their souls like hellhounds, as soon as they were parted from their bodies. And what they were so eager for was to torment them. And they hate them still now they have them in their power; and therefore will spend eternity without ceasing in tormenting them with the utmost strength and cruelty of which devils are capable. They are, as it were, continually and eternally turning those poor damned souls that are in their hands.

And those damned souls will not only be hated and tormented of devils, but they will have no love or pity to each other, but will be to one another like devils; they will to their utmost torment one another; they will be like fire to each other, as brands in a fire burn one another. Here all those principles which are contrary to love will rage and reign without any restraining grace to keep them within bounds. Here will be unrestrained pride, and envy, and revenge. Here will be contention in its perfection, and without any such thing as making peace. They will be left to bite and devour one another forever, as well as forever to bear the wrath of God. Those wicked men in hell who had been companions together while on earth, and had a sort of carnal friendship for each other, will have no appearance of friendship now, but perfect, continual, and undisguised hatred. As they promoted each other's sin, so now they will promote each other's punishment. They were the instruments of ruining each other's souls on earth in blowing up each other's lusts; now they will blow the fire of each other's torment. They ruined each other in sinning, setting bad examples to each other, poisoning one another by wicked talk; and now they shall be as much engaged in tormenting one another as they were in tempting one another.

And their hatred and envy will be a torment to themselves. God and Christ whom they will hate most, and to whom their souls will be as full of fierce hatred as an oven is full of fire, will be infinitely above their reach, dwelling in infinite blessedness and glory which they cannot diminish. And they will be tormenting themselves with a fruitless envy of the saints and angels in heaven, whom they shall not be able to hurt, or approach; and shall have no pity from them or from any; for in hell is hatred only, and no pity. And thus they will be left to spend their eternity together. Now consider, all ye who are out of Christ, who were never born again, and never had any blessed renovation of your hearts implanting a spirit of divine love there, leading you to choose that happiness which consists in holy love as your best and sweetest good, and to spend your life in struggling after happiness. Consider your misery. For this is the world to which you are under condemnation, and so the world to which you belong by the sentence of the law, and the world in which you are in danger every day of having your abode fixed; and if you are not greatly changed by God's almighty power, in a short time will inherit instead of a portion in that world of love of which you have heard. Consider it is indeed thus with you. These are no cunningly devised fables. They are the great and awful truths of God's word, and things which in a short time you will certainly know to be true. How therefore can you rest in such a state as you are in, and go about from day to day so careless and so negligent of your precious soul? Seriously consider these things, and be wise for yourself before it is too late, before your feet stumble on the dark mountains, and you fall into that world of wrath and hatred where is eternal weeping, and wailing, and gnashing of teeth, with spiteful malice and rage against God and Christ, and one another, and gnashing of teeth with horror and anguish of spirit.

Use III may be of *Exhortation* in two branches.

First. Let the consideration of what has been said of heaven stir you up earnestly to seek after it. If heaven be such a blessed world, then let this be our chosen country, and the inheritance we seek. Let us turn our course this way. It is not impossible that this glorious world may be obtained by us. It is offered to us. Though it be so excellent and blessed a country, yet God stands ready to give us an inheritance there, if this be the country we choose, and upon which we set our hearts, and spend our time chiefly in seeking it. God gives men their choice. They may have their inheritance where they choose it, and may obtain heaven if they will seek it by patient continuance in well-doing, Rom. 2:7. We are all of us, as it were, set here in this world as in a large wilderness with divers countries about it, with several ways or paths leading to those different countries, and we are left to our choice what course we will take. If we heartily choose heaven, and set our hearts chiefly on that blessed Canaan, that land of love, and love the path which leads to it, we may walk in it; and if we continue so to do, it will certainly lead us to heaven at last. Let what we have heard of the land of love excite us all to turn our faces towards that land, and bend our course thitherward. Is not what we have heard of the happy state of that country and the many delights which are in it enough to make us thirst after it, and to cause us with the greatest earnestness and steadfastness of resolution to press towards, and to spend our whole lives in traveling in the way which leads thither? What joyful news might it well be to us when we hear of such a world of perfect peace and holy love, to hear that there is an opportunity for us to come, that we may spend an eternity in such a world.

Is not what we have heard of that blessed world enough to make us weary of this world of pride and malice and contention and perpetual jarring and strife, a world of confusion, a wilderness of hissing serpents, a tempestuous ocean where there is no quiet rest, where all are for themselves, and self-interest governs, and all are striving to set themselves up, and little regarding what becomes of others; all together seeking worldly good which is the bone of contention among them, where men are continually envying and calumniating and reproaching one another and multitudes otherwise injuring and abusing one another, a world full of injustice, where there is abundance of opposition and cruelty without any remedy? Eccles. 4:1, "So I returned and considered all the oppressions that are done under the sun; and behold the tears of such as were oppressed, and they had no comforter; and on the side of their oppressors there was power; but they had no comforter." A world where there is so much falsehood and treachery, fickleness and inconstancy, hypocrisy and deceit; where there is so little trust to be had in men, and where even good men have so many failings which tend to render them unlovely and uncomfortable. Truly this is an evil world, and so it is like to be. It is in vain for us to expect that this world will be any other than a world of pride and enmity and strife, and so a restless world. The times may hereafter be mended, yet those things will always be found in the world as long as it stands. Who would content himself with a portion in such a world? What man acting wisely and considerately would concern himself much about laying up a store in such a world as this, and would not rather neglect the world, [and let it go to them that would take it, and] apply all his heart and all his strength to lay up treasure in heaven, and to press towards that world of love? What will it signify for us to hoard up great quantities here in this world? How may the thought of having our portion here in such a world as this be sinking to a man when there is an interest in such a glorious world offered? and especially when if we have our portion here, when we have done with this world, we have our eternal portion in hell, that world of hatred, a world of the wrath of God, and cruelty and malice of devils and damned spirits.

We all of us naturally desire rest and quietness; and if we would obtain, let us seek that world of peace and love of which we have heard. Here is doubtless a sweet rest to be had. Heb. 4:9, "There remaineth therefore a rest to the people of God." If we obtain an interest in that world, then when we have done with this we shall leave all our cares and troubles, our fatigues and perplexities and disappointments forever. We shall rest from those storms, we shall rest from our wearisome travel. Rev. 14:13, "Blessed are the dead which die in the Lord from henceforth; yea, saith the Spirit, that they may rest from their labors." You who are poor, and think yourselves despised by your neighbors, and little esteemed among men, do not much regard this, do not give yourselves much concern about the friendship of the world; but seek heaven where is no such thing as contempt, where none are despised, all are highly esteemed and honored, and dearly loved by all. You who think you have met with many abuses, and much ill treatment from others, care not for it; do not hate them for it but set your heart in heaven, a world of love; press towards a better country.

Here for direction how to seek heaven,

1. Do not let out your heart after the things of this world and indulge

yourself in a pursuit of earthly things. This is the reverse of seeking heaven. This is to go the contrary way, which leads directly from heaven and not towards it. If you would seek heaven, your affections must be taken off from the pleasures of the world. You must not indulge in sensuality; you must take off your heart from the profits of the world, and not spend your time and strength only in heaping up the dust of the earth. You must mortify a desire of the honors and vainglory of this world, and become poor in spirit, and lowly of heart.

2. You must in your meditations and holy exercises be much in conversing with heavenly persons and enjoyments. You cannot earnestly and constantly seek heaven without having your thoughts much there. Therefore turn the current of your thoughts and meditations towards that world of love, and that God of love who dwells there, and towards Christ who is ascended and sits there at the right hand of God; and towards the blessed enjoyments of that world. And be much in conversing with [God and Christ,] without which heaven is no heaven. Phil. 3:20, "Our conversation is in heaven."

3. Be content to pass through all difficulties in the way to heaven. Though the path is before you, and you may walk in it if you really choose it, yet it is a way which is strait, and there are many difficulties in the way; the whole way is ascending. That glorious city of light and love is, as it were, on the top of an high hill, an elevation which is exalted above the hill, and there is no arriving there without traveling uphill. Though this be wearisome, yet it is worth your while to come and dwell in such a glorious city at last. Be willing therefore to comply with this labor. What is it in comparison of the sweet rest which is at the end of your journey? Be willing to cross the natural inclination of flesh and blood, which is downward. Continue crossing this tendency; it will grow easier and easier, and you will be paid by more and more of the pleasant prospect which you will have the higher you rise, and a nearer view of the glorious city on the top of the hill, besides the glorious reward which you will have when you arrive there.

4. In all your way let your eye be to Jesus who is gone to heaven as your Forerunner. Look to him; behold his glory there in heaven to stir you up the more earnestly to be there. Look to him, and observe his example.

Consider how by patient continuance in well-doing, and in patient enduring of great sufferings, he went before to heaven. Look to him, and trust in his mediation, in his blood, with which he has entered into the holiest of all, as the price of heaven. Trust to his intercession in heaven before God. Trust to his strength by his Spirit sent from heaven to enable you to press on and surmount the difficulties which are in the way to heaven. Trust in his promises of heaven to those who love and follow him, whom he has confirmed by entering to heaven himself as the Head and Representative and Forerunner of such.

5. And lastly. If you would be in the way to the world of love, you must live a life of love. But I would make this a distinct exhortation. And therefore

Second. The second exhortation is to all, to seek that they may live a life of love, a life of love to God and love to men. We all hope to have a part in heaven, that world of love of which we have heard, and that in a little time. Surely then we should endeavor to use the same temper of mind. Here let several things be considered as motives.

1. This is the way to be like the inhabitants of heaven. You have heard how they love one another; and therefore they, and they only, are conformed to them who live in love in this world. In this way you will be like them in excellence and loveliness, for their holiness and loveliness consists in being of such an excellent spirit. And this will be the way to make you like them in happiness and comfort. For this happiness and joy and rest lies in loving the inhabitants of that world. And by living in love in this world the saints partake of a like sort of inward peace and sweetness. It is in this way that you are to have the foretastes of heavenly pleasures and delights.

2. This is the way to have a sense of glory of heavenly things, as of God and Christ, and holiness, and heavenly enjoyments. A contrary spirit, a spirit of hatred and ill will greatly hinders a sense of those things. It darkens the mind and clouds such objects, and puts them out of sight. A frame of holy love to God and Christ, and a spirit of love and peace to men greatly disposes and fits the heart for a sense of the excellence and sweetness of heavenly objects. It gives a relish of them. It, as it were, opens the windows by which the light of heaven shines in upon the soul.

3. This is the way to have clear evidences of a title to heaven. There are no evidences of a title to heaven but in feeling that which is heavenly in the heart. But by what has been said, it appears that heavenliness consists in love. Therefore the way to have clear evidences of a title is to live a life of love, and so seek the continual and lively exercises of such a spirit. You will find that this will cast out fear and give a strong hope of heaven, and be, as it were, an exercise of heaven in your hearts.

4. By living a life of love, you will be in the way to heaven. As heaven is a world of love, so the way to heaven is the way of love. This will best prepare you for heaven, and make you meet for an inheritance with the saints in that land of light and love. And if ever you arrive at heaven, faith and love must be the wings which must carry you there.

Index

All works are by Jonathan Edwards.

Jonathan Edwards, widely considered America's most important Christian thinker, was first and foremost a preacher and pastor who guided souls and interpreted religious experiences. His primary tool in achieving these goals was the sermon, out of which grew many of his famous treatises. This selection of Edwards' sermons recognizes their crucial role in his life and art.

The fifteen sermons, four of which have never been published before, reflect a life dedicated to experiencing and understanding spiritual truth. Chosen to represent a typical cycle of Edwards' preaching, the sermons address a wide range of occasions, situations, and states, corporate as well as personal. The book also contains an introduction that discusses Edwards' contribution to the sermon as a literary form, places his sermons within their social and cultural contexts, and considers his theological aims as a way of familiarizing the reader with the "order of salvation" as Edwards conceived of it. Together, the sermons and the editors' introduction offer a rounded picture of Edwards the preacher, the sermon writer, and the pastoral theologian.

Wilson H. Kimnach is professor of English at the University of Bridgeport. Kenneth P. Minkema is executive editor of *The Works of Jonathan Edwards.* Douglas A. Sweeney is assistant professor of church history at Trinity Evangelical Divinity School.

Yale University Press New Haven and London
http://www.yale.edu/yup/